COMPANIONSHIP IN GRIEF

ALSO BY JEFFREY BERMAN

Joseph Conrad: Writing as Rescue

The Talking Cure: Literary Representations of Psychoanalysis

Narcissism and the Novel

Diaries to an English Professor: Pain and Growth in the Classroom

Surviving Literary Suicide

Risky Writing: Self-Disclosure and Self-Transformation in the Classroom

Empathic Teaching: Education for Life

Dying to Teach: A Memoir of Love, Loss, and Learning

Cutting and the Pedagogy of Self-Disclosure (with Patricia Hatch Wallace)

Death in the Classroom: Writing about Love and Loss

COMPANIONSHIP IN GRIEF

Love and Loss in the Memoirs of C. S. Lewis, John Bayley, Donald Hall, Joan Didion, and Calvin Trillin

JEFFREY BERMAN

University of Massachusetts Press
Amherst and Boston

Printed in the United States of America

LC 2010008985
ISBN 978-1-55849-804-4 (paper); 803-7 (library cloth)

Designed by Sally Nichols
Set in Poetica and Goudy Oldstyle
Printed and bound by Thomson-Shore, Inc.

Library of Congress Cataloging-in-Publication Data

Berman, Jeffrey, 1945–
Companionship in grief : love and loss in the memoirs of C. S. Lewis, John Bayley, Donald Hall, Joan Didion, and Calvin Trillin / Jeffrey Berman.
p. cm.
Includes bibliographical references and index.
ISBN 978-1-55849-804-4 (pbk. : alk. paper) — ISBN 978-1-55849-803-7 (lib. cloth : alk. paper)
1. Loss (Psychology) in literature. 2. Autobiography—Authorship. 3. Grief in literature. I. Lewis, C. S. (Clive Staples), 1898–1963. II. Bayley, John, 1925– III. Hall, Donald, 1928– IV. Didion, Joan. V. Trillin, Alice Stewart. VI. Title.
PN56.L58B47 2010
809'.93353—dc22
2010008985

British Library Cataloguing in Publication data are available.

For Julie

Sorrow brought us together; joy keeps us together.

CONTENTS

ACKNOWLEDGMENTS

Companionship in Grief is my sixth book published by the University of Massachusetts Press, and I'm grateful to everyone associated with the Press: Bruce Wilcox, Director; Clark Dougan, Senior Editor; Carol Betsch, Managing Editor; and Anne R. Gibbons, copy editor par excellence. They have all become part of my extended family. I'm also grateful to the two anonymous outside readers who offered so many constructive comments on strengthening the manuscript. In addition, I'm indebted to the distinguished American poet and literary critic Sandra M. Gilbert, the author of several groundbreaking books on the literature of bereavement, for alerting me to important theoretical and critical studies of contemporary grief memoirs. David E. Balk, the editor-in-chief of the indispensable *Handbook of Thanatology*, called my attention to the "continuing bonds" theory of bereavement. My colleague Professor Martha Rozett read the manuscript carefully and offered helpful suggestions for revision, as did Charlotte Goodman, Professor Emerita of English, Skidmore College. I'm grateful to Donald Hall for his candid responses to an early version of chapter 3 that I mailed to him. Finally, I wish to thank Julie Nark for her labor of love in reading the manuscript and for her presence in my life.

COMPANIONSHIP IN GRIEF

INTRODUCTION

"The Lost Other Is an Ongoing Part of Our Existence"

I never imagined I would write a book about deceased spouses. But then again, I never imagined I would lose my beloved wife.

Barbara died on April 5, 2004, after a twenty-month struggle with pancreatic cancer. Immediately after her death I began writing a memoir about our life together after her diagnosis on August 12, 2002, one day after our thirty-fourth wedding anniversary. Writing about Barbara was both an act of will and an example of following one's obsession. As soon as I completed *Dying to Teach* (2007), I began a new book, *Death in the Classroom* (2009), a study of how my undergraduate students responded to Love and Loss, a course I taught in the spring of 2006. Like the fabled Scheherazade of the *Thousand and One Nights*, who must keep on telling stories to remain alive, I find myself writing books about death, partly to work through my grief, partly to commemorate and honor my wife's memory, partly to remain securely attached to her, partly to understand my changing relationship to her, and partly to help others—my students and my readers—understand and cope with their own losses. Thus this book.

Most of the books and articles I read during Barbara's illness focused on dying, death, and bereavement. After her death I became curious about how other memoirists write about their own deceased spouses. How do memoirists portray love, loss, and bereavement? Why is it so difficult for the bereft to let go of their grief—and how does grief change over time? How does one speak for the dead? What do their stories teach us about caregiving? Can these memoirs offer wisdom or comfort to those readers who have also lost their spouses? What role does writing play in bereavement? What do these memoirs teach us about recovery from spousal loss, including the possibility of falling in love again? These questions confront all memoirists of spousal loss.

Some memoirs, such as C. S. Lewis's *A Grief Observed* (1961), reveal little about the spouse's life or death. Finding myself curious about Lewis's marriage late in his life to Joy Davidman and her life before meeting him, I tried to learn everything I could about her. I was not content to rely on what Lewis's many biographers—and her own biographer as well—wrote about her. I decided to read her own writings, including her two novels, *Anya* (1940) and *Weeping Bay* (1950), as well as her theological treatise, *Smoke on the Mountain* (1954). It is probably only an accident—a serendipitous one—that all the deceased spouses in my study were themselves writers. One may infer a great deal about authors from their books. And so I found myself reading everything I could about the deceased spouses, not only to learn more about their lives but also to see how they were represented in the memoirs written about them. No matter how faithfully memoirists portray their spouses, they nevertheless construct them as characters, seeing them from the memoirists' unique points of view. Sometimes these constructions are strikingly different from the spouses' own self-representations.

My title comes from Donald Hall's observation in his memoir *The Best Day the Worst Day* (2005): "Poetry gives the griever not release from grief but companionship in grief" (118). So, too, do memoirs about deceased spouses offer us companionship in grief. Companionship implies relationship, and we see a double grief: the dying person's grief and also the survivor's grief. In the case of sudden, unexpected death, the survivor feels more grief than the dying person. Thomas Mann observed in *The Magic Mountain*: "It is a fact that a man's dying is more the survivors' affair than his own" (532). The grief becomes triple if we include the reader, who empathizes with the memoirist's anguish.

Companionship in grief also implies the special camaraderie that develops between writer and reader. Lewis, Bayley, Hall, Didion, and Trillin became my companions in grief. I found myself regarding them, and their deceased spouses, as allies, friends, and teachers. I felt less lonely and grief-stricken while reading their stories. Reading spousal loss memoirs alerts us not only to *anticipatory grief*, the term thanatologists use to describe the grief that occurs before impending death, but also *anticipatory recovery*. Working through one's grief is both an individual and collaborative process, and spousal loss memoirs are an important resource on which we can draw for knowledge and recovery.

Companionship in grief often changes into companionship in joy as memoirists of spousal loss accept the reality of their losses and find comfort and consolation in memory as well as in the present moment. This change may be imperceptible, may require years to occur, and may be subject to unexpected reversals. Just as the bereft may notice with surprise that they haven't cried for days or weeks, something may happen to trigger new tears: seeing a video of their spouses smiling radiantly, coming across one of their old letters, or finding one of their possessions last seen when they were healthy. Whenever I find myself grief-stricken or self-pitying, I recall C. S. Lewis's hard-won observation in *A Grief Observed* that "passionate grief does not link us with the dead but cuts us off from them" (54). One need not share Lewis's orthodox Christian religious views to appreciate insights such as this. His writings are filled with other revelations over love and loss, as when he states in a letter written to a friend who had recently lost his own wife, "it is never sadness—a proper, straight natural response to loss—that does people harm, but all the other things, all the resentment, dismay, doubt and self-pity with [which] it is usually complicated" (*Collected Letters* 3:560). I feel my own grief lifting whenever I finish rereading *A Grief Observed*.

Why do memoirists write about their deceased spouses? I suspect that many if not all memoirists need to maintain their attachment to their spouses. This was certainly one of my strongest motives for writing about Barbara. I could not prevent her from dying—no amount of love could keep her alive—yet I could not let her go. I sought to re-create her life in loving words. This does not imply magical thinking—I knew she was dead and that I would never see her again. But it does imply my disagreement with Freud's theory of bereavement, which, until the mid-1990s, remained the dominant view among clinicians and academics.

One of Freud's earliest statements on loss appears in his 1916 essay "On Transience," where he states emphatically that mourners must detach themselves from the lost love object. "Mourning, as we know, however painful it may be, comes to a spontaneous end. When it has renounced everything that has been lost, then it has consumed itself, and our libido is once more free (in so far as we are still young and active) to replace the lost objects by fresh ones equally or still more precious" (*S.E.* 14:307). He was no less unambiguous in his magisterial 1917 essay "Mourning and Melancholia," which is essential reading for anyone who wishes to learn more about bereavement. Indeed, two of the memoirists in my study, Donald Hall and Joan Didion, both turn to this brief essay—it is only fifteen pages long—in an effort to understand their own grief. An extension of his 1914 essay "On Narcissism," "Mourning and Melancholia" is Freud's most influential theorizing on grief, and he offers here a detailed description of depression, including its link to mourning. To avoid melancholy, Freud speculates, the living must give up all connection with the dead. "Reality-testing has shown that the loved object no longer exists, and it proceeds to demand that all libido shall be withdrawn from its attachments to that object" (*S.E.* 14:244). The withdrawal of libido, or "decathexis" of energy, is necessary so that the "ego becomes free and uninhibited again." Otherwise, the psychoanalyst warns, using one of his most suggestive metaphors, the "shadow of the object" will fall upon the ego, resulting in depression. "Mourning and Melancholia" casts much light on the psychological dynamics of depression and suicide, in which the ego's aggression toward an object—another person—is internalized, resulting in murderous self-aggression.

Freud was no stranger to mourning. In 1920 his daughter Sophie Halberstadt died at the age of twenty-six, and three years later her son Heinz died of miliary tuberculosis at the age of four and a half. According to the biographer Ernest Jones, Freud was devastated by his grandson's death. "It was the only occasion in his life when Freud was known to have shed tears. He told me afterward that this loss had affected him in a way different from any of the others he had suffered. They had brought about sheer pain, but this one had killed something in him for good" (Jones, *Life and Work* 3:96). It was out of character for the stoical Freud to cry, and he believed that the only way to survive a crushing loss was to renounce all ties to the dead.

Freud views bereavement in terms of his early libido theory, not in terms of the internal system of object relations theorized by later psychoanalysts. To his credit, he did not pathologize grief, but he felt that it disappeared quickly in "normal" mourning. In *Notes upon a Case of Obsessional Neurosis* (1909), better known as the story of the Rat Man, Freud tells his patient that "a normal period of mourning would last from one year to two years, a pathological one . . . would last indefinitely" (*S.E.* 10:186). He concedes in "Mourning and Melancholia" that "people never willingly abandon a libidinal position, not even, indeed, when a substitute is already beckoning to them," but he nevertheless concludes that "normally, respect for reality gains the day" (*S.E.*14:244). The "work of mourning" occurs when "each single one of the memories and expectations in which the libido is bound to the object is brought up and hypercathected, and detachment of the libido is accomplished in respect of it" (*S.E.* 14:245)—like erasing a computer's hard drive of all its data.

For decades clinicians accepted Freud's view of mourning. For example, in the first edition of *Grief Counseling and Grief Therapy* (1982), J. William Worden agrees with Freud and lists one of the "tasks of mourning" as "withdrawing emotional energy from the deceased and reinvesting it in another relationship." In the third edition (2002), however, Worden reverses himself and concludes that Freud was mistaken about the mourner's need to shatter the relational bond with the deceased. "We now know that people do not decathect from the dead but find ways to develop 'continuing bonds' with the deceased" (35). Worden now suggests, contrary to Freud, that one of the tasks of mourning "is to find a place for the deceased that will enable the mourner to be connected with the deceased but in a way that will not preclude him or her from getting on with life. We need to find ways to memorialize the dead, that is, to remember the dead loved one—keeping them with us but still going on with life" (35).

Other contemporary theorists and clinicians agree with Worden's revised position. Stephen Shuchter and Sidney Zisook argue that it is not only undesirable but also impossible for many people to break their attachment with the dead. "The continued emotional or spiritual existence of the dead spouse becomes one of the most powerful means of containing the potentially overwhelming emotions of grief" (303). The task of mourning, they conclude, is to "find a way of continuing the relationship with their dead spouse that allows both an 'appropriate' experience of grief and a continuing involvement in living" (303). Psychoanalytically oriented clinicians have adopted a new paradigm of mourning, one that recognizes, as Marilyn McCabe explains in *The Paradox of Loss*, "both that the lost other is an ongoing part of our existence, and that the *processes* of relationship continue to be reintegrated, transferred, rejuvenated, and transformed. These relational processes are part of a verbal and nonverbal, tacit and conscious narrative that helps us reconstruct our selves and our lives in the experience of profound loss" (13; emphasis in original).

One of the major proponents of the new "continuing bonds" theory is Dennis Klass, who, along with Phyllis R. Silverman and Steven L. Nickman, edited the noteworthy 1996 volume *Continuing Bonds*, which emphasizes an attachment theory approach to bereavement. The editors cite playwright Robert Anderson's statement, expressed after the death of his first wife, that "death ends a life, but it does not end a relationship, which struggles on in the survivor's mind toward some resolution which it never finds" (17). Klass, Silverman, and Nickman point out that there was little clinical or empirical basis for Freud's theory of bereavement. Rather, he generalized from his own experience. His belief that renunciation was all left him ill prepared for future losses. "After important deaths, Freud seemed unable to find new attachments and unable to find a sense of transcendent connection that he seemed to think necessary if his bond with the deceased were to be continued" (6). Based on their own research, Klass, Silverman, and Nickman conclude that "survivors hold the deceased in loving memory for long periods, often forever, and that maintaining an inner representation of the deceased is normal rather than abnormal" (349). Hope Edelman points out in *Motherless Daughters* that 80 percent of the 154 motherless women surveyed for her book indicated they were still mourning their mothers, even though the deaths had occurred an average of twenty-four years ago (23). Many feminist literary critics, David Kennedy suggests in his book *Elegy*, have also questioned the Freudian theory of bereavement, preferring instead a model based on attachment (85).

Clinicians continue to debate whether the bereaved should let go of or hold onto their attachment to the deceased, and the jury is still out whether the old Freudian decathexis approach or the new continuing bonds approach is more helpful in overcoming grief. Some researchers believe that the continuing bonds theory has become a new clinical orthodoxy that is as misguided as the Freudian decathexis theory it replaced. Because it is not easy to test clinically which approach is better for a survivor's well being, the debate is likely to continue. Some people may do better breaking their attachments to the deceased while others may do better maintaining their attachments. There may also be a middle position between these two extremes. For example, thanatologists Margaret Stroebe and Henk Schut argue for what they call a "dual process model" of bereavement in which the bereaved oscillate between letting go of and holding on to their attachments. Successful coping implies, for Stroebe and Schut, an "alternation between loss- and restoration-oriented coping, the process of juxtaposition of confrontation and avoidance of different stressors associated with bereavement. At times the bereaved will be confronted by their loss, at other times they will avoid memories, be distracted, or seek relief by concentration on other things" (215–16). As we shall see, the memoirists in my study maintain their attachments to the deceased while attending to the everyday realities of life—including writing, which is one of the most challenging activities.

A relational model implies that we share all emotions, not simply grief. Robert C. Solomon, a philosopher who has written several books on the importance of emotions, suggests that "grief, laughter, and happiness are all emotions that are most meaningful when they are shared. This is not the prevalent view, at least in much of our own culture" (*True to Our Own Feelings* 72–73). Solomon also points out that grief is not simply a way of bemoaning loss but "*also a way of keeping the love alive*" (74; emphasis in original). Solomon agrees with Daniel Goleman's belief in "emotional intelligence," as set forth in his best-selling book of that title, but unlike Goleman, he argues for an expanded meaning of the term, "that is, the essential conceptual and evaluative components of emotions, their insights, and not just their 'regulation'" (164). Academics are famously dismissive of emotion, subordinating it to the intellect. They would be surprised by the statement of one of the twentieth century's greatest mathematicians, logicians, and philosophers, Alfred North Whitehead: "Ninety percent of our lives . . . is governed by emotion. Our brains merely register and act upon what is telegraphed to them by our bodily experience. Intellect is to emotion as our clothes are to our bodies: we could not very well have civilized life without clothes, but we would be in a poor way if we had only clothes without bodies" (188).

I can imagine no better way to maintain our attachment to the dead, our continuing *emotional* bond, than by writing about them. Even if the loved object exists only in memory, that precious memory must be preserved for those who are alive and those who are not yet born. Far from being escapists, memoirists engage in reality-testing when they write about their deceased spouses, for they create a verbal portrait of their loved ones that others may read and remember, and from which they may draw inspiration. Writing my memoir about Barbara became not only my major "task of mourning" but also a sacred death ritual, one that I practiced every day for the eighteen months it took me to write *Dying to Teach*. Writing about one's deceased spouse allows the memoirist to bring the spouse back to life verbally, while at the same time forging new attachments to others. Memoirs of spousal loss are emotionally charged—I can think of no literary genre more fraught with intense and at times explosive feeling—and those readers who are themselves bereft may find themselves weeping. And yet they may find that their tears are not only of sorrow but also of joy as they recall, in pain and in pleasure, the time when their loved ones were present in their lives.

I begin my study with *A Grief Observed*, for it is not only the most famous memoir of spousal loss but also the one to which later memoirists refer. Along with Tolstoy's *The Death of Ivan Ilych*, *A Grief Observed* is probably the most cited story in bereavement studies. Insights abound in this slender volume. Lewis reminds us that grief is not a state of mind but a process, and he chronicles the different emotions he experiences, ranging from anger and depression to joyful acceptance. I didn't experience a crisis of religious faith when my wife died, as he did when his wife died, only because I had no religious faith to lose. But like him, I struggled with the dark emotions of grief that threatened to obliterate the many joyous memories Barbara and I shared together during our marriage. As a secular Jew, I had difficulty sympathizing with Davidman's rejection of her Judaism and her conversion to combative evangelical Christianity, yet I admire her courage and strength in accepting her death, which ended their brief but deeply fulfilling marriage. I also admire Lewis's unwavering devotion to her, including his decision to write about her death. An exemplary caregiver, as we can see from his letters, he was not afraid to disclose the unruly emotions that would be judged as spiritually incorrect, including despair and anger toward God. As a professor he could be abrupt and condescending, yet suffering deepened his compassion, and he was never too tired or self-preoccupied to offer heartfelt advice to those who wrote him for counsel. Unsympathetic to psychoanalysis, which he felt addresses psychological issues at the expense of more important spiritual ones, he nevertheless had a keen understanding of the mind, as when he observes, "I have learned now that while those who speak about one's miseries usually hurt one, those who keep silent hurt more" (*Collected Letters* 3:1102). Lewis reminds us that however much we may wish to imagine ourselves as larger than life tragic figures, suffering interminably for our lost loved one, like Heathcliff in *Wuthering Heights*, we must avoid the Victorian process of mummification. We honor the dead not by grieving for them but by affirming our companionship in joy with them.

Following Lewis, I turn to John Bayley's three memoirs about his wife, Iris Murdoch, whose brilliant novelistic career was cut short by Alzheimer's disease. Both Murdoch and Bayley were distinguished writers, the former one of the most honored English novelists of the twentieth century, the latter an eminent literary critic and the Wharton Professor of Literature at Oxford. Both were skeptical of autobiographical writing; the idea of autobiography "is utterly unattractive to me as an art form," Murdoch wrote, "and also somehow morally sickening" (qtd. in Conradi, *Iris Murdoch* 529). Given their distaste for personal writing, it is ironic that Bayley wrote a trilogy of memoirs about his wife's illness: *Elegy for Iris* (1999), *Iris and Her Friends* (2000), and *Widower's House* (2001). There are other ironies worth noting. "How boring bereaved people are. They have only one subject," Murdoch wrote in a 1953 diary entry after the death of a close friend (qtd. in Conradi, *Iris Murdoch* 340). In her 1974 novel *The Sacred and Profane Love Machine*, a character observes that "bereavement is a darkness impenetrable to the imagination of the unbereaved, and later forgotten when the bereaved one recovers" (30–31). Disproving these two statements, Bayley brings rare insight to the plights of the bereaver and caregiver—and his writings are never boring.

Bayley's three memoirs are extraordinary in many ways. He offers us the survival strategies for long-term caregiving, including taking both short-term and long-term views of life. He also knows about the survival value of a comic vision of life: "Humour seems to survive anything" (*Elegy for Iris* 51). Bayley would almost certainly agree with Amos Oz's observation in *A Tale of Love and Darkness* (2003): "If you have no more tears to weep, then don't weep. Laugh" (75). Other survival strategies include retreating into one's memory and fantasy life, which become not only pleasurable forms of escape but also essential for the caregiver's health. As his wife's illness worsens, he must not only speak and write for her but also manage every detail of her life. He shows us how writing is a form of caregiving—and how they both require an ethics of caring. *Elegy for Iris* describes a forty-four-year marriage that depended, paradoxically, on separation: "Apartness in marriage is a state of love, and not a function of distance, or preference, or practicality" (127). Alzheimer's shatters this apartness, creating a suffocating togetherness that becomes at times unbearable for the caregiver. Bayley's memoirs reveal an unflinching portrait of the cruel ravages of dementia, a disease that is often more devastating for the caregiver than for the patient. Bayley portrays himself throughout the memoirs as self-effacing and often clueless, yet he remains an admirable figure, a caregiver who remains attentive to his wife's physical and psychological needs while at the same time transmuting her past and present life into the stuff of art.

We learn less about Iris in the second memoir, *Iris and Her Friends*, and more about Bayley's motives for writing, including the desire to prevent her from becoming an empty character, a "she" devoid of consciousness. His worst moments occur toward the end of the memoir, when he fears he has lost his muse: "I can do nothing without her. Without her, I shall have nothing to write, and nothing to do" (265). But this fear proves to be unfounded, as we see in the final volume of the trilogy, *Widower's House*, a comic description of his post-Iris years. Notwithstanding his new self-pity, he remains an ironist and paradoxicalist, surprising us with statements such as "how much I had suffered lately from [friends'] kindness, and from goodness" (18). Alternating between a farcical and somber tone, the memoir describes how he is pursued by two women who do their best to attend to his emotional, physical, and sexual needs. The narration of his sexual misadventures is hilarious—and unexpected in a book about bereavement. Portraying himself as a widower under siege, he ends the memoir by falling in love with an old friend who has also lost a spouse. She, too, has been living in grief's aftermath. He feels no existential guilt about remarriage, partly because his new wife was also a close friend of Iris, and partly because, as he tells us, the spirit of Iris is always with them.

"Art is created against death," Donald Hall states in his 1978 book *Goatfoot Milktongue Twinbird* (16). Hall would probably agree with Auden's observation that "writing begins from the sense of separateness in time, of 'I'm here to-day, but I shall be dead to-morrow, and you will be active in my place, and how can I speak to you?'" (*English Auden*

305–6). Nowhere is this better seen than in *The Best Day the Worst Day*, Hall's memoir about his life with fellow poet Jane Kenyon. A constant theme throughout Hall's long career is the therapeutic value of work, in his case, writing, which produces for him a state of "absorbedness" that allows him temporarily to forget the fears and worries that might otherwise paralyze him. Nineteen years younger than Hall, Kenyon began as an undergraduate in his poetry course at the University of Michigan, then became his wife, and, during their twenty-three-year marriage, grew to be his literary equal. During her final days, as she lay dying from leukemia, she and Hall worked on selecting her posthumous collection of verse—he was her teacher, mentor, husband, editor, and caregiver, nursing both the poet and her poetry. In 1998, three years after her death, he published his haunting volume of poems aptly called *Without*, which he dedicated to her memory. Then came his memoir *The Best Day the Worst Day* in 2005. "It took me half my life, more than half, to discover with Jane's guidance that two people could live together and remain kind" (111).

Hall excels as a poet and a prose writer, and *Without* and *The Best Day the Worst Day* are unrivaled in conveying the intimacy of two lovers who are losing each other. Unlike C. S. Lewis and John Bayley, who don't reveal their dying wives' thoughts and feelings, Hall does. For this reason, his memoir is more emotionally charged than theirs, more agonizing to read. *The Best Day the Worst Day* also explores Kenyon's long history of mood disorders. In affirming the adaptive implications of manic depression, Hall champions her creativity, in the process revealing his deep empathic understanding of her life and art. There are several parallels between Hall and Bayley. They both know the survival value of humor; Hall can find irony and comedy during the darkest moments of his and Kenyon's lives. He is no less inspirational than Bayley: *The Best Day the Worst Day* offers insights into bereavement that will prove helpful to the bereft. Kenyon and Murdoch remain, for Hall and Bayley, respectively, muses in life and in death. Like Bayley, Hall informs us, near the end of his memoir, that he has fallen in love with a new woman. The announcement is brief, cryptic, and awkward, suggesting that it is not easy, existentially or aesthetically, to reveal that one has found a new companion after the death of a beloved spouse.

Unlike Bayley's trilogy of memoirs and Hall's *The Best Day the Worst*

Day, Joan Didion's celebrated memoir *The Year of Magical Thinking* (2005) reveals little about her nearly forty-year marriage to John Gregory Dunne. What we do learn suggests that it was not an emotionally intimate union. To discover more about how they viewed marriage, I turn to their many fictional and nonfictional books, especially Dunne's, which offer us fascinating insights into their marriage. Like Bayley, Didion read all of her spouse's books after his death in an effort to make sense of their life together, and if we follow her footsteps, we reach a deeper understanding of their marriage, including its many tense and embattled moments. Based on Didion's comments in *The Year of Magical Thinking* and Dunne's comments in the autobiographical *Vegas* (1974) and *Harp* (1989), their marriage was often conflicted, more so than the other marriages in the memoirs under study. In *The Year of Magical Thinking* Didion denies there was competition between the two writers, but in *Harp* Dunne talks about how they were both artistic "scavengers" exploiting material from anyone's life, including their spouse's, for a story.

In a striking example of life imitating art, for years Dunne had used his writings to rehearse his death from cardiac failure, a problem that proves fatal to many of the fictional characters with whom he most closely identifies. These fictional deaths are sudden and unexpected, like his father's death from cardiac failure in his early fifties—and, years later—his own death from the same cause. Some of these fictional deaths from cardiac arrest foreshadow with eerie accuracy his own death decades later. Stunned by the news in his mid-fifties that he would die unless he had immediate bypass surgery, Dunne mined this rich material in several of his fictional and nonfictional stories. However gloomy he was about the possibility of a catastrophic cardiovascular event, he recognized the artistic possibilities of using this material in his writing. A close reading of Dunne's and Didion's books reveals that each had a characteristic "beast in the jungle": fear of cardiac arrest for the former; free-floating anxiety combined with a dread of foreboding for the latter.

Writing becomes for Dunne a counterphobic act, which helps explain his need to return repeatedly in book after book to the subject of cardiac death. His stories also reveal his insights into bereavement, a subject that Didion began to research after his death in an effort to understand whether her own spousal grief is "normal" or "pathological." Like Hall, she turns to Freud's "Mourning and Melancholia" to understand the link between bereavement and clinical depression, though she remains far more wary of psychoanalysis than Hall. Like Jane Kenyon, Didion writes candidly about her own history of depression. She includes in *The White Album* (1979) a passage from her psychiatric profile when she entered the outpatient clinic of a California hospital for an attack of vertigo and nausea in 1968. The profile describes her as a "personality in process of deterioration with abundant signs of failing defenses and increasing inability of the ego to mediate the world of reality and to cope with normal stress." Interestingly, the characterization merges with her own self-characterization in *The Year of Magical Thinking*—though no one would call what she experiences "normal stress." Her memoir remains, of all those that focus on the deceased spouse, the most self-blaming, despite the fact there was nothing she could have done to prevent her husband's sudden death.

Calvin Trillin's memoir *About Alice* (2006) could not be more different from those written by C. S. Lewis, John Bayley, Donald Hall, and Joan Didion. Unlike them, he doesn't describe the impact of his wife's illness on his life or any of the emotions he experienced following her death at age sixty-three on September 11, 2001. There is not a word about his companionship in grief or his year of magical thinking, if he had one. Instead, he offers us less a portrait than a poignant glimpse of a remarkable woman who was his wife, the mother of his two daughters, and his muse, the woman he "wrote everything for."

Trillin observes in *About Alice* that many grateful readers wrote him letters after her death expressing the belief they knew Alice. But they didn't know her, he maintains. A "moderate" self-discloser, as he describes himself in his book *Family Man* (1998), he generally mentions his wife and two daughters only in his writings on food, travel, and lighthearted domestic dramas. He quotes her as describing herself as an "incorrigible, even ridiculous optimist," and that's how he portrays her in *About Alice* (69), but in her own writings she comes across as much more cautious and subdued, hopeful about life but with a heightened awareness of the precariousness of health. This aspect of her life does not come out in her husband's writings, but it is evident everywhere in her own writings. Unlike her husband, she gravitated toward painful personal subjects that most writers avoid—and what subject could awaken more dread than metastatic cancer? She survived lung cancer, though she was given only a 10 percent chance of recovery at the time of her diagnosis in the late 1970s. Ironically, the radiation therapy that saved her life was also responsible for weakening her heart twenty-five years later, and she died of congestive heart failure while awaiting heart transplant surgery. *About Alice* is a story of love, death, and gratitude for the extra twenty-five years husband and wife had together.

Four of the five memoirists in my study are men. This is not surprising if we consider that, as William Zinsser reports in *Inventing the Truth*, "eight autobiographies have been written by men for every one written by a woman" in the twentieth century (21). That so many men, and so few women, should write memoirs about spousal loss *is* surprising when we consider that there are many more widows than widowers. Why are most memoirs about spousal loss written by men? I'm not sure. Except for conspicuous exceptions such as Elisabeth Kübler-Ross, the overwhelming majority of clinicians and scholars who have written about death, dying, and bereavement are also men, and most of the researchers I cite are men.

If space allowed, I would have included in my study the writings of the renowned American poet and literary critic Sandra M. Gilbert. Her memoir about her husband's death while recovering from routine prostate cancer surgery, *Wrongful Death* (1995), followed by her volume of poetry exploring her stages of grief, *Ghost Volcano* (1997), both deserve further study. She has continued to explore literary representations of death, editing a book of elegies titled *Inventions of Farewell* and then authoring her groundbreaking book *Death's Door* (2006), in which she acknowledges that she wrote *Wrongful Death* and *Ghost Volcano* with a "testimonial passion that took me by surprise. Thus in the memoir I became a witness as well as the commentator I'd have been in a literary-critical work; in the poems I became not just a witness, as poets often are, but a journalist of my own sorrow, carefully dating and placing a number of my verses as I rarely had in the past" (xix). I suspect that all of the writers in my study would agree with Gilbert's need to "*claim* my grief and—almost defiantly—to *name* its particulars because I found myself confronting the shock of bereavement at a historical moment when death was in some sense unspeakable and grief—or anyway the expression of grief—was at best an embarrassment, at worst a social solecism or scandal" (xix; emphasis in original). I identify with her testimonial passion as well as her continuing need to write about death.

"For all who mourn dead spouses, lovers, partners," Gilbert writes from anguished personal experience in *Inventions of Farewell*, "the world seems to have been split apart, with massive absence replacing what had been passionate presence" (231). The spousal loss memoir is part of a long and growing tradition of elegies and grief memoirs. In his famous 1949 memoir *Death Be Not Proud*, John Gunther writes about his seventeen-year-old son's death from brain cancer. Simone de Beauvoir's 1984 book *Adieu* describes her long relationship with Jean-Paul Sartre, whose death she chronicles in the book. Several writers memorialize a parent's death: to cite only two examples, Philip Roth's *Patrimony* is a moving account of his father's death, and *Bequest and Betrayal* is Nancy K. Miller's story about her mother's death. Douglas Dunn's 1985 *Elegies* consists of thirty-nine short poems that commemorate his first wife, who died in 1981 at the age of thirty-seven. Ted Hughes's *Birthday Letters*, posthumously published in 1998 on the thirty-fifth anniversary of Sylvia Plath's suicide, dramatizes his tormented feelings about their marriage. Poems like "Blackbird" reveal the bitter legacy—or illegacy—of suicide: "You were the jailor of your murderer—/Which imprisoned you./And since I was your nurse and protector/Your sentence was mine too" (162). Ruth Stone's 1991 volume *Who Is the Widow's Muse?* pays tribute to her husband, who committed suicide in 1959. "In my thirty years of knowing you,/cell by cell in my widow's shawl," Stone writes in her 2002 poem "Getting to Know You," "we have lived together longer/in the discontinuous films of my sleep/than we did in our warm parasitical bodies" (*What Love Comes To* 309). Paul Monette's *Borrowed Time* and Mark Doty's *Heaven's Coast* both memorialize gay partners who died of AIDS. All of these memoirs and poems are elegiac in mood and portray a wide spectrum of emotions ranging from sorrow to joy.

Two memoirs focus on the deaths of professors. Mitch Albom's enormously popular *Tuesdays with Morrie* explores the life lessons gleaned from his sociology professor Morrie Schwartz's battle with Lou Gehrig's disease, while Randy Pausch's *The Last Lecture* chronicles his struggle with pancreatic cancer. A computer science professor at Carnegie Mellon, Pausch is relentlessly optimistic, which perhaps accounts for the book's commercial success: "I'm dying and I'm having fun," he writes near the end of his story. "And I'm going to keep having fun every day I have left. Because there's no other way to play it" (179). Both of these books have a pedagogical focus, recalling Montaigne's observation: "If I were a maker of books I should compile a register, with comments, of different deaths. He who should teach men to die, would teach them to live" (84).

Many literary scholars have pointed out that the memoir has become the dominant narrative genre of our time. "This is the age of the memoir," William Zinsser declares at the beginning of *Inventing the Truth*. "Never have personal narratives gushed so profusely from the American soil as in the closing decade of the twentieth century. Everyone has a story to tell, and everyone is telling it" (3). This popularity, Zinsser cautions, has a dark side. "The national appetite for true confession has loosed a torrent of emotions that are little more than therapy, the authors bashing their parents and wallowing in the lurid details of their tussle with drink, drug addiction, rape, sexual abuse, incest, anorexia, obesity, codependency, depression, attempted suicide, and other fashionable talk-show syndromes" (5). Memoirists of spousal loss confront some of these problems, yet those in my study avoid sensationalism. As F. Scott Fitzgerald observes ruefully in his autobiographical *The Crack-Up* (1956), "There are always those to whom all self-revelation is contemptible, unless it ends with a noble thanks to the gods for the Unconquerable Soul." One cannot magically banish self-pity from one's life or art following the loss of the most important person in one's life, but one can remain aware of it—and wary of it. To guard against self-pity, memoirists use irony, paradox, and self-lacerating humor, all of which allow them to escape, if only momentarily, from the self-absorption that often accompanies loss.

Other literary scholars share Zinsser's dismissal of memoirs that are "little more than therapy." Sven Birkerts is sympathetic to the memoir while conceding that the genre is symptomatic of our therapeutic self-help culture. "Were you abused, neglected, discriminated against; did you turn in your pain to pills, drink, or satanic cults? Write a memoir!" I agree with his conclusion that "we cannot allow the many to wreck things for the few" (7). Surely there is a distinction between well-crafted memoirs and lurid confessions. Many literary critics scorn "self-help" books, objecting to their oversimplifications and psychobabble. Nevertheless, the bereaved need all the help they can get. Memoirs can be well crafted *and* offer insights into love and loss that may prove clinically helpful to readers. Even Birkerts acknowledges this: "My own memoir was very much a coming-of-age saga, and the writing process turned out to be a kind of detached psychotherapy (though, alas, it did not eliminate either the need for or interest in the more expensive kind)" (55). Thomas Larson, the author of *The Memoir and the Memoirist*, similarly observes that writing was therapeutic to him during a crisis: "I don't think it's an overstatement to say that, during the mid-1980s, I got myself through the pain and back to sanity by writing" (5). Bereavement remains the "single most important and universal emotional crisis to which our patients will be exposed (Wiener et al. 53), and the death of a spouse remains the most life-changing event on the "social readjustment scale" devised by Thomas Holmes and Richard Rahe. Barbara and I saw a psychotherapist during her illness to help us cope with our fears of dying, but after her death, reading and writing about bereavement became my main therapy.

Paradoxically, I was so absorbed in writing *Dying to Teach* that I found myself released from grief, at least for most of the time. In order to avoid thinking about grief, Collin Murray Parkes suggests paradoxically, we have to think about it (41). I have long believed in the idea of "writing as rescue," the title of my early book on Joseph Conrad. One of my favorite quotations comes from Conrad's late novel *Chance*: "To be busy with material affairs is the best preservative against reflection, fears, doubts—all these things which stand in the way of achievement. I suppose a fellow proposing to cut his throat would experience a sort of relief while occupied in stropping his razor carefully" (340). I didn't write *Dying to Teach* to feel better—I would have written it even if it felt like I was banging my head against the wall—but I did feel better, an unexpected and welcome side effect. In fact, after I finished the memoir, it was harder *not* to write about Barbara. That is why I immediately began another book. Significantly, nearly all of the memoirists of spousal loss also acknowledged feeling better as a result of writing. No one reported feeling worse. This is consistent with the groundbreaking research of James Pennebaker, who has demonstrated conclusively in a series of carefully designed studies that writing about emotional experiences produces significant improvements in one's physical and mental health.

Both psychotherapy and literature, the talking cure and the writing cure, respectively, are more closely interconnected than most people realize. Both involve what Thomas Attig calls "relearning the world." Both involve, as narrative psychologists point out, telling and retelling stories, examining experience from multiple points of view, exploring complex and often contradictory motivation, analyzing one's assumptive world, and revising interpretations to discover healthy and constructive ways to engage reality. Both involve, in short, reauthoring and restorying our lives. As Robert Neimeyer has suggested, one of the new strategies for grief therapy is using narratives to "facilitate the re-authoring of the self in the wake of loss" (180). Neimeyer cites two examples of narrative techniques that are relevant for grief therapy, personal journals and unsent letters. A third example, for those who are able to engage in more ambitious writing projects, is a spousal loss memoir. A memoir is a "prophylactic against forgetting," as Thomas Larson observes (96), a way to capture the truth of one's feelings at a particular time.

And yet to acknowledge—and enjoy—a therapeutic benefit of writing about loss is, curiously, to incur the suspicion of those literary critics who believe that writing is more about wounding than healing. This grim view may be seen in some of the books published in the last twenty-five years on the elegy, a close cousin of the spousal loss memoir. In *Mourning and Panegyric* (1988), Celeste Marguerite Schenck dismisses Ellen Zetzel Lambert's statement in *Placing Sorrow* (1976) that the pastoral elegist can "win his release from suffering" (xiii). The title of Melissa F. Zeiger's 1997 book *Beyond Consolation* reveals her belief that the eulogy does not lead to resignation or comfort. In *Poetry of Mourning* (1994), Jahan Ramazani disagrees with Peter Sacks's statement in *The English Elegy* (1985) that one function of the elegy "is to set free the energy locked in grief or rage and to organize its movement in the form of a question that is not merely an expression of ignorance but a voicing of protest" (22). According to Ramazani, "The modern elegist tends not to achieve but to resist consolation, not to override but to sustain anger, not to heal but to reopen the wounds of loss" (xi). And yet in the coda he makes a telling admission: "But I fear that, despite melancholic modernism, this book may have been driven to its quasi-redemptive close by the narratological imperatives of consolation" (361).

"So what does the memoirist want?" Gore Vidal asks in his preface to

The Norton Book of American Autobiography. "Proof that he was there, that wherever he was, is" (9). A similar answer is true for memoirists of spousal loss. They want—and create—the proof that their deceased spouses were there, fully alive and healthy, enriching the memoirists' lives in innumerable ways. The memoirists could not prevent their spouses from dying—they did not write what Kathlyn Conway calls "triumph narratives" characteristic of so many illness stories—but they showed they could write stories that honor their spouse's memory. The memoirists also demonstrate the link between loss and creativity. "Grief needs an outlet," Hope Edelman writes; "creativity offers one. Some psychiatrists see mourning and creativity as the perfect marriage, with the thought processes of one neatly complementing the other" (265). Nowhere is the marriage between mourning and creativity better seen than in the five marriages discussed in this book. Transforming sorrow into joy, absence into presence, the spousal loss memoirists create a lasting bond that connects the living with the dead, a bond from which future generations may draw hope, inspiration, and strength.

ONE

C. S. LEWIS AND JOY DAVIDMAN

"Never Have I Loved Her More than since She Was Struck Down"

Clive Staples Lewis, known to his relatives and friends as "Jack" and to the rest of the world as C. S. Lewis, was one of the most prolific and influential writers of the twentieth century. He was the most famous "Christian apologist"—that is, defender of the Christian faith—of the century. A Renaissance man, he wrote dozens of books on a wide variety of subjects: literary criticism (including medieval and Renaissance literature), theology, poetry, fiction, science fiction, mythology, fantasy, children's stories (including the hugely popular *Chronicles of Narnia*), aesthetics, allegory, and philology. A fellow and tutor in English literature at Oxford until 1954, when he was elected chair of Medieval and Renaissance Literature at Cambridge, he wrote most of his books not for the specialist but for the common reader. "For one stretch during World War II," James T. Como writes, "his was the second most recognized voice (after Churchill's) on the BBC" (xxi). He made the cover of *Time* magazine on September 8, 1947, for the publication of his 1942 book *The Screwtape Letters*; he was cited as "one of the most influential spokesmen for Christianity in the English-speaking world." Joe R. Christopher observed in 1987 that "Lewis is the rare example of a writer almost all of whose sixty-some books are in print twenty years after his death" (127). Lewis's books have been translated into dozens of languages and have sold millions of copies—the *Narnia* books alone have sold more than 100 million copies. His 1950 children's story *The Lion, the Witch, and the Wardrobe* was made into a Disney film in 2005. Lewis scholarship has been an academic growth industry that shows no signs of recession. The same is true of his Christian writings, which have an enduring popularity that would have stunned him.

My first experience with C. S. Lewis occurred in 2004, shortly before Barbara's death, when I read *A Grief Observed*, his heartrending memoir about the death of his beloved wife, Joy Davidman. I then taught the book in 2006 in a course called Love and Loss. *A Grief Observed* has become a classic in the literature of bereavement: memoirists who write about spousal loss often refer to this slender volume, which can be read in a couple of hours. The book piqued my interest, for although we learn a great deal from it about the nature of grief following spousal loss, we learn little about Davidman's life prior to their marriage in 1956 or their life together until her death from bone cancer in 1960. At the time of their marriage he was fifty-seven; she, forty-one. He survived her by only three years, dying on November 22, 1963, the same day President John F. Kennedy was assassinated—and the same day that Barbara and I had our first date together when we were college freshmen. (It was also the death day of Aldous Huxley, the author of *Brave New World*.) *A Grief Observed* dramatizes Lewis's religious crisis following her death, but it leaves us in the dark about the kind of person she was, why they were attracted to each other, and their impact on each other. An intensely private man, Lewis published the memoir in 1961 under the pseudonym "N. W. Clerk," referring to his wife simply as "H," the initial of her first name, Helen, which she did not use. Why the secrecy? How did her death affect him? Why did he write the book? What role did writing play in his recovery from grief? And why has *A Grief Observed* exerted such a profound influence on later memoirists who write about spousal loss?

Born in New York City in 1915 to secular Jewish parents, Joy Davidman was academically precocious. She did her undergraduate work at Hunter College, graduating at the age of nineteen, earned a master's degree in English at Columbia University, and then taught high school English in New York City from 1935 to 1938. A gifted poet, she won the prestigious Yale Series of Younger Poets Award in 1938 for her volume *Letter to a Comrade*, which contained a foreword by Stephen Vincent Benét, who prophetically observed that one finds in her poems "plenty of indignation here, but not a willingness to accept frustration" (7). One year later *Letter to a Comrade* received the Russell Loines Award of the National Institute of Arts and Letters; the other winner was Robert Frost. In 1939 she worked as a screenwriter in Hollywood for Metro-Goldwyn-Mayer, writing four screenplays, none of which were used.

The experience left her cynical and disillusioned about popular culture. In 1942 she married the writer William Lindsay Gresham, with whom she had two children, David and Douglas. Her anthology *War Poems of the United Nations* was published in 1943. Her impressive first novel, *Anya*, about a young Jewish girl living in Soviet-dominated Ukraine at the end of the nineteenth century, appeared in 1940, and her second novel, *Weeping Bay*, set in a small French Canadian fishing village, was published a decade later. In 1948 she converted to evangelical Christianity, an experience that she describes in her 1951 essay "The Longest Way Round." In 1954 her last book appeared, *Smoke on the Mountain*, a reinterpretation of the Ten Commandments. Inspired by C. S. Lewis, who was largely responsible for her conversion, she wrote the book not long after meeting the man with whom she would soon spend the rest of her life.

Joy Davidman was a complicated and contradictory woman, a true believer who committed herself wholeheartedly first to atheism, then to Communism, and finally to Christianity. Each conversion repudiated her preceding belief system. For example, in *War Poems of the United Nations* she waxed poetic over the Soviet Union. "The Soviet policy of fostering the culture of each republic and independent region has enabled not only the Russian but also the Ukrainian, Georgian, Armenian, Kazak, Turkamen and Tatar peoples (to mention only a few) to enjoy an unprecedented flowering of the arts" (189). Within a few years she denounced Stalin's totalitarianism and repudiated her own involvement with the American Communist Party. In her novels, she recognized and embraced the messy ambiguity of everyday life; in her poetry anthology and religious writings, she reduced complex truths to black and white. There is nothing politically correct about *Anya* and little that is unambiguous about *Weeping Bay*, but *Smoke on the Mountain* insists on a religious purity that even the most devout believers would find challenging.

Davidman evoked strong feelings in those who knew her. Her relationships with her parents, brother, first husband, and friends were often turbulent and unstable. Much of what she preached in her writings she did not practice. One would never suspect from reading *Anya*, written when she was an atheistic Jew, that in a few years she would write another novel affirming the divinity of Jesus. Nor would one suspect from reading *Smoke on the Mountain*, which argues sternly against divorce and remarriage, that she would be divorced and remarried two years after completing the book, which was written while her first marriage was falling apart. The second marriage itself was controversial and, to some people, scandalous. She and Lewis were secretly married at the Registry Office in Oxford in a civil ceremony on April 23, 1956, ostensibly so that she and her two young children could remain in England. Many of Lewis's friends felt at the time that the brash American had manipulated the naive English bachelor into marriage. Then, when she lay dying in a hospital, they were married in a religious ceremony on March 21, 1957. Immediately following the religious ceremony, her cancer inexplicably went into remission. The story of their marriage is the stuff of melodrama, and yet there is no doubt that the union was joyous, the newlyweds affirming that their time together was nothing short of a miracle.

The marriage did not become famous until long after their deaths. Their life together became the subject of a 1986 award-winning British television film called *Shadowlands*, starring Joss Ackland and Claire Bloom. The BBC television film was adapted for the stage in London and New York in 1990–91 and was made into a major film directed by Richard Attenborough and costarring Anthony Hopkins and Debra Winger, both of whom received Oscar nominations. Despite this media attention, neither the film nor dramatic versions tell us much about Davidman's life before she met Lewis. We discover more about her in Lyle W. Dorsett's 1983 biography *And God Came In*. In celebrating her conversion to evangelical Christianity, however, he offers readers a highly biased point of view, one that tends to ignore the darker aspects of her personality. To learn more about this unusual woman, we may turn briefly to her writings, which reveal the many different sides of her character.

Anya

Dedicated to her mother, "who told me the story of Anya," Davidman's first novel begins in 1848 when the eponymous heroine is twelve years old, living in the Jewish section of Shpikov, a small town in Russian-dominated Ukraine. *Anya* is not autobiographical, but there are many parallels between the novelist and her fictional character: Anya's pride, vanity, willfulness, defiance, and unconventionality are reflections of her creator's personality. The early chapters of Anya's life focus on her parents' efforts to find a suitable husband for her, but it will not be easy for her to accept the severe constraints imposed on obedient Jewish girls. As the novel demonstrates, marriage during this time is motivated by economic rather than romantic considerations. "We are old," the parents think to themselves, "and soon we shall be very old; your father cannot forever keep the store when his bones ache in winter, and I, your mother, wish to sit in peace by my window. In peace we could sit, and die in honor, if our daughter had a husband" (27).

Anya brings her parents little peace even when she reluctantly accepts the proposal negotiated by the shadchan, the marriage broker, to wed the conventional Yankov, whom she does not love, and to forget about the disreputable Shimka, to whom she is attracted. To sabotage the union, she flirts with a Russian general, bringing shame upon her family and thus ending the engagement. Davidman's Lawrentian description of Anya riding the general's horse evokes her sexual awakening. "When the horse moved, Anya gripped its ribs with her legs, which felt warmer, and the beast's muscles ripped mellowly under her thighs" (57). Both Anya's father and fiancé are furious about the broken engagement. Yankov calls her an "adulteress" and a "harlot," and when she taunts him by declaring that Shimka has touched her body, he forces himself on her in an act that is close to rape. Afterward, when he realizes that he has penetrated a virgin, he screams that she made him do it, to which she unexpectedly replies, "'Yes. I made you do it,' . . . and she was surprised because she saw that this was true. She had meant him to take her; she had wanted to reduce her enemy to a ridiculous and abject squirming. She had forced him into the ridiculous antic of lust" (68).

Anya's desire to humiliate Yankov, even if it means humiliating herself, comes close to sadomasochism, and there are other such moments with different characters. During one of her early encounters with the sensual Shimka, she derives pleasure from inflicting pain upon her fellow Jews. "The presence of Jews, the outraged whispering of Jews, were as a sauce to her pleasure, and when by chance she came with Shimka into a lane empty of beholders their intimacies seemed to her mechanical and unreal. It is possible that Shimka was for her only the whip with which she lashed her people" (20). A few pages later we learn that "to give pain was pleasure, and it was pleasant also to be the breathless victim of such pain" (25). Years later, when she runs off with a Russian colonel of cavalry, she welcomes rough sex. "Then Muralov, with his face made at once coarse and fine by passion, set the fleshy heel of his hand upon her mouth and really beat her across the belly and thighs. But some obscure compunction in him kept him from hurting her very much, and the marks were gone in four days, so that at the time she liked it more than she suffered. She loved the look of his mouth, which he had forgotten to control" (210).

Anya knows how far she can go, however, without becoming self-destructive. She agrees to marry the meek Israel Spiegelglass, comically named "Cookeh" or "Cookeleh," whom she knows she can control, and with whom she quickly has a child, ironically named Yankov. Davidman's humorous description of the way in which the shadchan manipulates the helpless Cookeleh into marriage with Anya, who is close to an outcast at this point in the story, is masterful. "The greatest joy a cat has with a mouse is in luring its desires, offering it an avenue of escape, and after a moment flicking the mouse over on its back with a delicately balanced paw: if it is a fat mouse, a juicy meal, the tantalizing pleasures of this game make the cat's mouth run over with water. And thus it was with Schloime and the young man Cookeleh" (100). Anya is the cat with nine lives, able to survive any situation. And Davidman is the feline novelist, tantalizing readers as her character survives one harrowing ordeal after another. Anya feels no desire on her wedding night, "only a kind of cold eagerness to have the troublesome beginning of her married life over with" (128). She dispenses with the cumbersome sheitel, or wig, which respectable married Jewish women customarily wear, preferring instead to allow everyone to see her thick locks of hair. For a few months she seems to enjoy domestic contentment, but she finds herself drawn irresistibly to passionate men who make no emotional demands on her. She refuses to allow any man—her husband, her lovers, or Shimka, with whom she has a brief affair near the end of the novel—to dominate her. "No man shall have power over me," she thinks: "I shall not lie weeping for any man to comfort" (72).

Anya remains true to this inner vow. She leaves her husband three times, spending less than a month with the Russian colonel, a year with a grain merchant, and seven months with Shimka, who unexpectedly dies. Each time she returns to Cookeleh, she accepts his reproaches and easily resumes her married life as if nothing has happened. Defying conventional morality and propriety, she remains strangely unmoved when, returning home from the affair with the Russian colonel, she learns that her infant daughter has died three days earlier.

How does Davidman feel about Anya? For a first novel, the narrative distance is remarkably steady. She sees Anya with both sympathy and criticism: she is never too close to her character, as often happens in first novels, which tend to be autobiographical, nor is she too distant from her. Davidman's heroine is complex, often contradictory, and always fascinating. There is never a moment when Davidman idealizes or demonizes her protagonist. Nor does she shrink from describing Anya's unexpected rages and savage words, her defiance of society one moment followed by her craving for social acceptance the next moment, her contempt toward her hapless husband followed by gratitude when he allows her to return after her affairs with other men. There are moments when Davidman penetrates so deeply into Anya's consciousness that we wonder whether the novelist is writing about her own ambivalence toward love. "Love is lust, and hatred is lust. Love wishes to enslave the body of the beloved, that he may lie beneath the feet; hate wishes to commit passionate outrage upon the hated body. Love aspires to lie as a slave beneath the onslaught of the lover, and hate makes one submit in ecstasy to any defilement" (77–78).

Long before the rebirth of the feminist movement in the 1960s, Davidman seems to know what women want—satisfaction—and she shows what Anya is prepared to do to gain that satisfaction. Anya is an early portrait of a liberated woman, and although neither marriage, motherhood, nor illicit passion permanently satisfies her, she never gives up the search for self-fulfillment. Nor does she allow herself to be defeated by events that would break other women, such as the death of her first daughter, several miscarriages, and the loss of the community's respect. She is, finally, a survivor, an Anna Karenina who does not kill herself. As the story ends, she is still beautiful, still attractive to men, still hopeful about the future. Whether or not she believes in her confession and repentance after she returns home for the final time—"I have sinned. I have crawled in dust. I am filthy in the sight of the Lord" (292)—she convinces her husband to accompany her to America, the land of milk and honey. And she will go there with her young child, fathered by Shimka, a child she audaciously names "Avrom," after Abraham, the father of the Jewish people.

Can one infer from *Anya* that the novelist would convert to Christianity less than a decade after the publication of the novel? The evidence is inconclusive. The novel brings to life many of the colorful traditions of late nineteenth-century Russian Jewry, and it captures some of the darker details of Jewish life, such as Shimka's ambivalence toward his own religion. "The persecuted are arrogant, and the Jews had a terrible reason for such pride; the persecuted are also intolerant" (16). Anya shares this ambivalence, as does Davidman. There are many moments in the novel when Anya appears to be a Jewish anti-Semite, hating her own people whose customs and laws she rejects. In turn, the Jews regard her as a pariah, deepening her hatred. She feels no grief after her mother's death, and when the period of sitting shivah on the floor in mourning is over, she "took up the work of the household; she found it soothing, and it kept her from too much hate of the Jews" (85). Again and again she fears and mistrusts "the Jews," as if they are a single people. She expresses no interest in accepting or rejecting the Jewish God, and there is never a moment when she ponders the existence of an afterlife.

We cannot equate the author with her eponymous character, nor can we conclude that Anya's ambivalence toward her Jewishness foreshadows Davidman's conversion to Christianity. *Anya* is not a portrait of the artist as a young woman. We can say, however, that Davidman understands Anya's restlessness, her refusal to be like other Jewish wives and mothers, her willingness to incur the wrath of her people to follow her own interests. However we feel about Anya, she never gives up the search for the land of milk and honey, and she has the energy, resourcefulness, and determination to pursue the promised land wherever the path to it may lead.

"The Longest Way Round"

What would Anya's life be like in the United States? Would she embrace the land of milk and honey, or would she find life in the blossoming New World similar to that in the decaying Old World? Would she soon be disillusioned with American materialism and secularism? Would she find herself devoted to a new ideology or political movement? We can only speculate on the answers to these questions, but we know that Davidman became increasingly disillusioned with her country around the time *Anya* was published. It is hard to imagine the secular Anya converting to Christianity, but the story of Davidman's own conversion appears in her essay "The Longest Way Round," published in *These Found the Way*, a study of thirteen converts to "Protestant Christianity." Davidman's thirteen-page essay offers a wealth of information about her early uncritical acceptance of her parents' Jewish atheism, her gradual dissatisfaction with materialism, her flirtation with Communism, and her conversion to Christianity. She opens the essay by referring to a mystical experience when she was fourteen, when the "meaning of all things was revealed and the sacrament at the heart of all beauty lay bare." She sadly rejects the vision, however, because she was a "well-brought up, right-thinking child of materialism" for whom God did not exist (13). Her Jewish parents had come to the United States as children from small villages in eastern Europe; her father "retained the ethics of Judaism, the only 'real' part of it, and got rid of the theology," a position that Davidman later rejects as untenable, since she doesn't believe that a "*rational* morality" is possible (14; emphasis in original). "With no revealed law, no conviction of sin, no weekly reminder of shortcomings, no humility before God, no wonder at mystery, no hope of heaven, no help of grace—what can the best atheist do but turn Pharisee?" (15).

Davidman never comments on the irony that in converting from Judaism to Christianity, she was moving in the opposite direction from that of her paternal grandfather, who, as David Wesley Soper points out, "died of pneumonia contracted while preaching Judaism to the Gentiles on the streets of Manhattan's Lower East Side" (*These Found the Way* 78). After reading H. G. Wells's *Outline of History*, Davidman declared her atheism at the age of eight and found herself during the Great Depression believing "in nothing." She was outwardly a "hardy, cocksure young atheist," which was a "mask, a surface personality for dealing with the world" ("The Longest Way Round" 16)—not unlike, perhaps, Anya, who, reminiscent of T. S. Eliot's Prufrock, puts on a face to meet the faces that she meets. Behind Davidman's persona, however, was a "girl with vague eyes, who scribbled verses—scribbled them in a blind fury, not knowing what she wrote or why, and read them afterward with wonder" (16). Reading C. S. Lewis's *Pilgrim's Regress* and, years later, *The Screwtape Letters* and *The Great Divorce*, she came to see an undiscovered country beyond any earthly home, and she found herself in her early twenties wanting to do something with her life. The world was, she writes sardonically, out of joint, and so she joined the Communist Party. Her motives, she concedes, were mixed: "Youthful rebelliousness, youthful vanity, youthful contempt of the 'stupid people' who seemed to be running society, all these played a part" (19).

Communism appealed to Davidman's social conscience, her desire for solidarity with others, her desire to transform the world, but she slowly discovered, to her horror, that Marxist orthodoxy demanded strict allegiance to brutal policies. "By nature I am the sort of woman who nurses sick kittens and hates to spank her bad little boys; yet as a Marxist I would have been willing to shoot people without trial" ("The Longest Way Round" 21). She makes no reference to writing *Anya*, nor does she reveal that she used the party name "Nell Thulchin," which, as Soper informs us, was the name of the small Ukrainian village where her mother had lived as a child and the setting for *Anya* (*These Found the Way* 90). She does mention her marriage to William Lindsay Gresham in 1942 and the birth of their two sons. Motherhood left her with little time for the Communist Party. She found herself at a crossroads after her husband's "nervous breakdown," which she never describes in detail. "All my defenses—the walls of arrogance and cocksureness and self-love behind which I had hid from God—went down momentarily. And God came in" (23). Feeling "more alive than I had ever been," she found herself forgiving some of her enemies, praying to God—"I must have been the world's most astonished atheist"—and returning to the writings of C. S. Lewis, from whom she learned, slowly, "how I had gone wrong" (23–24).

As Dorsett indicates, there is much that Davidman omits in "The Longest Way Round." She doesn't discuss, for example, her stormy relationship with her parents and brother, who disapproved of her conversion. Nor does she discuss the deteriorating relationship with her alcoholic husband, who made little attempt to conceal from his wife his marital infidelity. Nor does she reveal the depths of her early commitment to the Communist Party. She not only tried to convert her friends to Communism but she also "espoused the Party line with the enthusiasm of a true believer" (Dorsett 47). Within a few years she embraced Christianity with the same evangelical fervor. A devout Christian himself, Dorsett welcomes her religious conversion, but he never comments on her all-or-nothing personality.

Along with her children, Davidman was baptized in 1948 in the Presbyterian church of Pleasant Plains near her home in Dutchess County, New York. She concludes "The Longest Way Round" with two wishes: to deepen her mystical knowledge of God, and to allow that knowledge to change her everyday life. Confessing that she has a "good deal of pride and anger" to overcome, she ends on a Voltarean note: to care for her husband, children, garden, and home—"and, perhaps to serve God in books and letters as best I can" (26).

Weeping Bay

Literary service to God came quickly in the form of *Weeping Bay*, her second and final novel. Reading it, I never would have guessed it was penned by the author of *Anya*, a novel that reveals no interest in religious or spiritual concerns. No one would consider *Anya* a Jewish novel, despite its wealth of details authenticating Jewish life in late nineteenth-century Russia, but *Weeping Bay* is an unabashedly Christian novel, written to proclaim the author's impassioned faith in Jesus. Set in Canada's Gaspé Peninsula, located at the eastern tip of the province of Quebec, the novel reflects Davidman's journey to Christianity that will lead to her momentous meeting with and marriage to C. S. Lewis.

Unlike *Anya*, which chronicles the life of a single character, *Weeping Bay* is less interested in character for its own sake than in dramatizing the forces that lead to dehumanization, despair, and premature death. The novel has a religious and political agenda that cannot be missed. Davidman never uses words like "evangelical Christianity," but her unrelenting opposition to Roman Catholicism is unmistakable. Church, state, and factory conspire to resist any attempt to improve the appalling social, political, and economic conditions in the poor industrial and fishing community. In its Dickensian outrage over the oppression and poverty of workers, *Weeping Bay* recalls *Hard Times*. It also recalls novels like Upton Sinclair's *The Jungle*, which publicized the inhumane treatment of American workers in meat packing plants. There is a muckraking zeal about *Weeping Bay* in its protest of the capitalist exploitation of workers, which leads to widespread suffering, especially among the most vulnerable members of society, children, who are starving because their parents don't earn enough money to feed them, and young women, who must resort to dangerous nonmedical abortions because of the unavailability of birth control. The novel attacks Roman Catholicism for its many excesses, including the construction of an extravagant church that has bankrupted the town, and its practice of selling indulgences, in which mourners are forced to contribute large sums of money to prevent the deceased from languishing in purgatory. The "flames of Purgatory are real flames," a priest declares, "yet they have this difference from the flames of this world, that they are extinguished not by water but by money" (78).

The visionary character in *Weeping Bay* is not a representative of the reactionary Roman Catholic Church, the corrupt town government, or the exploitive business community but a mysterious "carnival man" who embodies Davidman's faith in Jesus. (Her choice of a carnival man may have been influenced by *Nightmare Abbey*, William Gresham's 1946 novel about carnival people that was made into a film starring Tyrone Power and Joan Blondell.) "A lean, dry, brown, outlandish stick of a man" who speaks in slurred French, he is neither a town resident nor a tourist (*Weeping Bay* 148). Rather, he is a "crazy" but "cheerful" man who delights in singing songs fraught with religious allusions. He talks gently to children, inviting them to see the exotic attractions in the carnival, and he seems to know intuitively when people are in trouble. The carnival man has a profound impact on the novel's hero, Hervé Kirouac, a man of mythic physical strength and a volatile temper who has lost his religious faith.

Anya and *Weeping Bay* are strikingly different, yet there are intriguing commonalities. *Anya* ends with the eponymous heroine's decision to journey to America, the promised land, a journey that foreshadows Davidman's decision a few years later to cross the Atlantic in the opposite direction to relocate in England. *Weeping Bay* ends with Hervé's decision to devote himself to improving his people's material conditions, which reflects Davidman's idealistic commitment first to the Communist Party and then to Christianity. The "honest anger at injustice and misery," about which Davidman writes in "The Longest Way Round" (22), characterizes the narrative voice in *Weeping Bay*. In both *Anya* and *Weeping Bay* Davidman remains sensitive to women's issues, advocating birth control and the legalization of abortion. There is one passage in *Weeping Bay* that may suggest the novelist's own struggle between conformity and rebellion. During an angry exchange between Hervé and his wife, Davidman makes a telling observation. "If Hervé had known much about the inside of a woman's head, he would have seen then how near she was to speaking it; how, in all their battles, it was herself, her own rebelliousness, her own yielding that she feared. But those were not things that a man and woman could know about each other" (166–67). Dedicated to her father, "who helped me find out," *Weeping Bay* reveals Davidman's rebellion against the Jewish religion into which she was born and the movement to evangelical Christianity that she came to embrace.

Smoke on the Mountain

Where there is smoke, there is fire, and Davidman's last book reveals a firebrand author who uses incendiary rhetoric to announce the approaching Armageddon. Dedicated to C. S. Lewis, whose authority she invokes repeatedly to support her argument, *Smoke on the Mountain* is highly polemical and—to those who do not share her religious assumptions—highly problematic. In its impassioned language it resembles D. H. Lawrence's *Studies in Classic American Literature*, demanding nothing less than a radical change in every aspect of one's life. Subtitled *An Interpretation of the Ten Commandments*, *Smoke on the Mountain* announces the author's assault on those who fail to honor both the spirit and the letter of the Decalogue. The book contains eleven chapters, each of the first ten corresponding to a Commandment, and the final one proclaiming that Christians will be saved only through a complete "surrender to God."

C. S. Lewis remarks in the foreword to the English edition of *Smoke on the Mountain* that "every story of conversion is a story of blessed defeat." *Smoke on the Mountain* is a 139-page conversion story, though the author never discloses the story of her own defeats, blessed or otherwise. To begin with, Davidman never reveals that she was Jewish, though ironically, even as she celebrates the "good news" of the New Testament, the book's tone and rhetoric evoke the thundering prohibitions of the Old Testament. She never reveals that she was an atheist, though she repeatedly denounces atheists, whom she defines in the broadest way. "The man who says, 'One God,' and does not *care*, is an atheist in his heart. The man who speaks of God and will not recognize the presence of God burning in his mind as Moses recognized him in the burning bush—that man is an atheist, though he speak with the tongues of men and angels, and appear in his pew every Sunday, and make large contributions to the church" (23). She never reveals that she was once a member of the Communist Party, believing in its humanitarian promises, though now she rejects even those small material changes that can alleviate suffering. "Whatever men have made, that they may worship; there are men who worship modern plumbing and hope to redeem China and India with the flush toilet" (35). Now, she finds every opportunity to denounce the Soviet Union for its totalitarianism without acknowledging her own mistaken judgment. She never reveals her husband's "nervous breakdown," as she refers to it in "The Longest Way Round," though she now rejects "Freudian psychiatry," which she ridicules for its mistaken emphasis on psychological rather than spiritual illness. "The unconscious mind is a favorite modern scapegoat; whatever may *really* be in it, many of us have mastered the trick of excusing, as 'unconscious drives,' behavior whose true motives we know only too well" (112).

One problem with *Smoke on the Mountain* is not its vision of Christianity, which is similar to Lewis's, but its narrow, judgmental criticisms of nearly everyone, Christian and non-Christian alike. As a novelist, Davidman demonstrates a sympathetic imagination that allows her to appreciate the ambiguous and ambivalent motives of her characters. Her affection for Anya never blinds her to the character's many weaknesses, and her affection for Hervé Kirouac and his family is never in doubt. It is true that she is merciless in her characterizations of the priests, but she is sensitive to those men and women who suffer the cruel effects of poverty, disease, and ignorance. As a Christian apologist, however, Davidman is combative, relentlessly hypercritical, and absolutist. She urges us to "remember the twin duties of compassion toward others and severity to ourselves" (94), but she often fails to heed this excellent advice. Sometimes she comes across as wildly idealistic, as when she tells us that we should be free to love our families with "complete unselfishness" (67), an assertion she must know as a novelist is impossible.

Another problem with *Smoke on the Mountain* is its either-or thinking. "In the last analysis," she writes, "there are only two things to worship—the true power and the false power; God or devil; God or self" (23–24). Her fondness for aphoristic binaries invigorates her prose but muddles her logic: "Yet surely Christianity was not meant to save the world for us; it was meant to save us from the world" (36). She equates humanism with materialism and then implies that both lead inevitably to atheism, which she condemns as morally bankrupt. "There is no logical reason why a materialist shouldn't poison his nagging wife, if he can get away with it" (79). In *Weeping Bay* she was sympathetic to the need for birth control, extolling the beauty of sex apart from its procreative function, but in *Smoke on the Mountain* she rails against those women who decide not to have children.

Still another problem with *Smoke on the Mountain* is its holier-than-thou vision of morality, which does not countenance a "white lie." Acknowledging that certain white lies may be morally defensible, as when a person lies to protect an innocent person from a murderer, she nevertheless concludes that "most of our white lies are told, not for charity, but for laziness and cowardice—to save the work of thinking up a real answer, or to avoid a trivial social discomfort" (110). What she does not tell us, as Dorsett notes without commentary, is that she made up two poets and their verse when she was compiling *War Poems of the United Nations*. "Feeling certain such writing should exist even if she could not find it, the imaginative editor invented Megan Coombes-Dawson and Hayden Weir. To give Weir a stamp of glamorous authenticity, he was described as a heroic soldier who died in battle early in World War II" (43).

One of the most curious sections of *Smoke on the Mountain* is chapter 7, "The Adulterous Generation," in which she offers her withering critique of contemporary marriage. "The Christian definition of adultery seems quite clear and hard. While you have a husband or wife still living, taking a new partner is adultery—and a sin" (84). She then adds that adultery comes in many forms. "There is the casual love affair, indulged in because a momentary temptation is strong, or because 'everybody does it, and I don't think it matters.' There is the intense, passionate, long-drawn-out triangle (or even quadrilateral), adorned with conflict and heartbreak. And there is the legalized form, with its rapid and light-hearted changing of partners in the courts. All these, in practice, come to much the same thing: a corruption of the heart, a destruction of the home, an end to love" (85). Her opposition to divorce is largely unqualified. "Our Lord's command about marriage was as sharp and straight as a sword. Your wife is your wife for good, he said; you can't get rid of her, except for adultery (and only one Gospel permits even that exception) and a divorced woman is committing adultery if she remarries. Now this is a difficult doctrine, as the disciples were the first to point out" (88).

There is no reason Davidman needs to tell us in *Smoke on the Mountain* that her husband was an alcoholic and an adulterer, and that she had put up with his vices for several years. Nor does she need to tell us that he was planning to marry her cousin Renée around this time. But one might expect Davidman to temper her opposition to divorce because shortly after the book's publication, she wrote to Lewis and told him that she and her children were moving to England, her marriage to Gresham now over. Davidman began her correspondence with Lewis in 1950, and the correspondence blossomed into friendship when she visited him for the first time in England in September 1952, where she lived for six months. She returned briefly to the United States in 1953 when she realized her marriage was over, and she then departed for London later that year with her children. With Lewis's help, she and her children moved to Oxford, where her friendship grew into love. Surely she must have known when she was writing *Smoke on the Mountain* that she was placing both Lewis and herself in a difficult situation by arguing against a divorced woman's right to remarry in the Anglican Church. "Lewis believed," as Dorsett points out, "the official position of the Church of England made remarriage impossible. The Church maintained that marriage was indissoluble and therefore remarriage after divorce constituted adultery" (112). Given, then, Davidman's strong opposition to divorce, it is inconsistent, if not disingenuous, that she quotes in *Smoke on the Mountain* one of Lewis's most controversial suggestions: "If people do not believe in permanent marriage, it is perhaps better that they should live together unmarried than [that] they should make vows they do not mean to keep. It is true that by living together without marriage they will be guilty (in Christian eyes) of fornication. But one fault is not mended by adding another: unchastity is not improved by adding perjury" (90).

The story of their marriage became stranger in 1956 when Davidman and her two young sons were living in England. The British Home Office decided not to renew their permit to remain in the country, and her only solution was to marry Lewis, which would make her and her children British citizens. Most of his friends, such as J. R. R. Tolkien, were unaware of the civil ceremony, and they were stunned when he placed an announcement of the marriage in the personal column of the *Times* eight months later, on Christmas Eve, 1956. Many of his friends felt that he had been pressured into marriage. Roger Lancelyn Green and Walter Hooper report that at the time of the marriage, "The smart thing to say [in Oxford] was, 'Do you know what's happened to C. S. Lewis? He's been surprised by Joy!'" (330). George Sayer insists in his biography that Lewis told him he was not in love with Davidman at the time and that it wasn't a real marriage (222–23), a statement that the editor of Lewis's *Collected Letters*, Walter Hooper, confirms: "Lewis made it clear that he did not regard this as a true marriage" 3:643). And yet Davidman's son Douglas Gresham insists that his mother and Lewis were romantically involved as early as 1954. "The subsequent secret marriage of convenience in 1956 is made much of as a charitable gesture on Jack's part, but no matter what he may have told his friends and colleagues, either then or later, this 'unmarriage' became very quickly a real marriage in both Jack's mind and Mother's" (Gresham 67).

Perhaps the truth lies between these two extremes. Lewis wrote in a 1957 letter, "There is no great mystery about my marriage. I have known the lady a long time: no one can mark the exact moment at which friendship becomes love" (*Collected Letters* 3:834). When, a few months later, she was diagnosed with bone cancer and told she had little time left, Lewis petitioned the bishop of Oxford to sanction the marriage on the grounds that William Gresham had been married and divorced before he met Davidman, thus invalidating her marriage in the eyes of the church. The bishop rejected the petition, but Lewis found another minister, a former student, who agreed to marry them in a religious ceremony. They were married at her hospital bedside—and almost immediately her cancer went into remission.

Nor was her recovery the only surprise. As Douglas Gresham reports, there were two other strange occurrences immediately after his mother married Lewis:

> A strange and terrifyingly beautiful thing began to happen. Jack became a victim of a condition known as osteoporosis, the etiology of which is mostly unknown; his bones began to lose their calcium and become weak and spongy. This disease is incurable, treatable only with increased calcium intake and drugs to try to assist the body to absorb calcium from dietary sources. The condition is non-fatal, but causes extreme agony, and Jack was often in great pain. At the same time, Mother's decalcified cancer-consumed thigh bone, of which only a few shattered fragments remained, began to regenerate, to rebuild itself, to find some source of available calcium and regrow into a healthy femur. Another unusual occurrence was that on one occasion when Mother was in terrible pain, so much that she really felt that she could not stand it any longer, Jack prayed that he might be permitted to bear the burden of this cross and accept the pain while Mother's analgesic drugs had time to take effect. At once, he began to experience indescribable agony in his legs and for a while Mother was relieved of her pain. (Gresham 80–81)

Lewis and Davidman attributed both phenomena to a spiritual miracle, the power of prayer to heal the believer. Their religious friends invoked the same explanation. The second phenomenon, the transfer of pain from wife to husband, is the easier of the two to explain scientifically: the well-documented placebo effect, the power of the mind to effect changes in the body. But how does one explain the spontaneous regeneration of Davidman's thigh bone and the sudden development of Lewis's osteoporosis? In a letter written on November 6, 1957, Lewis saw a possible connection between his wife's "new bone" and his own bone disease: "I was losing calcium just about as fast as Joy was gaining it, a bargain (if it was one) for [which] I am very thankful" (*Letters of C. S. Lewis* 280). Were the two developments merely coincidence? Were they a double example of the placebo effect, one leading to renewed health, the other to illness?

Lewis's friends were happy for the new couple, but many of them found Davidman to be abrasive and rude. Some of the criticisms can be attributed to the cultural differences between Americans and the

British, differences that became even greater because she was a New Yorker with an explosive temper. Significantly, everyone is in agreement that Davidman and Lewis experienced a close and happy marriage for the three years they lived together; even Sayer, who disliked her, acknowledges this, adding, "Joy told a correspondent [her brother] that Jack was a 'wonderful lover' and that she was glad she had not had a mastectomy, because he very much enjoyed caressing her breasts" (227). Illness only heightened Lewis's attraction to her, as he observed in a letter to a friend: "Never have I loved her more than since she was struck down" (Sayer 222). Peter Bayley reports the following comment that Lewis made to him and Neville Coghill: "'Do you know, I am experiencing what I thought would never be mine. I never thought to have at sixty what passed me by in my twenties.' He was smiling and seemed gentle and jubilant with love. I like to think that the great interpreter of chivalrous, honourable, generous, and chaste love, in his palmary studies of Chaucer, other medieval writers, and Spenser, should have come toward the end of his life to such felicity" (86).

There is no evidence of any marital tension between Davidman and Lewis, no evidence that she rebelled against his patriarchal view of marriage, which he defined unapologetically in a 1940 letter, ten years before he began corresponding with her. "My own feeling is that the Headship of the house is necessary to protect the outer world against the family. . . . What do nine women out of ten care about justice to the outer world when the health, or career, or happiness of their own children is at stake? That is why I want the 'foreign policy' of the family, so to speak, to be determined by the man; I expect more mercy from him" (*Letters of C. S. Lewis* 185).

Davidman never published any books or articles during her marriage to Lewis. This is surprising only because she had defined her identity at the beginning of her career as a writer, first as a poet, then as a novelist, later as a correspondent for the communist magazine *New Masses*, and finally as a Christian writer. She was apparently content to serve as her husband's literary adviser and editor. "She likened herself," writes Dorsett, "to Scribner's Maxwell Perkins, the astute editor to whom the literary world was indebted for bringing out the best in F. Scott Fitzgerald, Alan Paton, Ernest Hemingway, Thomas Wolfe, and Ring Lardner" (115). Serving as a Maxwell Perkins was no small feat, and she undertook the job with the seriousness and intensity that were characteristic of her entire life. Even before they were married, she helped him in countless ways, from answering the deluge of letters he received each day from admirers throughout the world, to helping him overcome one of his rare experiences with writer's block. She was the driving force behind his 1956 book *Till We Have Faces*, which he dedicated to her. The title of his 1955 spiritual autobiography, *Surprised by Joy*, refers both to the state of his mind arising from his deep religious faith and to the new woman in his life. Green and Hooper state that Lewis began writing *Surprised by Joy* in 1948, before he met Joy Davidman, but he must have been struck by the double meaning of the title of his book: the arrival of so much joy late in his life.

To my knowledge, Lewis never commented publicly on his role in Davidman's conversion, but he made a revealing statement to Sheldon Vanauken, who, like Davidman, converted to Christianity largely as a result of reading Lewis's religious writings: "My feeling about people in whose conversion I have been allowed to play a part is always mixed with awe and even fear: such as a boy might feel on first being allowed to fire a rifle. The disproportion between his puny finger on the trigger and the thunder & lightning [which] follow is alarming. And the seriousness with which the other party takes my words always raises the doubt whether I have taken them seriously enough myself. By writing the things I write, you see, one especially qualifies for being hereafter 'condemned out of one's own mouth.' Think of me as a fellow-patient in the same hospital who, having been admitted a little earlier, [could] give some advice" (qtd. in Vanauken, 134). I find Lewis's voice enormously appealing here, humble, respectful, wise, and compassionate. He was sensitive to the implications of influencing another person's life, particularly when his writings led to the adoption of a radically new belief system. This was the public role that Lewis, an intensely private man, came to play as a result of his own conversion to Christianity.

Surprised by Joy

As with Davidman, there is a striking discontinuity between Lewis's early and later life. He did not begin his career as a Christian; like

Davidman, he was an atheist for many years. For a writer who rejected the modern tendency to learn about authors' lives through their books—as late as 1957 he wrote to a friend, "Aren't you sick of modern biographies? I don't want in the least to know about anyone's *vie intime*" (*Collected Letters* 3:903)—he is startlingly autobiographical in *Surprised by Joy*. And for a writer who in his early books rejected the importance of the affective world, his spiritual autobiography is emotionally charged. He acknowledges in the preface that he feels uncomfortable narrating the story of his conversion. "The story is, I fear, suffocatingly subjective; the kind of thing I have never written before and shall probably never write again. I have tried so to write the first chapter that those who can't bear such a story will see at once what they are in for and close the book with the least waste of time" (7–8). Authors are seldom as solicitous of their readers as Lewis is, and one can only imagine his shock had he known about the far more suffocatingly subjective memoir *A Grief Observed* that he would publish only six years later. *Surprised by Joy* is Lewis's most autobiographical book before *A Grief Observed*, and it is essential for an understanding of his later memoir, for not only does he describe his development from atheism to Christianity, a process that paralleled Davidman's conversion, not in its details but in its outcome, but he also explores the mysterious nature of his "Joy" experience, which helps us to understand the intense feelings he came to associate with love and loss.

The opening chapter of *Surprised by Joy* contains an epigraph from Milton's *Paradise Lost*—"happy, but for so happy ill secured." The epigraph highlights the precarious nature of Lewis's childhood security. After describing the temperamental differences between his mother's cheerful and tranquil personality and his father's emotional volatility, he observes that these two influences "bred in me long before I was old enough to give it a name a certain distrust or dislike of emotion as something uncomfortable and embarrassing and even dangerous" (11–12). His early years were happy, with "good parents, good food, and a garden (which then seemed large) to play in" (13). He mentions his brother and "ally," Warren, three years older, with whom he was to be close for the rest of his life. He then singles out three childhood experiences that played a transformative role in his life. The first experience he describes as "itself the memory of a memory": "As I stood beside a flowering currant bush on a summer day there suddenly arose in me without warning, and as if from a depth not of years but of centuries, the memory of that earlier morning at the Old House when my brother had brought his toy garden into the nursery." Acknowledging that he cannot find the words to describe this experience, he calls it a sensation of desire, adding, "But desire for what?" (22), a question he could not answer then and has difficulty answering now. Before he knew what had happened, "the desire itself was gone, the whole glimpse withdrawn, the world turned commonplace again" (22). The second experience occurred while reading Beatrix Potter's *Squirrel Nutkin*, when he glimpsed the "Idea of Autumn": "It sounds fantastic to say that one can be enamoured of a season, but that is something like what happened; and, as before, the experience was one of intense desire" (23). The third experience, also literary, came when he read Longfellow's *Saga of King Olaf.* Hearing "a voice that cried/Balder the beautiful/Is dead, is dead," he is uplifted "into huge regions of northern sky," a desire that vanishes almost immediately.

Lewis invites those readers who have no interest in understanding these three experiences to read no further—he sounds like a battle-hardened professor here, dismissing those students whose boredom might infect their susceptible classmates. The unifying theme behind each of these three experiences, he tells the readers who remain in his classroom, is "that of an unsatisfied desire which is itself more desirable than any other satisfaction," an experience he calls "Joy," which he then defines in a peculiar way: "I call it Joy, which is here a technical term and must be sharply distinguished both from Happiness and from Pleasure. Joy (in my sense) has indeed one characteristic, and one only, in common with them; the fact that anyone who has experienced it will want it again. Apart from that, and considered only in its quality, it might almost equally well be called a particular kind of unhappiness or grief. But then it is a kind we want" (*Surprised by Joy* 24). Joy is thus, for Lewis, a moment of intense desire, a longing that is always beyond one's grasp. Joy is not an end in itself but suggestive of a higher reality, a timeless and spaceless reality, a divine incarnation.

Immediately after describing these three visionary experiences, Lewis spends the rest of the chapter writing about the central traumatic loss of his childhood, the death of his mother in 1908, when he was nine. The news of her illness was almost as wrenching as her death a few months later. "And then my father, in tears, came into my room and began to try to convey to my terrified mind things it had never conceived before. It was in fact cancer and followed the usual course; an operation (they operated in the patient's house in those days), an apparent convalescence, a return of the disease, increasing pain, and death. My father never fully recovered from this loss" (*Surprised by Joy* 24). Warren Lewis reports that his mother died on his father's birthday, August 23: "There was a Shakespearean calendar hanging on the wall of the room where she died, and my father preserved for the rest of his life the leaf for that day, with its quotation: 'Men must ensure their going hence'" (*Letters of* C. S. *Lewis* 3).

Lewis was painfully aware that his wife's approaching death seemed terribly similar to his mother's death decades earlier. As he wrote to an American friend in 1957, "I am newly married to a dying woman. Every moment is spent at her bedside. I am sure we may count on your prayers; add your prayer for help and guidance in the difficult responsibility of bringing up two orphan stepsons. I have only one qualification if it is one; these two boys are now facing the very same calamity that befell my brother and myself at about the same age" (*Letters of* C. S. *Lewis* 276). One cannot exaggerate the importance of this childhood calamity, for Lewis lost not only his mother but his father as well. "Usually when a parent dies, the child really loses both parents—one to death and the other to mourning": John E. Schowalter's observation in "Parent Death and Child Bereavement" (175) is strikingly true of Lewis's situation. He remained estranged from his psychologically depressed father, who became an absent presence, until shortly before his death. Children are generally more resilient than their parents in reacting to loss, but Lewis knew from his own experience that childhood grief is complicated, problematic, and sometimes permanent. "They say that a shared sorrow draws people closer; I can hardly believe that it often has that effect when those who share it are of widely different ages. If I may trust my own experience, the sight of adult misery and adult terror has an effect on children which is merely paralysing and alienating" (*Surprised by Joy* 25). It is impossible to know which loss was greater for Lewis to bear, the death of his mother or the transformation of his father into a bitter, distraught man, one who "spoke wildly and acted unjustly." The only person Lewis could trust and seek comfort in was his brother—they were "two frightened urchins huddled for warmth in a bleak world" (25).

"Grief was overwhelmed with terror," Lewis reveals as he was taken into the bedroom where his mother lay dead. "To this day I do not know what they mean when they call dead bodies beautiful" (*Surprised by Joy* 25). Perhaps this explains his decision not to describe in *A Grief Observed* his wife's body at the moment of death. His aversion to the "absurdity of mourning clothes" and to his mother's funeral contributed, he adds, to his "distaste for all that is public, all that belongs to the collective: a boorish inaptitude for formality" (*Surprised by Joy* 26). He concedes that some people might view his mother's death as his first religious experience, but they would be mistaken, he counters. He had prayed for her recovery, but that didn't prevent her death. Years later, after his religious conversion, he concluded that when his mother died he had approached God "without love, without awe, even without fear" (26). His mother's death spelled the end of his childhood security and happiness: "It was sea and islands now; the great continent had sunk like Atlantis" (27). We learn more about his loss of security in a letter he wrote to a friend on December 31, 1953. Commiserating with her loss, he writes, "I can well understand how in addition to, and mingling with, the void and loneliness, there is a great feeling of unprotectedness and a horror of coping with all the things—the harsh, outer world—from which you have hitherto been shielded. I first met this 'cold blast on the naked heath' at about 9, when my Mother died, and there has never really been any sense of security and snugness since. That is, I've never quite succeeded in growing up on that point: there is still too much of 'Mammy's little lost boy' about me" (*Collected Letters* 3:398).

Lewis returns to his joy experience several times in his spiritual autobiography, each time elaborating on its meaning to him. "Joy is distinct not only from pleasure in general but even from aesthetic pleasure. It must have the stab, the pang, the inconsolable longing" (*Surprised by Joy* 74). In his view, joy is always associated with loss—the two are inseparable. Before his conversion, first to theism in 1929, at the age of thirty-one, when he began to believe in a transcendent God, then to Christianity two years later, when his belief changed to an immanent God, he experienced moments of joy while listening to Wagner's music or reading Norse and Celtic mythology. These experiences, however, were different from the original joy experience. He never discloses the extent of his sexual experience before marriage, but he is careful to point out that joy cannot be reduced to sensual pleasure. "Joy is not a substitute for sex; sex is very often a substitute for Joy. I sometimes wonder whether all pleasures are not substitutes for Joy" (161). He has no sympathy for Freud's theory of sublimation, in which sexual impulses are rechanneled or redirected into more socially acceptable outlets, such as art, athletics, or business. Lewis was no puritan about sex, and later he intimated that he and his wife had a fulfilling sexual life together, but sex does not occupy a major role in his vision of life.

In "Checkmate," the penultimate chapter of *Surprised by Joy*, Lewis reveals the epiphany that for the first time illuminates his lifelong search for joy. One cannot pursue joy directly, he discovers; to do so would be like pursuing "not the wave but the wave's imprint on the sand" (207). It is as if all the images and sensations of joy confessed to him that they could provide no help in fulfilling his quest. "All said, in the last resort, 'It is not I. I am only a reminder. Look! Look! What do I remind you of?'" (207). They remind Lewis not of a specific pleasure or object or person he desired but of a "road right out of the self, a commerce with something which, by refusing to identify itself with any object of the senses, or anything whereof we have biological or social need, or anything imagined, or any state of our own minds, proclaims itself sheerly objective" (208–9). This pure objectivity, which he calls the "naked Other, imageless (though our imagination salutes it with a hundred images), unknown, undefined, desired" (209), leads him away from the world of appearances to the "Absolute, which is the utter reality," the living reality of Christianity. Lewis's long journey, first as an atheist, then as a theist, was suddenly over; now another journey began, one that he deemed infinitely more challenging than anything he had previously experienced.

For those who, like myself, cannot grasp or accept Lewis's Christian explanation of joy, other explanations must suffice. Those who are psychologically oriented will be struck by the association in his spiritual autobiography between joy and maternal love. He loses his mother immediately after announcing his visionary experiences of joy, and from then on he identifies joy with the stab and pang of inconsolable longing. Echoing Job's lament, "That which I greatly feared had at last come upon me," Lewis records the "steady, unrelenting approach of Him whom I so earnestly desired not to meet" (*Surprised by Joy* 215). He was, the night he prayed to God for the first time, the "most dejected and reluctant convert in all England." He then compares himself wryly to the Prodigal Son, "who is brought in kicking, struggling, resentful, and darting his eyes in every direction for a chance of escape" (215), an apt birth metaphor that evokes maternal love and loss.

C. S. *Lewis's Correspondence*

C. S. Lewis's voluminous correspondence—there are more than four thousand pages in the three volumes of his *Collected Letters*, and that doesn't include many letters found in his other collections—gives us a sense of his caregiving responsibilities as well as his reaction to his wife's illness. Grief never prevented him from answering the many letters from well-wishers who inquired into his wife's health. Reading these letters, one can only admire his compassion, patience, and devotion. He was a true teacher, sharing with others the knowledge gleaned from suffering. He was also a faithful correspondent, conscientious in writing to those who asked him for advice. His letters yield many insights into his character.

One of the people who wrote him frequently was an American whom the editor of *Letters to an American Lady*, Clyde S. Kilby, identified simply as "Mary." Walter Hooper, the editor of *Collected Letters*, reveals her full name, Mary Willis Shelburne, an American widow who often wrote Lewis about her financial anxiety. He not only answered her letters but also helped her out financially, sending her a monthly stipend. In his letter to her on November 16, 1956, Lewis describes his wife's failing health. "You may as well know (but don't talk of it, for all is still uncertain) that I may soon be, in rapid succession, a bridegroom and a widower. There may, in fact, be a deathbed marriage. I can hardly describe to you the state of mind I live in at present—except that all emotion, with me, is periodically drowned in sheer tiredness, deep lakes of stupor" (*Collected Letters* 3:808). Lewis's preoccupation with his wife's illness did not limit his empathy for others, as we can see in his January 4, 1957, letter to Shelburne: "I must try not to let my own present unhappiness harden my heart against the woes of others! You too are going through a dreadful time" (*Collected Letters* 3:823). Six weeks later he informs her that he has known the woman he married "a long time" and that "no one can mark the exact moment at which friendship becomes love." He then adds an important detail: "You can well understand how illness—the fact that she was facing pain and death and anxiety about the future of her children—would be an *extra* reason for marrying her or a reason for marrying her sooner" (3:834; emphasis in original).

Lewis mentions Joy Davidman's name for the first time in his July 3, 1957, letter, in which he responds ruefully to a rumor of his own death: "What on earth is the trouble about there being a rumour of my death? There's nothing discreditable in dying: I've known the most respectable people do it!" (*Collected Letters* 3:865). A revealing postscript to his April 15, 1958, letter to Shelburne suggests that most of his correspondents are female, not all of whom were thrilled to learn about his marriage: "By the way, you are one of the *minority* of my numerous female correspondents who didn't gradually fade away as soon as they heard I was married!" (*Collected Letters* 3:935; emphasis in original).

Lewis's letter to Shelburne written on October 18, 1959, signals the worsening of his wife's health. "Will you redouble your prayers for us? Apparently the wonderful recovery Joy made in 1957 was only a reprieve, not a pardon. The last x-ray check reveals cancerous spots returning in many of her bones. There seems to be some hope of a few years life still and there are still things the doctors can do. But they are all in the nature of 'rearguard actions.' We are in retreat. The tide has turned." And yet he still maintains his religious faith. "Of course God can do again what He did before. The sky is not now so dark as it was when I married her in hospital. Her courage is wonderful and she gives me more support than I can give her" (*Letters to an American Lady* 85). In a July 15, 1960, letter, he reports his wife's death. "Joy died on the 13th. I can't describe the apparent unreality of my life since then. She received absolution and died at peace with God" (*Collected Letters* 3:1171).

Lewis's correspondence reveals many details of his wife's illness and death that do not appear in *A Grief Observed*. Three years before his marriage, he remarked to an American who was complaining about her son-in-law, "Are you giving full weight to the very raw deal he has had in marrying a girl who has nearly always been ill? Men haven't got your maternal instinct, you know. To find a patient where one hoped for a helpmeet is so much more frustrating for the husband than for the wife" (*Collected Letters* 3:360). Lewis had this "maternal instinct," and he never complained about his own caregiving responsibilities. No matter how ill his wife was, he wrote about their marital happiness. "You [would] hardly believe how much happiness, not to say *gaiety*, we have together—a honeymoon on a sinking ship," he wrote on February 13, 1957 (*Collected Letters*, 3:832). Three weeks later, on Ash Wednesday, he writes to a nun, "The disease is of course cancer; by which I lost my mother, my father, and my favourite aunt. She knows her own state of course: I [would] allow no lies to be told to a grown-up and a Christian. As you can imagine new beauty and new tragedy have entered my life. You [would] be surprised (or perhaps you would not?) to know how much of a strange sort of happiness and even gaiety there is between us" (*Collected Letters* 3:837). To the novelist Dorothy Sayers he wrote on June 25, 1957, "My heart is breaking and I was never so happy before: at any rate there is more in life than I knew about" (*Collected Letters* 3:862).

Davidman's letters reveal her own courage and happiness during their marriage. Sometimes, when her husband was too ill to answer a correspondent, she would reply instead, as when she wrote a woman on May 27, 1957, who was also battling cancer. "One thing I'd like to say since you mention that you've been threatened with cancer. Before I had it, I had all the usual fear and horror of it; but since then I've found that it's possible to live with your cancer and still get a great deal of happiness out of life. The pain, perhaps, is usually exaggerated. I've had three operations, a frightful time with deep X-rays, three months encased almost completely in plaster and the complication of a broken leg—and all this had involved a great deal of pain at times; but the pain came more from the treatments than from the disease, and was on the whole less than I would have expected. At the moment I've no pain at all! I'm not going to play Pollyanna about the blasted disease—it's just that, bad as it is, one can take it without complete disintegration" (*Collected Letters* 3:857). A letter she wrote to Mary Shelburne on June 6, 1958, conveys perhaps the greatest change as a result of illness. "I was very proud; I liked the superior feeling of helping others, and for me it is much harder to receive than to give but, I think, much more blessed. Then, too, it's only since I've been ill and helpless that I've realised just how good people in general are, when they have a chance. So many people have taken trouble over me, and gone out of their way to give pleasure or help! It's very heartwarming—and humbling, for I remember how cynical I used to be about humanity and feel a salutary shame" (*Collected Letters* 3:952).

Lewis's letters around the time of his wife's illness are especially important in giving us an insight into the challenge of maintaining hope in the presence of death. One letter, written on May 12, 1957, describes a phenomenon that was true not only of his wife but also of my own: sometimes an improvement in a cancer patient's physical health leads to a worsening of psychological health. "Joy is at home, completely bedridden. Though the doctors hold out no ultimate hope, the progress of the disease does seem to be temporarily arrested to a degree they never expected. There is little pain, often none, her strength increases and she eats and sleeps well. This has the paradoxical (but come to think of it, natural) result of giving her lower spirits and less peace. The more *general* health, of course the stronger the instinctive will to live. Forbidden and torturing hopes will intrude on us both. In short, a dungeon is never harder to bear than when the door is open and the sunshine and bird song float in" (*Letters of* C. S. *Lewis* 276; emphasis in original). There is no evidence that Davidman or Lewis required psychological counseling during her illness, as Barbara and I did; their Christian faith were antidotes to whatever inclination toward depression they may have felt.

Lewis was candid about the sexual element of his marriage, though he seems to have been less open about this to his female correspondents. He told Dorothy Sayers, in a letter written on December 24, 1956, the same day an announcement of his marriage appeared in the *Times*, that his dying wife will return home if she makes an unexpected recovery. "You will not think that anything wrong is going to happen. Certain problems do not arise between a dying woman and an elderly man. What I am mainly acquiring is two (nice) stepsons" (*Collected Letters* 3:819). And yet in his August 24, 1957, letter to Dom Bede Griffiths, a former student who had become a Benedictine monk, he speaks with pleasure about the sensual element of his marriage. "Tho' she is still a cripple her *general* health is better than I have ever seen it, and she says she has never been happier. It is nice to have arrived at all this by something which began in Agape, proceeded to Philia, then became pity, and only after that Eros. As if the highest of these, Agape, had successfully undergone the sweet humiliations of an incarnation" (*Letters of* C. S. *Lewis*, 277–78; emphasis in original). Lewis expressed here an idea that he would develop in greater detail in *The Four Loves*. In a letter written on September 23, 1960, two months after his wife's death, he confided to

Sheldon Vanauken, "Like you, I can't imagine real Eros coming twice. I still feel married to Joy" (*Collected Letters* 3:1187). He makes his most revealing sexual disclosure to Dom Bede Griffiths in December 20, 1961: "One thing is perhaps worth recording. I prayed that when I buried my wife my whole sexual nature [should] be buried with her, and it seems to have happened. Thus one recurrent trial has vanished from my life—an enormous liberty. Of course this may be only old age—we must not, as Bunyan says [in *The Pilgrim's Progress*], 'mistake the decays of nature for the advances of grace.' But the liberty is a fact. It is wonderful to be able to think unreservedly and gratefully of the act of love without the least reawakening of concupiscence" (*Collected Letters* 3:1303).

Two of Lewis's letters to friends, one to Arthur Greeves written on August 30, 1960, the other to Chad Walsh written on October 18 of that year, convey one of his wife's final statements to him that does not appear in *A Grief Observed*: "You have made me happy" (*Collected Letters* 3:1181, 1199). It's not likely that he forgot to include this memorable detail. Did he omit these words because some readers might find them self-serving? Perhaps, yet he must have reflected on and cherished her dying words to the end of his own life.

A Grief Observed

Written outside of Lewis's comfort zone, *A Grief Observed* might also be called *A Grief Experienced*, for he is both observing and experiencing the darkest emotions. He had offered his theological interpretation of the necessity of suffering in his 1940 book *The Problem of Pain*, but he was not speaking then from personal experience. Now he was, and the result is his most personal and anguished book, a dark night of the soul about which he had never written. In a letter to Dorothy L. Sayers on June 25, 1957, he had stoically declared that "we learn to love what we know we must lose" (*Collected Letters* 3:862). But now that he had indeed lost his beloved wife, everything else in his life threatened to collapse, including his major support system: Christianity. In losing his wife, he lost all the Joy in his life, leaving him mired in darkness and despair.

In the many letters describing his wife's illness and death, Lewis displays extraordinary composure, not allowing himself to succumb to anger, grief, or self-pity, but in his memoir he opens the floodgates of emotion, which at times threaten to sweep him and his readers way. Given the near-heroic self-control in his correspondence, one may wonder whether he deliberately evokes emotion for literary effect in the memoir. Reading his stepson's autobiography, however, dispels such a suspicion. "He could not hide it from me, nor did he try, for I shared his grief," Douglas Gresham admits. "Many a time when approaching him, light-footed as I have always been, I stopped and backed silently away when I saw that he was racked with pain, sometimes physical, sometimes emotional, but too high a matter for me in either case. No-one knew how Jack suffered in those last three years" (Gresham, 133). Describing himself as susceptible to emotional contagion, Gresham found himself avoiding his stepfather. "I could not talk to Jack about Mother, for I knew that if I did, he would weep and so also would I, and although now I feel that this might have been good for both of us, then it would have been anathema for me to cry openly, for as an English schoolboy I found it difficult to show my emotions" (133–34). Lewis confirms this observation in *A Grief Observed*, disclosing that he "cannot talk to the children about her" because they look at him as if he were "committing an indecency." They are "longing for me to stop," he continues. "I felt the same after my own mother's death when my father mentioned her. I can't blame them. It's the way boys are" (9).

Lewis knew that many readers would be emotionally unable to comprehend, much less appreciate, the searing emotions of *A Grief Observed*. He was right about the ambivalent response of many readers, and he was understandably reluctant to identify himself as the author of the book. As Thomas Talbott points out:

> Some admirers of Lewis have found the honesty in *A Grief Observed* disturbing; others, such as George Musacchio, have found it impossible to believe that their hero, C. S. Lewis—this "rational and insightful Christian writer"—should have been "so shattered" by his wife's death or "plunged so near to despair." They have therefore invented the fiction that *A Grief Observed* is itself a work of fiction. But it is simply naive to suppose that Lewis could not have experienced his own "mad midnight moments" or even, in response to great trauma and sleep deprivation, have experienced an emotional breakdown of sorts. (194)

Biographers offer conflicting accounts of how the manuscript was submitted for publication. According to A. N. Wilson, the book was submitted under the pseudonym "N. W. Clerk" to the publishing house of Faber and Faber, whose managing editor, T. S. Eliot, found the manuscript distasteful. "Several people were consulted, and no one seemed sure that N. W. Clerk, whoever he was, should be allowed to burden the world with unhappiness." Eliot then asked Charles Monteith, a younger director of the firm and a former student of Lewis at Oxford, to read the manuscript. Once Monteith recognized Lewis's handwritten corrections on the typescript, "everything else fell into place" (Wilson 285). Biographers Roger Lancelyn Green and Walter Hooper offer a different account, stating that the typescript was submitted under the name "Dimidius," Latin for "halved" or "divided in two," an allusion to Lewis's friend Charles Williams, who referred to a Christian cynic as "Thomas Didymus Sceptic." Eliot then wrote Lewis saying that he and his wife were moved by the work but suggested a different pseudonym, a "plausible English pseudonym" that would "hold off enquirers better than Dimidius" (Green and Hooper 405–6). However grief-stricken Lewis was when the book first appeared in 1961, he slyly chose initials for his pseudonym, "N. W.," which in Anglo-Saxon means "I know not who," apt initials for a pseudonym. According to Sayer, the book did poorly until it was republished posthumously under his own name in 1964.

There is no disagreement that *A Grief Observed* began as a series of journal entries Lewis wrote shortly after his wife's death. He filled four notebooks with entries, apparently not realizing in the beginning that these writings would form a publishable book. To protect his wife's identity, he refers to her as "H." He tells us, at the beginning of the last chapter, that he has resolved to keep the memoir brief, giving us what is surely one of the most unusual reasons for limiting a book's length. "This is the fourth—and the last—empty MS. book I can find in the house; at least nearly empty, for there are some pages of very ancient arithmetic at the end by J. I resolve to let this limit my jottings. I *will* not start buying books for the purpose" (59; emphasis in original).

Part of the power of *A Grief Observed* lies in Lewis's ability to allow all of the voices within him to express themselves. The commonsensical voice sternly reminds him that he must continue his life without sadness or complaint: he was happy before he met his wife, and he has "plenty of what are called 'resources'" (4). The self-pitying voice wishes to wallow and indulge in pain despite the feeling of self-disgust. The Christian voice insists that he must accept the wisdom and goodness of God's plan however incomprehensible it may be. And the angry voice cries out that God has abandoned him in his hour of need. This is the strongest and, aesthetically, the most powerful voice, dominating the first two chapters. "When you are happy, so happy that you have no sense of needing Him, so happy that you are tempted to feel His claims upon you as an interruption, if you remember yourself and turn to Him with gratitude and praise, you will be—or so it feels—welcomed with open arms. But go to Him when your need is desperate, when all other help is vain, and what do you find? A door slammed in your face, and a sound of bolting and double bolting on the inside" (5–6). Now that Joy is no longer in Lewis's life, these inner voices threaten to shatter and disintegrate his core self, resulting in a dizzying multiple personality.

A Grief Observed is, in short, dialogical, examining the nature of grief from multiple perspectives and in different voices. Lewis is never so self-absorbed that he cannot imagine how others must see him. He views himself critically and, at times, hypercritically, as when he imagines that he is a pathetic cautionary tale to others: "To some I'm worse than an embarrassment. I am a death's head. Whenever I meet a happily married pair I can feel them both thinking, 'One or other of us must some day be as he is now'" (11). Whatever authority he gained as a teacher, writer, and scholar seems to have disappeared, leaving him forlorn, bereft, and defenseless. In revealing his pain and vulnerability, Lewis never retreats into impersonal academic language or theological platitude. *A Grief Observed* is a consummate work of art: the writing is intimate, spontaneous, conversational, and eloquent, as if the words poured out of him, uncensored and unedited—like a Mozart score. The dark chords of Lewis's composition are occasionally lightened by gallows humor, as when he declares that perhaps the bereaved "ought to be isolated in special settlements like lepers" (11).

Lewis portrays Joy as the stronger of the two, intellectually, spiritually, and physically. "Her mind was lithe and quick and muscular as a leopard. Passion, tenderness, and pain were all equally unable to disarm it. It scented the first whiff of cant or slush; then sprang, and knocked you over before you knew what was happening. How many bubbles of mine she pricked! I soon learned not to talk rot to her unless I did it for the sheer pleasure—and there's another red-hot jab of being exposed and laughed at. I was never less silly than as H.'s lover" (*A Grief Observed* 4–5). Throughout the book he reverses gender roles: she appears more masculine in her intellect, he more feminine in his emotionality, but then he imagines her response to this characterization. "I once praised her for her 'masculine virtues.' But she soon put a stop to that by asking how I'd like to be praised for my feminine ones. It was a good *riposte*, dear." Nevertheless, he states that there was "something of the Amazon" about her (48). Gone is his 1940 patriarchal belief that the husband is the "Headship" of the house, replaced by a matriarchal vision in which the wife protects the husband from internal and external attack. She is his rock and protector, and he cannot imagine his future life without her presence. Only once does he wonder how she might have reacted to his book. "What would H. herself think of this terrible little notebook to which I come back and back? Are these jottings morbid?" (*A Grief Observed* 9). He never returns to these questions.

Nor does Lewis reveal any specifics about his wife's life, either before or during their marriage. He never discloses in the memoir, as he does in many of his letters, that she was born Jewish and converted to Christianity in her thirties. In an April 30, 1959, letter to Dom Bede Griffiths, for example, Lewis describes his wife as a "Semitic genius," a "Jewess by birth" who holds two views that would interest Griffiths—and, presumably, readers of *A Grief Observed*: "That the only living Judaism is Christianity. Where her own people still have religion it is archaic, pedantic, and—so to speak—sectarian" and "That we Goyim misread much of the O.T. because we start with the assumption that its sacred character excludes *humour*" (*Collected Letters* 3:1042–43; emphasis in original). Although he shares in abundant detail his religious crisis following her death, he does more telling than showing when he describes their life together, as when he summarily refers to the "old life, the jokes, the drinks, the arguments, the lovemaking, the tiny, heartbreaking commonplace" (25). Later he admits that she was "not a perfected saint" but rather a "sinful woman married to a sinful man; two of God's patients, not yet cured" (42), yet he is far more willing to describe in concrete detail his own sinfulness than hers.

All of Lewis's biographers have commented on the married couple's intense happiness, a relationship seemingly devoid of tension or mistrust. It appears to have been a story-book marriage, too good to believe if it appeared in a work of fiction. Death ended the three-year honeymoon. They had much in common—prodigious intellectual curiosity, a passion for reading and writing, and similar conversionary experiences. But their differences were even more striking: a late middle-aged confirmed English bachelor, deeply private and reserved, married to a woman seventeen years his junior, born and raised in New York City, Jewish by birth, brash and outspoken by temperament. Lewis was a social and political conservative, opposed to contraception and the legalization of abortion, both of which Davidman advocates in *Weeping Bay*, published at the same time she began corresponding with him. How were they able to become so close, so quickly, when these differences threatened to separate them? Complicating their marriage were her two young sons, both of whom were separated for the first time from their biological father and now living in a strange country, so different from their own. Douglas remained close to his mother and new stepfather, but David did not, and most of Lewis's references in his letters indicate that they had a strained relationship.

Davidman began as Lewis's disciple, but did she defer to his judgments as his wife? Most of Lewis's friends felt that she had manipulated him—so brilliant intellectually yet so naive personally—into marriage. She never taunted her husband, as Anya taunts hers, but did Lewis fear that marrying an American divorcée with two young children was more than he bargained for? How did the two of them work out the delicate question of marital power? "No man shall have power over me," Davidman writes about Anya; "I shall not lie weeping for any man to comfort" (72). Ironically, Lewis was the one who wept for his wife when she became ill.

In his 1946 book *The Allegory of Love*, Lewis observes that marriages during the medieval age had "nothing to do with love"; rather, all marriages were "matches of interest, and, worse still, of an interest that was continually changing. . . . Any idealization of sexual love, in a society where marriage is purely utilitarian, must begin by being an idealization of adultery" (13). Lewis's sober view of medieval marriage paralleled Davidman's cynical view of modern marriage. "Love is lust," Anya thinks, "and hatred is lust. Love wishes to enslave the body of the beloved, that he may lie beneath the feet; hate wishes to commit passionate outrage upon the hated body. Love aspires to lie as a slave beneath the onslaught of the lover, and hate makes one submit in ecstasy to any defilement" (*Anya* 77–78). Davidman had come a long way since the publication of *Anya* in 1940, yet her first marriage did little to improve her vision of embattled male-female relationships. Lewis tells us in *A Grief Observed* that throughout their too-brief marriage he "feasted on love, every mode of it—solemn and merry, romantic and realistic, sometimes as dramatic as a thunderstorm, sometimes as comfortable and unemphatic as putting on your soft slippers. No cranny of heart or body remained unsatisfied" (7). One possible explanation for this idealized feast is that both partners were starved for love. His words do not sound like those of a man manipulated into marriage.

Curiously, what both husband and wife had in common, as their stories and letters reveal, is a fascination for sadomasochistic fantasies. Biographer Alan Jacobs remarks on Lewis's "sadomasochistic tendencies as a young man" (287), tendencies that may be seen in the following passage from *The Four Loves*: the sexual act "can invite the man to an extreme, though short-lived, masterfulness, to the dominance of a conqueror or a captor, and the woman to a correspondingly extreme subjection and surrender. Hence the roughness, even fierceness, of some erotic play; the 'lover's pinch which hurts and is desire'" (*Four Loves* 145). This is strikingly close to the descriptions in *Anya*, when Davidman's protagonist engages in rough sex, including taunting a man into raping her.

Lewis does not disclose any details of their marriage, nor does he disclose that his wife was a talented writer, but he does not hesitate to describe his own writing, including the motivation behind his book. "I not only live each endless day in grief, but live each day thinking about living each day in grief. Do these notes merely aggravate that side of it? Merely confirm the monotonous, tread-mill march of the mind round one subject? But what am I to do? I must have some drug, and reading isn't a strong enough drug now. By writing it all down (all?—no: one thought in a hundred) I believe I get a little outside it. That's how I'd defend it to H. But ten to one she'd see a hole in the defence" (10). The last sentence raises two questions: what is Lewis holding back in *A Grief Observed*, and what "holes" would his wife see in his argument? He assures us that he shall "put in nothing fictitious (or I hope I shan't)" in the book, yet in the next sentence he asks what is for him a troubling question: "But won't the composition inevitably become more and more my own? The reality is no longer there to check me, to pull me up short, as the real H. so often did, unexpectedly, by being so thoroughly herself and not me" (18). As he begins the fourth notebook, he admits that writing has had its desired effect: "In so far as this record was a defence against total collapse, a safety-valve, it has done some good" (59). There is no doubt in his mind about this. Years earlier, in 1944, he had exhorted his friend Arthur Greeves to practice the writing cure: "Cheer up, and whenever you are fed up with life, start writing: ink is the great cure for all human ills, as I have found out long ago" (*Collected Letters* 1:187). He puts the cure to good use in *A Grief Observed.*

Lewis reveals little about his wife's preparation for death or his feelings about her while she was alive. He writes about his own grief and anger, not hers, and he never intimates she feared God had abandoned her, as he feared God had abandoned him. Presumably she did not experience these dark emotions because her faith was never in doubt. After disclosing he has lost his mother, father, and now wife to cancer, he remarks that he is comforted by the fact that toward the end of her life H. had largely overcome her fear of the disease. "H. herself, dying of it, and well knowing the fact [that his parents died from cancer], said that she had lost a great deal of her old horror at it. When the reality came, the name and the idea were in some degree disarmed" (*A Grief Observed* 12). There is never a moment when he suggests she was fearful of dying or death. She appears to accept her impending death with religious faith and philosophical stoicism; she seems to be aware of the futility of protest, anger, or indignation. She senses his fear of loss and tries to comfort him. "She once said to me, 'Even if we both died at exactly the same moment, as we lie here side by side, it would be just as much a separation as the one you're so afraid of.'" Lewis then adds, "Of course she didn't *know*, any more than I do. But she was near death; near enough to make a good shot" (14; emphasis in original). He reveals only one moment shortly before death when she protested her fate: "Have I forgotten the moment of bitterness when she cried out, 'And there was so much to live for'"? (17)—it is his question mark, not hers. On the penultimate page he reports one of their last conversations. "Once very near the end I said, 'If you can—if it is allowed—come to me when I too am on my death bed.' 'Allowed!' she said. 'Heaven would have a job to hold me; and as for Hell, I'd break it into bits.' She knew she was speaking a kind of mythological language, with even an element of comedy in it. There was a twinkle as well as a tear in her eye" (75). Her impassioned words here evoke the ending of *Wuthering Heights*, when Heathcliff, believing he sees the spirit of his beloved Catherine Earnshaw, dead for eighteen years, exclaims that nothing will prevent him from being reunited with her in the next world.

Lewis spares readers of *A Grief Observed* from most of the details of his wife's suffering, even when those details reveal her acceptance of death. Warren Lewis reports in his June 21, 1960, diary entry, written about three weeks before her death, that her pain had become unbearable. "Nurse, this is the end, I know I'm dying," she exclaimed one morning. "But even then the old courage was still there," Warren adds; "almost the last thing she said before falling into a drug-induced coma was, 'I've got enough cancers now to form a Trades Union of the darned things.' And to the doctor she said, 'Finish me off quick, I won't have another operation'" (qtd. in Green and Hooper 398).

Lewis describes in *A Grief Observed* two important changes occurring to him in the months immediately following his wife's death. The first is his crisis of faith, which arises not from the question of God's existence, which he never doubts, but from the possibility that by allowing Davidman to die, God betrays Himself as a "Cosmic Sadist," a "spiteful imbecile" (30). This accusation, he discloses in the next sentence, was made during the preceding evening, when he was overcome by grief. Lewis surely knew that readers familiar with his Christian writings would be shocked by this characterization, but he doesn't withdraw the charge. He finds the accusation illogical, however: "I think it is, if nothing else, too anthropomorphic. When you come to think of it, it is far more anthropomorphic than picturing Him as a grave old king with a long beard" (30). He returns to the question of God's sadism a few pages later, regaining his faith in a loving deity: "The more we believe that God hurts only to heal, the less we can believe that there is any use in begging for tenderness." He then makes a surprising comparison, one that might strike some readers as reductive: "What do people mean when they say, 'I am not afraid of God because I know He is good'? Have they never even been to a dentist?" (43).

What can *A Grief Observed* teach those readers who are, like myself, agnostics or atheists? "Little," Lewis might himself answer unhesitatingly, since his conclusion unambiguously affirms a loving and merciful Christian God who hurts only to heal. But non-Christians can find wisdom and comfort in *A Grief Observed.* The book courageously demonstrates the importance of doubt in one's belief system. Without doubt, faith becomes meaningless. Lewis's doubt is not as strong as that of Job, who demands that God explain the loss of his ten children, property, and health, and who at the end of the story is silenced by God's appearance as a whirlwind. Lewis's doubt, however, is strong enough to be convincing. As Adam Gopnik observes in a biographical essay on Lewis in the *New Yorker*, his faith in *A Grief Observed* "becomes less joblike and more Job-like: questioning, unsure—a dangerous quest rather than a querulous dogma." By acknowledging doubt, Lewis encourages his readers to question their own beliefs and disbeliefs. He would agree with Terence: Homo sum; humani nil a me alienum puto (I am human; I count nothing human foreign to me). If *A Grief Observed* demonstrates that doubt can assail the foremost Christian apologist of the century, those who are "free thinkers" may also be riddled with doubt, which is, after all, a sign of intellectual honesty.

The second change Lewis acknowledges in *A Grief Observed* involves the role of memory in bereavement. "What pitiable cant to say, 'She will live forever in my memory!' *Live?* That is exactly what she won't do. You might as well think like the old Egyptians that you can keep the dead by embalming them. Will nothing persuade us that they are gone? What's left? A corpse, a memory, and (in some versions) a ghost. All mockeries or horrors. Three more ways of spelling the word *dead.* It was H. I loved. As if I wanted to fall in love with my memory of her, an image in my own mind! It would be a sort of incest" (20). Incest is a startling word to use here, even metaphorically, for there is nothing forbidden or shameful about honoring the memory of a deceased loved one. Nor would sexual fantasies of a deceased spouse be incestuous—they would be masturbatory. Why, then, would the memory of his late wife be a form of incest? Lewis never answers this question, and his anger is so intense at this point that he would reject any attempt to comfort or console him over his loss.

Lewis does not anticipate Elisabeth Kübler-Ross's stage theory of dying, in which she discusses the various stages through which terminally ill patients pass—denial, isolation, anger, bargaining, depression, and acceptance. But he does show how grief and sorrow are not a state but a process, one in which talking and writing can be especially valuable. He rarely spoke sympathetically about psychoanalysis—"Keep clear of psychiatrists unless you know that they are Christians," he wrote a friend in 1947 (*Letters of C. S. Lewis* 211)—but he reveals in *A Grief Observed* that the best way to confront dark emotion is not to repress but to express it, holding back nothing—neither anger nor envy nor agony. It is not the tragic emotions that Lewis finds difficult to express but rather the "bath of self-pity, the wallow, the loathsome sticky-sweet pleasure of indulging it—that disgusts me" (4). Yet he knows that self-pity is also part of the story of love and loss, and he doesn't hesitate to include it in his book, even if it disgusts him or arouses disgust in his readers. Emotionally charged, *A Grief Observed* becomes more remarkable when we recall Lewis's statement in *Surprised by Joy* that he distrusts and dislikes emotion, which he finds uncomfortable, embarrassing, and even dangerous. Ironically, these two autobiographical works are among his most successful literary creations, precisely because of their expressive power.

Nearly every thanatologist is familiar with *A Grief Observed*, which is essential reading in grief counseling and bereavement studies. Lewis knows that grief affects the body as well as the mind and spirit. The opening paragraph of the book describes the physical symptoms of grief, which are sometimes indistinguishable from fear. "I am not afraid, but the sensation is like being afraid. The same fluttering in the stomach, the same restlessness, the yawning. I keep on swallowing" (3). He also knows that bereavement is a "universal and integral part of our experience of love. It follows marriage as normally as marriage follows courtship or as autumn follows summer. It is not a truncation of the process but one of its phases; not the interruption of the dance, but the next figure" (50). This statement is, for me, perhaps the single greatest insight into the nature of bereavement. Lewis knows that bereavement is not simply a feeling but a process that cannot be rushed. Whereas Tennyson states in *In Memoriam*, "'Tis better to have loved and lost / Than never to have loved at all," Lewis recognizes a more painful truth: love inevitably leads to loss. Bereavement may become pathological for some grievers, but for most people it is a normal process, one that must be accepted as the inevitable price of love.

Lewis follows up this insight with an even greater revelation, one that I have never seen expressed before: "The more joy there can be in the marriage between the dead and the living, the better. The better in every way. For, as I have discovered, passionate grief does not link us with the dead but cuts us off from them" (54). He remains securely attached to her, engaged in a silent dialogue with her, even though he knows he will never see her again. He rejects the idea of bereavement as companionship in grief, instead affirming companionship in joy between the living and the dead. The movement from pain to consolation, implicit in most elegies, is strikingly visible in Lewis's spousal loss memoir, but *A Grief Observed* goes beyond this in affirming joy. His vision of companionship in joy acknowledges that the dead cannot be brought back to life—not only is that a biological impossibility but it would also be painful to the deceased, since they would then need to die again. Significantly, Lewis's epiphany does not depend upon the Christian belief in the reunion with the dead, a belief he shares but does not emphasize in the book, in part because it is unscriptural.

Toward the end of *A Grief Observed* Lewis makes an observation that I also wondered about myself when I was writing *Dying to Teach*. Writing has allowed him to "feel better," yet at the same time he experiences a "sort of shame, and a feeling that one is under a sort of obligation to cherish and foment and prolong one's unhappiness." Why does he wish to remain unhappy? "Partly, no doubt, vanity. We want to prove to ourselves that we are lovers on the grand scale, tragic heroes; not just ordinary privates in the huge army of the bereaved, slogging along and making the best of a bad job" (53). Lewis's answer to this question, or rather self-accusation, is that to imagine ourselves as tragic heroes is to succumb to despair. "I seem to remember—though I couldn't quote one at the moment—all sorts of ballads and folktales in which the dead tell us that our mourning does them some kind of wrong. They beg us to stop it. There may be far more depth in this than I thought." He vows at the end to avoid the Victorian convention of "mummification," making the "dead far more dead" (55). His conclusion—one that I hope will be true for myself—is to remain in touch with the Joy in his life. "I will turn to her as often as possible in gladness. I will even salute her with a laugh. The less I mourn her the nearer I seem to her" (56). He ends *A*

Grief Observed with an image of Joy on her deathbed, exclaiming to the chaplain, "I am at peace with God." Lewis adds, "She smiled, but not at me. Poi si tornò all' eterna fontana" (76)—an allusion to the *Divine Comedy*, when Beatrice, seeing Dante for the last time, looks down on him, smiles, and "then unto the eternal fountain she turned."

TWO

JOHN BAYLEY AND IRIS MURDOCH

"In Widowhood You Lose Not Only Your Loved One but Much of Yourself"

John Bayley had written one novel and several books of literary criticism before his wife, Iris Murdoch, began developing Alzheimer's disease in the mid 1990s, but he was not a memoirist, nor did he seem interested in autobiographical writing. He appeared to share his wife's suspicion of self-disclosure; she insisted that her novels were about "fictional" characters rather than "real" people. Peter J. Conradi notes in his biography that she not only denied drawing her characters from real life but also found the practice immoral. He quotes a 1982 diary entry in which she expresses her distaste of the personal element of fiction. "Autobiography: 'to try to tell the truth about oneself'—why bother? So you are indifferent to truth? No—one struggles with truth versus falsehood all the time. But that effort would be pointless, one must just try to be good. Idea of autobiography is utterly unattractive to me as an art form—and also somehow morally sickening" (529). Bayley and Murdoch were fascinated by psychology, yet neither spent much time reading literature as disguised self-revelation. They kept their personal lives separate from their literary lives—they had no interest in being celebrities. For all of these reasons, it was unlikely that Bayley would write a memoir about his wife; in fact, he wrote three: *Elegy for Iris* (1999), *Iris and Her Friends* (2000), and *Widower's House* (2001).

They were, to be sure, two of England's most distinguished writers. In his critical study *The Saint and the Artist*, the British Conradi calls Murdoch "our most intelligent novelist since George Eliot" (5), a comparison that would not have entirely pleased her, since she was no fan of the nineteenth-century novelist. The author of twenty-six novels, two books on philosophy and ethics, and a book on Sartre, Murdoch was made a Dame of the British Empire in 1987. Her novel *The Sea, the Sea* received Britain's most prestigious literary honor, the Booker Prize, in 1978. She was also one of the century's key moralists, as Martha Nussbaum suggests: "Murdoch, more than any other contemporary ethical thinker, has made us vividly aware of the many stratagems by which the ego wraps itself in a cozy self-serving fog that prevents egress to the reality of the other" (36). In the afterword to his biography, Conradi cites Harold Bloom's pronouncement upon her death in 1999 that there are "no first-rate writers left in Britain" (595). John Bayley was no less gifted, an eminent literary critic and the Wharton Professor of Literature at Oxford. He wrote many books and was a regular reviewer for the *New York Review of Books*. Murdoch believed—with justification—that her husband was the "greatest literary critic in England since Coleridge" (qtd. in Conradi, *Iris Murdoch*, 403). John Fletcher called their marriage "one of the most fruitful literary and critical partnerships of our time, and remarkable in any time" (qtd. in Conradi, *The Saint and the Artist*, 18). It was also an unlikely marriage, partly because they were so different. The 2001 film *Iris*, starring Jim Broadbent, Judi Dench, and Kate Winslet, captures Bayley's eccentricity and humor as well as his love for and devotion to his wife, though it fails to convey his intellectual brilliance and originality. "'I intend to make my mark,' the young Iris had once said, long before I met her. Her genius lives in her books'" (*Widower's House*, 132). Murdoch indeed made her mark, as did Bayley, and their genius lives in their many books.

Bayley's 1961 book *The Characters of Love* (titled *The Character of Love* in the 1963 edition I am using) foreshadows the portrayal of love in his memoiristic trilogy, which chronicles a remarkable forty-four year marriage. *The Character of Love* is not only a "study in the literature of personality," as its subtitle accurately states, but also a portrait of the author's vision of love. The book exemplifies "in one way or another the understanding about love which I had picked up in the course of my relationship with Iris" (159). Focusing on Chaucer's long poem *Troilus and Criseyde*, Shakespeare's *Othello*, and Henry James's *The Golden Bowl*, Bayley announces his thesis in the chapter called "The Worlds of Love," where he argues that an author's "success with this theme is closely linked with his attitude towards his own characters—that author, in fact, is best on love who best loves his own creations" (14). Authors' love for their characters, Bayley implies, has little to do with their approval or disapproval of them but rather with a "delight in their independent existence as *other people*, an attitude towards them which is analogous to our feelings toward those we love in life; and an intense interest in their personalities combined with a sort of detached solicitude, a respect for their freedom" (15; italics in original).

Reading *Elegy for Iris*, *Iris and Her Friends*, and *Widower's House*, one is struck by the extent to which he succeeds in capturing the existence of a woman who has lost her memory. And he does this by contrasting the past, when Iris Murdoch was one of the most dazzling women of her age, with the present, when she no longer knows her history or identity. These flashbacks offer us insight into the richness and beauty of their lives, and emphasize the importance of memory, which serves as one of the few consolations for the caregiver.

Bayley's decision to write about Iris Murdoch's illness was not an easy one, for he had always been a private man, avoiding the glare of publicity. As Robert Weil points out, Bayley, an authority on Russian novelists, was "following Tolstoyan precedent in redefining society's fear of disease and mental illness, echoing the words of Ivan Ilych, who had 'searched for his accustomed fear of death and could not find it'" (251–52). But a key difference between the two writers is that unlike Tolstoy, who uses the veil of fiction to tell the truth about the reality of dying and death, Bayley writes autobiographically, opening two lives to public scrutiny. "Bayley's dramatic decision not only to come forward with a public announcement of his wife's illness, but also to write joyously and spiritually about his experiences in caring for her reflects his estrangement from a late twentieth-century society where old age is feared and where death has been sanitized by our mainstream culture" (Weil 252). To write joyously about grief is a daunting challenge. "How boring bereaved people are. They have only one subject," Murdoch wrote in a 1953 diary entry after the death of a close friend (Conradi, *Iris Murdoch* 340). To write joyously and *interestingly* about grief is a double challenge.

Elegy for Iris

Of the three memoirs, *Elegy for Iris*—titled in the UK *A Memoir of Iris Murdoch*—is by far the best known. It also reveals the most about their marriage. Eight years younger than Iris Murdoch and far less worldly and sophisticated, the twenty-eight-year-old Bayley fell in love with her at first sight when they met in 1953. She was his first and only love, though she had several lovers at the time. He is strikingly open and candid about her extensive sexual experience—and his own inexperience: "She sensed I had next to no knowledge of lovemaking" (57). She was not only attracted to males and females, and they toward her, but she had the ability to keep all of her relationships separate. They "fell into each other's arms" (32) the first time she visits his Spartan college room after a dance at St. Anthony's College, Oxford, where she was teaching, and they spent the night together talking without stopping.

As Bayley gets to know her better, he is at first astonished—and then dismayed—by the sheer number of her lovers. "And there seemed to be so many of them. Persons who were, in a sense, in my own position. Iris seemed deeply and privately attached to them all. No doubt in all sorts of different ways. I could only hope that she did not talk to any of the others in quite the way that she talked to me, chattered childishly with me, kissed me" (*Elegy for Iris* 45). In his biography, Conradi cites Murdoch's comment in a 1976 diary entry that emphasizes the centrality of love to her both as an idea and as a reality: "Like Socrates, perhaps, love is the only subject on which I am really expert?" (199). Knowing that she had several lovers, "whom she was apparently juggling at the same time," Bayley intuits, correctly, as it turns out, that "she usually gave her favours out of admiration and respect: for, so to speak, the godlike rather than conventionally attractive or sexual attributes in the men who pursued her. Men who were gods for her she also found erotic, but sex was something she regarded as rather marginal, not an end in itself" (55). No god himself, he cannot help wondering why she was attracted to him. Before their marriage she informs him of all her past lovers, startling him by her almost portentous tone. "There was so-and-so with whom she had first been to bed, and so-and-so and so-and-so who had wanted to marry her" (70). Later he tells us that "there have been moments when I found myself wondering how Iris got on in bed with lovers whose approach was more ambitious or more demanding than my own" (93).

Throughout his memoirs Bayley returns repeatedly to the paradoxes of human relationships, always surprising and delighting us with his unconventional wisdom. In the beginning, he had no interest in her affairs with others. "By some emotional paradox, being in love made me, at least at first, more incurious about this, not less. Iris existed for me as a wonderful solitary being" (9). We expect that as their marriage develops, Bayley and Murdoch will praise the intimacy of marriage, and while this was true for both of them, he unexpectedly affirms that one of the "truest pleasures of marriage is solitude" (*Elegy for Iris* 40). As close as they were intellectually, emotionally, and sexually, they still retained their separate identities and independence, their "otherness." Perhaps the central paradox of their life together was their "apartness," as he reveals in an extraordinary passage describing the early years of marriage:

> Already we were beginning that strange and beneficent process in marriage by which a couple can, in the words of A. D. Hope, the Australian poet, "move closer and closer apart." The apartness is a part of the closeness, perhaps a recognition of it; certainly a pledge of complete understanding. There is nothing threatening or supervisory about such an understanding, nothing of what couples really mean when they say (or are alleged to say) to confidants or counsellors that their partner doesn't understand them. This usually means that one partner understands the other all too well, or that both do, and doesn't rejoice in the experience. (44)

Bayley sees a paradox but not a contradiction when he speaks about the joys of solitude in marriage. "The one went perfectly with the other. To feel oneself held and cherished and accompanied, and yet to be alone. To be closely and physically entwined, and yet feel solitude's friendly presence, as warm and undesolating as contiguity itself" (*Elegy for Iris* 123). There is thus an implicit parallel between a novelist's love for his or her characters, a delight in their independent existence as other people, and a husband's love for his wife. Husband and wife can be intimate with each other while at the same time respecting their spouse's freedom, independence, and otherness. Whereas one might see separation and closeness as binaries, Bayley sees them as complementary, each necessary for the other. Ironically, Alzheimer's disease shatters this apartness, for the loss of Iris's memory, freedom, and independence increases her dependence on her husband, who finds, as her illness worsens, that he can no longer leave her alone even for a moment. "Life is no longer bringing the pair of us 'closer and closer apart,' in the poet's tenderly ambiguous words. Every day we move closer and closer together. We could not do otherwise. There is a certain comic irony—happily, not darkly comic—that after more than forty years of taking marriage for granted, marriage has decided it is tired of this, and is taking a hand in the game" (265–66).

This passage is significant for several reasons. First, Bayley reveals his acceptance of his wife's illness and his role as caregiver—an acceptance that is, until the end of *Elegy for Iris*, largely free of anger, bitterness, or resentment. (These dark emotions appear more frequently in his next memoir, *Iris and Her Friends*.) Second, he displays here and elsewhere what may be called an ethics of caring: it is hard to imagine a more loving or devoted caregiver, one who is exquisitely attentive to her needs. Iris remains a character of love, long after she has forgotten the nature of love, and although he doesn't comment on this, his love is constant for better and for worse, in good times and bad. Third, he demonstrates his ability to see the "comic irony" of their situation, indeed, the comic irony of life, filled as it is with existential absurdity. This vision of comic irony could not be more different from the crisis of faith Lewis experiences after his wife's death, when he refers to God as a "Cosmic Sadist," a "spiteful imbecile" (*A Grief Observed* 30). A freethinker, Bayley never experienced a crisis of faith during or after his wife's protracted illness.

Throughout *Elegy for Iris*, Bayley reminds us of Sisyphus pushing his rock up a mountain, only to watch it roll down again, at which point he turns around and resumes his unending task. Iris is certainly not an inanimate rock, not even when she loses the power of language and volition; rather, her presence serves as her husband's anchor, holding him steady. She is as much his lifeline, his support system, as he is hers. "One must imagine Sisyphus happy," Camus states at the end of "The Myth of Sisyphus" (91), and so one must imagine Bayley happy at the end of the story. The happiness rests on the knowledge that love inevitably ends with loss; that we are all alone in an absurd universe, devoid of God or an afterlife; and that we must create our own meaning and care for those we love. Illness, suffering, and death remind us of the importance of living as fully and deeply as possible. They also remind us of our responsibilities to each other, our connectedness to those we love. Bayley recognizes throughout the story, particularly at the end, that he is needed more than ever to allay his wife's anxieties of apartness. Finally, unlike Edgar in *King Lear*, who concludes that "ripeness is all," Bayley knows that "helplessness is all" (267), a recognition that only strengthens his determination to care for his wife as best he can.

Bayley sees other comic—not tragic—ironies in Iris's illness. "The eeriness of Alzheimer's beginnings is also its reassurance" (*Elegy for Iris* 214). He knows that he should be worried about the future, but he also knows that time has no meaning to the Alzheimer's patient. "The exasperation of being followed about the house now by Iris is as strong and genuine as is my absolute need for it" (238). Were she to leave him, he realizes, he would compulsively follow her. "As the condition gets worse, it also gets better. It seems to compensate each new improvement"—to which he concludes, laconically, "[I] should be more thankful for that" (239). Without confusing the roles of patient and caregiver, he can feel himself unconsciously developing Iris's symptoms. "Does the care-giver involuntarily mimic the Alzheimer's condition? I'm sure I do" (241). Bayley never comments on a paradox that remains implicit throughout the trilogy: although the dying patient can become an unbearable burden to the caregiving spouse, the patient also grants the caregiver a priceless gift—the opportunity to demonstrate love, compassion, and devotion.

Bayley is honest enough to admit that he has never seen Iris "objectively" (10). He might have added that we can never see anyone, especially ourselves, objectively, for we all have a bias. His early descriptions of her indicate that her appearance to him was constantly changing. She looks like a woman without a past or known present when he sees her for the first time on a bicycle, and he later recalls a friend's malicious statement that she is "like a little bull" (10). Not long afterward, when he sees her leaving from an Oxford tutorial, she appears devoid of sexual appeal. "That made the fact that I was in love with her much more exciting; and it also seemed highly satisfactory, for what, as I instantly realised, was a rather ignoble reason. Since she had no obvious female charms, she was not likely to appeal to other men" (15). Why she appeared to him so unattractive remains, he admits, a "complete mystery"; the truth was, he later discovers, to his dismay, that she was irresistible to both sexes. "It was my naive and now inexplicable assumption that she could appeal only to me, and to no one else, that stopped me seeing how fearfully, how almost diabolically attractive everyone else found her. They knew more about such things, I suppose" (15).

The willingness to acknowledge his naïveté and haplessness is one of the most endearing aspects of Bayley's character. Throughout the memoir he reveals both humility and self-effacing wit. He tells us at the beginning that unlike the hard-working Iris, he was "more naturally indolent" (*Elegy for Iris* 6). A few pages later he confesses to being a "clueless young creature" (16). After they were married, Iris would occasionally ask him for technical assistance with a novel, as when she inquired about the special diet for a character in *The Sea, the Sea*. Some of his suggestions found their way into the novel, but when it was awarded the Booker Prize, one of the judges, A. J. Ayer, remarked in his prize-giving speech that he had "enjoyed everything in the novel except for the food" (41). Describing a situation in which Iris's generous offer to allow two acquaintances to use her room resulted in their wanton destruction of one of her treasured possessions, Bayley observes that "I still grind my teeth when I think of it, even though they are not my own teeth any more, but false ones" (146). He sees himself not as Iris's equal, intellectually, artistically, or morally, but as an English teacher who writes "the odd critical study" (41).

Bayley readily admits his sexual inexperience and naïveté, his quirky humor and penchant for making a "decidedly mediocre impression" on others. Feeling overwhelmed with awe and admiration for Iris at the beginning of their relationship, he couldn't understand why she was interested in him. Nor could he entirely trust his initial impressions and perceptions of her, for there were times when he was unnerved by something as superficial as a flame-colored brocade that she wore at a party. "I felt in some way scandalised: dazzled but appalled at the same time. All my daydreams, my illusions and preconceptions about the bicycle woman seemed to have torn away and vanished back into a past which I would still very much have preferred to be inhabiting, given the choice. But I had no choice" (*Elegy for Iris* 27–28). He learned that he could trust his perceptions of her only when he rejected others' perceptions, which invariably were more conventional than his own. It did not take him long to discover that although her physical appearance was constantly transforming, like the mythical Proteus, who, not surprisingly, fascinated her and her fictional characters, her own character was solid, unchanging, essential.

In fact, it was Proteus, the shape-changing sea god in Greek mythology, who helped them resolve the only serious crisis during their courting years. They began dating in 1954, several years before the free love climate of the 1960s, and jealousy consumed Bayley whenever he brooded over Iris's sexual adventurousness with other men. He did not want to know about these affairs, but he could not stop himself from thinking about them. "The more I got to know Iris during the early days of our relationship, the less I understood her. Indeed, I soon began not to want to understand her. I was far too preoccupied at the time to think of such parallels, but it was like living in a fairy story—the kind with sinister overtones and not always a happy ending—in which a young man loves a beautiful maiden who returns his love but is always disappearing into some unknown and mysterious world, about which she will reveal nothing. Eventually, he makes some dire mistake, and she disappears for good" (*Elegy for Iris* 45). Iris *was* always disappearing, he adds, though she was always "quite open" about the men with whom she disappeared. As their relationship became more serious, he sensed that they would have to reach an understanding of this issue. He never uses words like "faithlessness" or "promiscuity" to describe her behavior at this time, nor does he require an all-or-nothing commitment from her. Her implicit belief in the nonexclusivity of love, at least before marriage, would have made it unlikely that she would agree to such a demand. Conradi notes in his biography that Murdoch "praised monogamy—of which she indeed had a happy experience—attacking the promiscuity which she forgot had marked her own youth" (538).

It was at this point that mythotherapy came to the rescue. "'Remember Proteus,' she used to say. 'Just keep tight hold of me and it will be all right.' Proteus had the power of changing himself into any shape he wished—lion, serpent, monster, fish—but when Hercules held tightly on to him throughout all these transformations, he was compelled in the end to surrender, and to resume his proper shape as the man he was" (*Elegy for Iris* 47). Bayley continued to hold on to her, and the crisis ended. The mythic parallels are inexact, for she continued to be attracted to other men, but he became less threatened by the possibility of losing her. There is no implication that she continued having sexual relations with other men after marriage, and their long marriage appeared to be conflict free, with each being devoted to the other.

The constancy of their love throughout the forty-four-year marriage offers a striking contrast to the ill-fated trysts and infatuations in Thomas Hardy's fictional world. Hardy is one of Bayley's favorite writers, and he refers to him often in the memoirs. He also wrote a book on Hardy in which he quotes a revealing passage from a short story called "Barbara of the House of Grebe": "a lover's heart after possession being comparable to the earth in its geologic stages . . . first a hot coal, then a warm one, then a cooling cinder, then chilly—the simile shall be pursued no further" (*An Essay on Hardy* 22). By contrast, to judge from Bayley's three memoirs, his marriage to Murdoch was sunny and warm, with no hint of storm.

Murdoch's statements on love are consistent with Bayley's portrayal of their own love. "Love is a kind of bombshell that breaks people's lives, really falling in love," she observes in an interview with Michael O. Bellamy. "It's obviously a dangerous condition, because it's so tremendously self-centered. To really love somebody in an unselfish way is not perhaps thoroughly natural to human beings; certainly in romantic love, in 'falling in love' love, one is tremendously selfish. One feels that everything in the world has gone away to the other person, but then this becomes a function of one's own will, too" (54). She and Bayley believed in the ideal of unselfish love, rarely found in Hardy's world but demonstrated throughout Bayley's memoirs. "The human task is to become unselfish, to unself," Murdoch said in an interview with Barbara Stevens Heusel (200). In Murdoch's comments on Plato in *Metaphysics as a Guide to Morals*, she contrasts two types of love and returns to the concept of unselfing. "A love relationship can occasion extreme selfishness and possessive violence, the attempt to dominate that other place so that it be no longer separate; or it can prompt a process of unselfing wherein the lover learns to see, and cherish and respect, what is not himself. There are many aspects to this teaching; for instance, letting the beloved go with a good grace, knowing when and how to give up, when to express love by silence or by clearing off. This negative heroism may be very enlightening, aided by the palpable satisfaction of having behaved well when one desired to behave otherwise" (16–17).

Reading Bayley's memoirs, one senses they worked through the feelings of selfishness or possessiveness that may have been present in their early relationship. Moving "closer and closer apart" meant that neither sought to dominate or possess the other. Bayley credits Iris with the ability to love unselfishly, along with the ability to empathize with friends' tempestuous emotions without experiencing these emotions herself. "She never participated in the drama of themselves put on by others, but she could feel intensely herself emotions of love, jealousy, adoration, even rage. I never saw these emotions myself, but I knew they were there. In my case, she could always take jealousy away simply by being with me" (*Elegy for Iris* 67).

Proteus may have saved Bayley's early relationship with Iris, but there was something distinctly unprotean about her character. Her essential goodness, perhaps even more than her extraordinary intellectual talent, formed the basis of their lifelong marital love. Her generosity, compassion, calmness, and wisdom formed the unchanging bedrock of her personality. Not even Alzheimer's changes that. She never displays any of the darker emotions that occasionally manifest themselves in Bayley's character, such as anger and jealousy. He always offers the most generous interpretations of her behavior, as when he tells us that her many sexual lovers were the "recipients of Iris's kindness. They had desired her, and not been rejected" (*Elegy for Iris* 72). He does not idealize Murdoch, but she does have a distinctly saintly quality, which is consistent with her philosophical and novelistic interest in Christian ethics. Religious without believing in formal religion, she embodies the Christ-like virtues of humility and tolerance. Her instincts are always kindly, and she is genuine in her relationships with others, without guile or selfishness. His early impression of her—"She was a superior being, and I knew that superior beings just did not have the kind of mind that I did" (11)—is borne out by everything she says, does, and writes. The only qualification the reader may add is that Bayley, too, is a superior being: theirs was a marriage made in heaven, in which neither of them, ironically, believed.

Elegy for Iris describes a husband and wife whose marital sympathy depended, paradoxically, upon separation. "Apartness in marriage is a state of love, and not a function of distance, or preference, or practicality" (127). Their differences were at least as striking as their similarities.

They had many literary and philosophical interests in common, but they kept their distance from each other. Murdoch rarely spoke with Bayley about the novels on which she was working, and he read them only after they were published. (*The Sea, the Sea* was an exception.) Early in their marriage she responded to his questions about her current novel, but he soon stopped asking. I found this detail curious, since authors often ask their spouses or friends for advice about their work in progress. It appears that neither needed the other for intellectual or artistic validation. Despite being perhaps England's leading novelist, Murdoch had little interest in reading contemporary fiction, a subject on which her husband was an authority. They differed on the question of religion and spirituality. Bayley could appreciate the spiritual power of a novel like *The Bell* though he had little understanding of or interest in spirituality. Yet he was always respectful of her spirituality even when it may have led her into dubious relationships.

There was little professional competition between them, but this may have been largely because of Bayley's decision to give up writing novels when Iris began her career as a novelist, an interpretation endorsed by biographer Conradi: "Following the success in 1955 of *In Another Country*, John ceased for thirty-five years writing novels: Iris's career was 'simply too meteoric'" (415). One of the first questions Murdoch asked him, before they knew each other, was whether he thought about writing a novel, and he was so surprised that he answered in the affirmative. "This was not strictly true," he confesses to us with characteristic honesty. "It was nearly true, and I determined on the spot . . . to make it true that very night" (*Elegy for Iris* 21). After *In Another Country* was published in 1955, he gave up writing fiction until the 1990s when Iris, beginning to develop memory problems, suggested that he write a story about a shadowy-looking woman whom they saw bathing while vacationing in Italy. Iris's suggestion was the impetus behind his novel *Alice* and the two others in the trilogy, *The Queer Captain* and *George's Lair*. "Although it was not until two or three years later that Iris's Alzheimer's symptoms became fully apparent, I have sometimes wondered if she knew that her own career as a novelist was nearly over. Was she encouraging me to start again?" (200). Bayley never explains whether he regretted giving up fiction writing nor why he resumed fiction writing decades later. He devotes little commentary to their separate but parallel writing careers.

In *Iris and Her Friends* he remarks on the paradox that the loss of her memory opened the floodgates of his own remembrance of the past, almost as if he now had to remember for the two of them.

Bayley is careful not to set himself up as the inerrant expert on his wife's fiction. He cannot refrain entirely, however, from setting critics straight when he believes they are wrong about her fiction, as when he rejects the charge that her novels are whimsical or sentimental. Nor does he seem reluctant to point out to her something about her novels of which she may not be entirely aware, as when he tells her about her sympathy with all forms of great art. "You are the only novelist I know who can make the whole world of art come into your novels without being laborious about it, or making it seem fancy"—to which she smilingly responds, "Well, thanks very much. I don't like to think about what happens when I do it. You're the critic, not me" (*Elegy for Iris* 120).

Murdoch was no Florence Nightingale, Bayley admits, but she cared for him when he became ill early in their marriage and developed glandular fever, which, like a "Victorian illness," "makes the patient weak, as if fading painlessly away" (*Elegy for Iris* 156). She nursed him to health while continuing to work on a novel. "She just looked after me, and as she did so, I could see from her face that her mind was far away, pursuing the plot of the story she was engaged on. She found no bother at all in getting on with it while I was ill, and indeed told me later that she owed the genesis of that particular tale to the quiet time my illness had brought us both. That gave me such satisfaction that I at once fell ill again" (158). He does not need to point out that the situation will be reversed decades later, when he cares for her during her extended illness, all the time with his own mind far away, pursuing the plot of the memoirs about their life together.

Murdoch was the least narcissistic person Bayley knew, but some of her literary mentors and lovers had colossal egos. One of these men inspires Bayley's most satirical prose. "There is the kind of literary personality, of the sort the Germans refer to reverently as a *Dichter*, who is organised on so impressive and heroic a scale that questions of modesty, image, and attitudinising can hardly be said to arise" (*Elegy for Iris* 164). The word *Dichter* means "poet" in German, and Bayley tells us that Iris had made "masochistic journeys" to see the "god-monster of Hampstead" (149). This is the only time he characterizes Murdoch as masochistic, though he later wonders aloud whether her trips to the "god-monster" of Hampstead were motivated by self-abasement. "Was she, almost as if in one of her own novels, the absent victim of a sacrifice in which she would have participated as a willing victim had she been present?" (149).

Who was the *Dichter*? Bayley does not identify him, but he tells us that he has authored a long novel called *Die Blendung*. One does not need sophisticated research skills to unmask the *Dichter* as Elias Canetti, the Bulgarian-born German writer whose 1935 novel, translated as *Auto-de-Fe*, aroused Nazi wrath, forcing the Jewish writer to flee to England, where he met and had an affair with Murdoch shortly before she began seeing Bayley. She dedicated her 1956 novel *The Flight from the Enchanter* to Canetti. The recipient of the Nobel Prize in Literature in 1981, he died in 1994, five years before Bayley published *Elegy for Iris*. There was no particular reason why Bayley did not name the author of *Die Blendung*—later in the memoir he does refer to him by name. Perhaps Bayley felt that he could be less inhibited by not naming the *Dichter*. "Squat, almost dwarfish, with a massive head and thick black hair, he looked like a giant cut short at the waist" (*Elegy for Iris* 165). He had a giant ego, too, as Bayley notes sarcastically when he describes meeting the *Dichter* at a literary party. Canetti asked Bayley what his attitude was toward *King Lear*, arguably Shakespeare's greatest and most tragic play, but it soon became apparent that the question was entirely self-motivated. "'Friends tell me that my book is unbearable,' he said. Fortunately, I knew this to be a reference to his long novel *Die Blendung*, and I nodded my head gravely. There was further silence. '*King Lear* is also unbearable,' he pronounced at last" (164). Bayley's response? "The mage was certainly mesmeric" (165).

No less unbearable were the scathing comments Canetti made about Murdoch in the final installment of his uncompleted autobiography, *Party in the Blitz*, published posthumously in German in 2003 and translated into English in 2005. Canetti accuses Murdoch of being "the bubbling Oxford stewpot. Everything I despise about English life is in her. You could imagine her speaking incessantly, as a tutor, and incessantly *listening*: in the pub, in bed, in conversation with her male or female lovers" (163) After ridiculing her as a novelist, calling her an "illegitimate writer" who never suffered for her art, Canetti then damns her as a lover:

"She lay unmoving and unchanged, I barely felt myself enter her, I didn't sense that she felt anything, perhaps I might have felt something if she had resisted in some form. But that was as much out of the question as any pleasure. The only thing I noticed was that her eyes darkened, and that her reddish Flemish skin got a little redder" (167). "Canetti's English memoirs caused a sensation when they first came out in Germany," reports Jeremy Adler in his afterword to *Party in the Blitz*. "His anger at what he considered the faults of English life might have been enough to ensure attention, but his broadside against the literary scene seemed designed to shock" (197). Puzzled by the brutality of Canetti's denunciation in print of a woman he often spoke highly about in his private life, Adler speculates that in *Party in the Blitz* he "turns her into a counter-image of his own self, attacking her with unrestrained ferocity, dismembering every thread of her being" (233). Peter Conradi suggests in his biography that Canetti symbolized to Murdoch the dark double from which she struggled to free herself. Murdoch told Bayley shortly before marriage that her close relationship with Canetti had ended and that he had given the two "his blessing," as she put it. And then, in a significant sentence, Bayley offers us an insight into her need to write about Canetti. "She continued to see him from time to time and her creative imagination continued to be enthralled by him, even though, as she told me, by writing about him in her own way she got him out of her system, and finally in a sense out of her novels, too" (*Elegy for Iris* 68–69).

Bayley returns to the *Dichter* near the end of *Iris and Her Friends*, relating a "vile Canetti nightmare" that shows how threatened he was by Iris's former lover. While returning with his wife from a close friend's funeral, Bayley admits for the first time in the memoir that he "longed for death" (255), largely because Iris's health had rapidly deteriorated. He imagines that she has become a tiresome old woman named Priscilla, with whom he is on bad terms. Suddenly he has a "dream, but it was also a story, a fiction, and it was hateful" (256). His need for this story, he confesses, is also hateful. "This absurd nightmare that I started to tell myself was like a revenge, engendered by the demons of solitude, a revenge taken on the mad stranger screaming and protesting beside me" (256–57). He then has a vision of a man on the road with a scythe over his shoulder. Bayley stops the car and Priscilla immediately "shimmered up to the strange man, all apology and London charm. She talked to him, smiled at him. He had a massive face and head, thick black hair. He was squat and sinister" (257). "Where had I seen that man?" Bayley asks. "He was Dr. Elias Canetti, the distinguished author, Nobel Prize winner" (257).

Bayley then discloses that before he married Iris, he was terrified that Canetti "would carry her off, like Pluto, into his own dark underworld. But Iris escaped in time, fortunately for me" (*Iris and Her Friends* 258). As the phantasmagoria continues, a "sweet-looking" woman invites Bayley and Priscilla inside a house, and he imagines leaving Priscilla with Canetti while he goes off with the other woman, who almost certainly is Canetti's wife. (In *Elegy for Iris* Bayley recalls Iris telling him that Canetti's wife, a woman with a "sweet face and air of patient, welcoming reserve," would sometimes be present in their apartment when her husband was making love with another woman [68].) Canetti approves of this because it allows him to take Iris into the "Dark Lord's Domain." Bayley then makes an observation about Iris's relationship with Canetti that does not appear in the earlier memoir. "When I first fell in love with Iris, she had told me of this strange and wonderful man, with whom she had been and still was in love. When he learned about my existence from some third party, he had forbade her to see me. Fortunately, she ignored that. But the shadow of Canetti seemed in those early days to stretch all the way from Hampstead to Oxford" (*Iris and Her Friends* 259).

Bayley's decision to publicize in *Iris and Her Friends* his lifelong fear that his wife might succumb to Canetti's frightening power reveals the power of a "childish fear" in a septuagenarian's unconscious mind. The fantasy also conveys Bayley's understandable anger over his present situation—being married to a once-extraordinary woman who has now become hideous. Canetti had once told Bayley that he could marry Iris; now he says, in the dream, "'I give you [her.]' I am giving you this madness, this mad woman. . . . To have and to hold, to love and to cherish" (260). The nightmare ends, and "humour, normality, love" (260) return, with husband and wife resuming their trip home, holding hands.

Unlike Canetti's "tell-all" autobiography, Bayley remains discreet in what he reveals about his life with Iris Murdoch. There are no sensationalistic self-disclosures, no lurid descriptions, no titillating erotic stories, no shocking revelations of their life together. Written in a spirit of loving-kindness, the memoir embodies an aesthetic of generosity. *Elegy for*

Iris celebrates a long and fulfilling marriage, one that brought happiness to husband and wife and allowed both to nurture their own and each other's creativity. Apart from Bayley's fear of the spectral Canetti, there were few if any dark secrets in their marriage, and both husband and wife appeared to be happy and self-content, the opposite of the tormented artists who torture others and themselves. If the plot of this sunny and stable marriage is insufficiently complex or tempestuous enough to compel the reader's interest, there is enough conflict in his heartbreaking portrait of her slow, irreversible journey into darkness. She remains a character of love and a loving character even as she loses her memory, identity, and personhood. The brilliance and originality of *Elegy for Iris* lie in its unflinching honesty about the cruel ravages of Alzheimer's disease, a disease that is in many ways more devastating for the caregiver than for the patient. The book offers an inspirational portrait of a caregiver who remains tirelessly attentive to his wife's physical and psychological needs while at the same time transmuting her life, past and present, into the stuff of art. Bayley doesn't analyze his motives for writing about her in *Elegy for Iris*, nor does he question how she would have responded to the book if she were still able to read. It is safe to say, however, that he writes not to get her out of his system, or, worse, to move on with his life, but to honor the woman who has spent a lifetime bringing insight, beauty, and pleasure to him and her readers.

Attuned to the subtle changes wrought by the illness, Bayley informs us in the beginning of the story that Iris remains "her old self in many ways." She can still autograph a book for an admirer, please others, enjoy her lifelong habit of swimming. She still loves to be teased, and she can even tell the difference between one of her husband's mirthful jokes, humor for its own sake, and his increasingly strained jokes that strike her as inauthentic, designed to allay her worry. Like most Alzheimer's sufferers, she knows dimly that something is wrong but doesn't know how to react to memory loss. As *Elegy for Iris* progresses, so does her disease. As a cloud of anxiety and dread settles over her life, darkening her once-sunny disposition, she pretends that nothing is wrong. The denial is reinforced by the anxious caregiver, who becomes infected by fear. During the early stages of the illness Bayley reads to her old favorites such as *Agamemnon* and other Greek plays in translation, but the reading only reminds her of the loss of identity, although, as he tells us, "reminder is hardly the word, for an Alzheimer's patient is not usually conscious in any definable way of what has happened. If it were otherwise, the process, however irreversible it becomes in the end, would have developed along different lines, in a different form. Some sufferers do remain conscious of their state, paradoxical as this seems. The torment of knowing that you cannot speak or think what you want must be intolerable, and I have met patients in whom such a torment is clearly visible. But when Iris talks to me, the result seems normal to her and to me surprisingly fluent, provided I do not listen to what is being said but apprehend it in a matrimonial way, as the voice of familiarity, and thus of recognition" (63).

The memoirist learns, in other words, to read his wife's words differently, not for their content and context, which make no sense, but for their clue to her affective state. For a person like Murdoch who has spent her entire life reading and writing, losing the ability to read and write while still otherwise remaining alive is perhaps the worst fate imaginable. Now Bayley must read for her, read to her, and indeed read her as if she were an undecipherable text. He must not only speak for her, because she cannot speak for herself, but he must also manage her, because she cannot manage herself. The loss of identity is reflected in the empty expression on her face. "The face of an Alzheimer's patient has been clinically described as the 'lion face'" (53). Bayley himself speaks like a clinician here, one who attends to a patient's outer and inner reality.

Bayley's instinctive ability as a caregiver is strikingly evident in an interview he gave to Joanna Coles that was first published in the *Guardian* (Manchester) in 1996 and reprinted in the 2003 volume *From a Tiny Corner in the House of Fiction: Conversations with Iris Murdoch*, edited by Gillian Dooley. Murdoch is present during most of the interview, and he is exemplary in his empathy, reassuring her that her writer's block is only temporary. "'It has occurred before, darling,' says Bayley, leaning towards her reassuringly. 'You've had periods of lying fallow, as one might say, rather like a field. Because what is really rather extraordinary about you darling, if I might say, is that you don't mind being interrupted, and you don't keep pompous writing hours. You simply write whenever you feel like it'" (246). (In *Elegy for Iris* he tells us that she never had writer's block earlier in her career [218].) His humor may be silly, but it doesn't fail to evoke mirthful laughter, as when he responds to Iris's request to pour her and the interviewer a cup of coffee: "'Pour? Oh, I thought you meant paw!' And he starts scrabbling at the air as if he's a cat, and we all laugh" (247). When Iris reveals a few moments later that she's "in a place from which I am trying to get out," which obviously distresses Coles and Bayley, he tactfully breaks the silence by asking the interviewer if she has written a novel. She confesses gloomily that she hasn't, to which he says, encouragingly, "It's well worth trying" (249). The interview ends with Bayley confiding privately to Coles, "We've been to see doctors you know and they say the old brain's very crafty. It can come up against a block and for a bit things seem a bit strange, but then it finds its way around things again" (249–50). Anyone reading the interview would agree with Coles that their relationship "is not only touching, it's still fresh and young, making sense of what marriage is for" (247).

Unlike other irreversible diseases, Alzheimer's generally does not cause unbearable physical suffering. The psychological suffering, however—anxiety, confusion, dread, and panic attacks—may be unbearable to patient and caregiver alike. Bayley describes these panic moments, when they both seem paralyzed by fear. Hearing others' stories may not always be comforting. A woman married to an Alzheimer's patient "cheerfully" remarks to Bayley that it was "like being chained to a corpse," and even though he politely agrees, not wishing to challenge her experience, he feels repelled by the suggestion that Iris's affliction could resemble that of the woman's husband. He is repelled, not because the simile is inaccurate but because he does not wish to see himself or his wife in such a self-dramatizing way. He then makes a telling observation about the need to see one's own situation as different from others'. "My own situation, I felt, was quite different from hers. It's not an uncommon reaction, as I've come to realise, among Alzheimer's partners. One needs very much to feel that the unique individuality of one's spouse has not been lost in the common symptoms of a clinical condition" (*Elegy for Iris* 49).

As a writer Bayley prefers understatement to overstatement, comedy to tragedy, irony to sentimentality. He never pretends to have more knowledge or patience than he has. We learn more about his life than about hers, but he sees Iris as the starring character of the story, the heroine, and himself in a supporting role. His writing has a metaphorical richness that never fails to impress us, as when he says that his mode of communication with Iris "seems like underwater sonar, each bouncing pulsations off the other, then listening for an echo" (*Elegy for Iris* 51). More interested in presenting paradoxes than in explaining them, he is a keen and reliable observer. He reports that Murdoch once told him that the question of identity puzzled her. "She thought she herself hardly possessed such a thing, whatever it was" (64). He then speculates that those with a strong identity may suffer more from Alzheimer's than those who, like his wife, were not egocentric. "Iris's own lack of a sense of identity seemed to float her more gently into its world of preoccupied emptiness" (65). Until the end of the book, he speaks lightly about his own emotions when caring for her, dwelling on the unexpected consolations of Alzheimer's for the patient and caregiver. "Nowadays she lies quietly asleep, sometimes giving a little grunt or murmur, often sleeping well past nine, when I rouse and dress her. This ability to sleep like a cat, at all hours of the day and night, must be one of the great blessings that sometimes go with Alzheimer's, converse of the anxiety state that comes on in wakefulness and finds worried questions such as 'When are we leaving?'" (73–74).

Those who write autobiographically must be able to see themselves as both participants and observers, always a challenge when one attempts to record one's hidden blind spots. Bayley is particularly effective in maintaining this double vision, and he does so through self-effacing humor. He tells us, for example, that in the "old days" he would sometimes throw a tantrum if something had not been done properly, blaming Iris, rightly or wrongly, for the problem. She would then become "calm, reassuring, almost maternal" and find a way to solve the problem. Few memoirists would record such a detail, and even fewer would then admit that they exploited this buried reflex as a way to manage an ill spouse. "If she has been following me all day, like Mary's bear, interrupting tiresome business or letter writing (very often letters to her own fans), I erupt in what can seem even to me an uncontrolled fit of exasperation, stamping on the floor and throwing the papers and letters on it, waving my hands in the air. It always works. Iris says, 'Sorry . . . sorry' and pats me before going quietly away. She will be back soon, but that doesn't matter. My tantrum has reassured her as no amount of my own caring, or my calming efforts to reply to her rationally, could have done" (*Elegy for Iris* 76).

Bayley never tells us what if anything Murdoch said to him about caring for her. Did she acknowledge at some point that she could no longer care for herself? Did she express sadness that their lives would never be the same? Was she angry at him for being healthy? Did she feel guilty that he was wearing himself out in caring for her? Did she express gratitude that he was so devoted to her? Bayley never raises any of these questions. Nor does he tell us in *Elegy for Iris* whether he began to wonder how his life would be different after her death—whether, indeed, he wished to outlive her? Or did he feel, to the contrary, that his life would end with hers?

What Bayley does tell us, however, is how he cared for his wife on a day-to-day basis. *Elegy for Iris* is not a how-to book, but it offers caregivers practical survival strategies for impossible situations. The main strategy he credits to the Reverend Sidney Smith, a contemporary of Jane Austen, who urged his depressed parishioners to "take short views of human nature—never further than dinner or tea" (53). (On the last page of the memoir Bayley spells the reverend's first name as "Sydney" as well as on p. 73 of *Iris and Her Friends.*) At first Bayley expresses this platitude seriously, but after awhile he repeats it as an "incantation or joke, which can raise a laugh if it is accompanied by some horsing around, a live pantomime of 'short views' being taken. It is not now intended to be rationally received, but it gets a smile anyway" (53). It also gets a smile from Bayley's readers, who recognize that words have little impact on Alzheimer's patients, apart from, perhaps, the loving tone in which they are expressed. And it is Bayley's loving tone that most affects his readers.

Still another survival strategy, one that Bayley practices on every page but on which he never comments, is the reverse: taking long views. That is, one recalls a long and rich life spent together. It is the consolation of memory. He engages in a secular version of counting his blessings, expressing gratitude for what was and, at least for him, what continues to be. Taking long views is what the memoirist does, writing about a past that continues to live in the writer's memory. These long views remind him how fortunate he and Iris have been. Blessed with a long and accurate memory, Bayley can reflect upon a lifetime of love, happiness, art, and achievement. Nothing in the future can destroy what they had in the past.

Another survival strategy is to be as physically close to the Alzheimer patient as possible. "A goose which cannot find other geese will attach itself to some object—another animal, even a stone or a post—and never lose sight of it. This terror of being alone, of being cut off for even a few seconds from the familiar object, is a feature of Alzheimer's. If Iris could climb inside my skin now, or enter me as if I had a pouch like a kangaroo, she would do so. She has no awareness of what I am doing, only an awareness of what I am" (*Elegy for Iris* 127). Some readers may be disturbed by these analogies, which appear dehumanizing, but they capture the dehumanizing features of Alzheimer's disease, which robs its victims of their humanness. Their new closeness is, for him, though not for her, suffocating, worlds apart from what their marriage used to be like, when they were separate but never separated. They are now, for the first time, truly together, suffocatingly close, though it is a closeness not to be wished for, as he suggests in a passage filled with heartrending irony. "We have actually become, as is often said of a happy married couple, inseparable—in a way, like Ovid's Baucis and Philemon, whom the gods gave the gift of growing old together as trees. It is a way of life that is unfamiliar. The closeness of apartness has necessarily become the closeness of closeness. And we know nothing of it; we have never had any practice" (126–27).

Still another survival strategy is humor, which never fails Bayley. "Humour seems to survive anything" (*Elegy for Iris* 51), and no matter how despondent or despairing he becomes, he finds some redeeming comedy in the situation. His humor is often corny but never cruel, and he directs it against himself rather than against Iris. "A burst of laughter, snatches of doggerel, song, teasing nonsense rituals once lovingly exchanged awake an abruptly happy response, and a sudden beaming smile that must resemble those moments in the past between explorers and savages, when some sort of clowning pantomime on the part of the former seems often to have evoked instant comprehension and amusement" (51). There are not many writers who can entertain us with their offbeat humor while at the same time enlightening us about its evolutionary significance. Unlike Elias Canetti, who pompously saw himself as King Lear, Bayley contents himself with being Lear's comic fool, whose words contain philosophical wisdom.

There is no preparation or practice for an illness like Alzheimer's, either for the patient or for the caregiver. Nor does Bayley have much practice in writing about his wife's life, either past or present. *Elegy for Iris* is his first memoir, and while his life has been steeped in reading, writing about, and teaching literature, nothing has prepared him for the challenge of imagining a "real character" whom he can no longer recognize. There is a chilling irony in Murdoch's injunction to him, during their courting years, to "Remember Proteus," for neither of them could have predicted in the mid 1950s that her metamorphosis would become so horrific forty years later. So too is there a disquieting irony when she urged him to "just keep tight hold of me and it will be all right" (*Elegy for Iris* 47). Bayley does keep tight hold of her, but it is not all right.

Elegy for Iris is not an overly self-conscious memoir, concerned with the theoretical difficulties of representing ineffable reality. Bayley is more a storyteller than a theorist, and he succeeds in showing how the story of his life with Iris Murdoch has changed irrevocably. He never worries about the conscious or unconscious distortions implicit in all autobiographies, the "lies of the autobiographer" that Andrew Hudgins writes about in *The Glass Anvil*. In Hudgins's view, the "lies of the autobiographer" are inevitable and include, in "ascending order of transgression from misdemeanor to felony," the following: (1) the "lie of narrative cogency," which "contracts, condenses, tightens memory"; (2) its opposite, the "lie of texture," which invents details to make the truth more believable; (3) the "lie of fictional convention," in which the truth is shaped into literary categories; (4) the "lie of emotional evasion," which is the "sin of omission"; (5) the "lie of the recreated self," in which autobiographers makes themselves look good; (6) the "lie of extended consciousness," which includes both the appropriation of other people's experiences and the application of adult knowledge to a childhood experience; (7) the "lie of interpretation," in which autobiographers formulate an interpretation that "tends to drive out other possibly valid interpretations and suppress ambivalence, ambiguity, and chance"; (8) and finally the "lie of impressionism," which is motivated by the desire to create an artistically coherent work. "The autobiography dances on the shifting middle ground between fact and fiction, reportage and imagination, actuality and art; and different writers will draw their lines on that ground in different places." Though the "lies of interpretation and impressionism bother me," Hudgins concedes, "they are essential. We read memoirs precisely to find out what one writer thinks his life means and how that life felt to the one who lived it" (93–106). Memoirists also heighten the dramatic significance of their stories for artistic effect, as Thomas Larson indicates in his study of the genre. "In my experience, nine out of ten memoirists will confess that they embellish their stories for dramatic effect. Nine out of ten will also admit that their memories of events have made their stories more dramatic than the original events themselves" (152–53). Both Hudgins and Larson remind us that however much we value objective truth, we always view reality—and ourselves—subjectively, a conclusion Bayley would doubtlessly endorse.

Bayley pauses periodically in his narration to comment on the impossibility of fully realizing Iris's character. His wife's absent presence calls into question his ability to remember and document her past. "Is it that I can think of her only as she now is, which is for me the same as she has always been? In any case, no description of anybody, however loving, can seem to do anything but veer away from the person concerned, not because it distorts his or her 'reality,' whatever that may be, but because the describer himself begins to lose all confidence in the picture of the person he is creating" (145). Bayley does not suggest a solution to this dilemma, but he doesn't allow the unrepresentability of reality to prevent him from doing his best to conjure the old Iris Murdoch back to life. Iris remains his muse in life, death, and the shadowy death-in-life netherworld of Alzheimer's disease.

Unlike cancer patients, whose lives change forever on the day of their diagnosis, Alzheimer's patients do not realize in a flash they are suffering from an irreversible, fatal disease. They may be troubled for months or years by failing memory, but as the symptoms worsen, and the fog of forgetfulness slowly descends upon them, they cannot realize the gravity of their situation. But the caregiver can. The first indication of Murdoch's illness came during a presentation she was giving in Israel in 1994, when she could not summon the words to answer questions from the audience. Everyone could tell there was something seriously wrong—everyone except Murdoch herself. "It was hard to say how conscious she was of her own difficulty, but the effect soon became paralysing, for the listener as well as for her" (*Elegy for Iris* 212). The slow decline began to accelerate, and she had trouble completing her last book, *Jackson's Dilemma*, which contains several internal inconsistencies that are a reflection of her loss of authorial control, itself a symptom of her illness. Bayley's realization produced at first only denial. "I was somehow sure that everything would carry on just as usual. In a sense, I was right. When the Alzheimer's patient loses touch with time, time seems to lose both its prospective and its retrospective significance" (*Elegy for Iris* 214). He began taking the shortest possible views, even shorter than those recommended by the Reverend Smith. Doctors' visits and medical tests confirmed that she was indeed suffering from Alzheimer's. He rejected friends' advice for Iris to take new experimental drugs that work only temporarily and then produce greater confusion and disorientation: "The friendly fog suddenly disperses, revealing a precipice before the feet" (219).

The final chapter of *Elegy for Iris* contains Bayley's diary entries from January 1 to Christmas 1997. Life is now so different from the past. They never felt a need for television, being too absorbed in their work, but now she watches children's "teletubbies" all day, staring at the screen as if in a trance. He does too. On March 30 he makes a "savage comment" about the grimness of their situation, to which she looks "relieved and intelligent," responding, "But I love you" (233). Always a paradoxicalist, he observes that as her condition gets worse, it gets better—better in the sense that she is no longer tormented by anxiety and dread. Despair sometimes overwhelms him, and he is tempted to shout to her, "It's worse for me. It's *much worse*!" (249; emphasis in original). He ends a May diary entry with the anguished words, "When are they going to let *me* out?" (249). He has become infected by her anxiety and dread, almost as much a victim as the Alzheimer's patient. "Alzheimer's obviously has me in its grip. . . . Does the care-giver involuntarily mimic the Alzheimer's condition? I'm sure I do" (240–41). At times he cannot prevent himself from going "berserk." Bayley offers a faithful description of compassion fatigue, a common problem among caregivers and hospice workers. As Carol Wogrin suggests, "Those who have enormous capacity for feeling and expressing empathy are the ones who tend to be at the highest risk of compassion stress" (385)—largely because the most effective therapists are the most vulnerable to emotional contagion. Frustration and rage overcome Bayley as he watches Iris spill the contents of a passenger's pocketbook while taking a bus back to Oxford after a brief vacation, and as he roughly gets her into a seat, he gives her a "surreptitious violent punch on the arm by which I am holding her" (255). These revelations lend authenticity to the memoir, reminding us that Bayley is human, not saintly. Every person has a limit, and he has reached his. We accept his rage because we know he has a right to feel that way; it is earned rage. We know that his anger does not invalidate his lifelong love for her. We also know, if we are honest with ourselves, that we cannot predict how we will act as caregivers. Above all, he remains devoted to her care. Their journey together, he realizes at the end, is nearly over. Twice Murdoch has told Peter Conradi that she is "sailing into the darkness." By the time *Elegy for Iris* ends, the journey is all but complete.

Iris and Her Friends

Iris and Her Friends is more somber and desperate than the preceding memoir, largely because Alzheimer's has taken its grim toll on husband and wife. She is now in the final throes of the illness, and there are few moments when she resembles her old self. The humor is now more trenchant than in *Elegy for Iris*, the author's mood and voice bleaker. *Iris and Her Friends* is less about the patient than it is about the caregiver who has also been rendered into a patient. We learn little about Murdoch's life that we have not seen in the earlier memoir; now the focus is almost exclusively on the memoirist himself. The artistic challenge Bayley confronts in the second memoir is more daunting than in the first one. How does a writer convey the emptiness and boredom of an Alzheimer patient without making the narrative empty and boring? Bayley solves the problem in *Elegy for Iris* by contrasting Murdoch's past and present lives. The book focuses far more on the past than on the present. We see the blossoming and maturation of love, the development of a celebrated union, the marriage of a future world-famous novelist and distinguished literary critic. Bayley never lets us forget the ghastly reality of his present situation, but the flashbacks enliven the story, reminding us that both husband and wife have lived a long and rich life together. By contrast, few of the flashbacks in *Iris and Her Friends* have anything to do with Murdoch. She is hardly a character at all, now ravaged by an illness that has transformed her into an insensible object—or so she seems most of the time. Nor does the title refer to Iris's "friends," who are largely absent from the memoir. Rather, the title refers to the consolations and comforts Alzheimer's brings to both patient and caregiver. "There may be rewards and alleviations on the way, for all parties. As well as anxiety in the patient, there may be a kind of merciful indifference, even lightness of heart, a shrugging off of responsibility for the things most of us feel we have to do every day—washing, dressing, keeping up appearances" (5).

Iris and Her Friends continues where *Elegy for Iris* ends, and the two could have been published as one long memoir. Bayley uses the same survival strategies in caring for his wife, but these compensations are now more solitary and unshareable. Once again he is a paradoxicalist, stating that the "certainty of things getting worse is our most unexpected friend; yet undoubtedly he is one" (12). Since Murdoch is incapable of speaking, writing, or, presumably, thinking about the past, it is Bayley's past that we see, his "pre-Iris" experiences. Thus he writes about his service in the British army during World War II, his early encounters with women, including one to whom he proposed marriage and who, to his relief, turned him down, and another woman whom he transmuted into a fictional character in his first novel.

If Bayley's major surprise while writing the first two memoirs was the importance of finding "friends" who would offer a welcome, indeed, life-saving respite from the intolerable strain of caregiving, no less surprising, even shocking, is the onrush of memories of the past. Here he rightly invokes Proust, who "dramatised the joy he received from that sudden flooding back of the past" (*Iris and Her Friends* 15). But he goes beyond Proust in exploring how the floodgates of his own memory are opened while his spouse's memory recedes. He cannot help wondering about this mysterious and unanticipated phenomenon. "Is it the absence of any such goings-on now in Iris's mind which stimulates the production of them in my own? As if my own brain chemistry were responding to deficiency in another brain, involuntarily seeking to compensate? All such ways of looking at it are probably equally misleading. Anything looked at in the mind vanishes by the act of looking? A kind of Heisenberg effect?" (63). Unable to determine whether this reciprocal relationship reveals causation or merely correlation, he is troubled by the pleasure of writing. "There creeps into recollection the complacency which is also a part of memory. I am pleased with myself not only for remembering but for having recorded it in the mind with such precision. Most memoirs and autobiography have a 'clever little me' feel about them somewhere" (129). He is also troubled by the possibility that he may be exploiting his wife's vulnerability, a concern he did not raise in *Elegy for Iris*. "I have a horrid feeling that I enjoy such things more and more now, because Iris does not, cannot, do so herself. It is not as if I am enjoying them for her, or trying to share my pleasure. More as if her inner desolation has stimulated my own receptivity, my own private powers of response" (129–30).

As with *Elegy for Iris*, but to a greater extent, *Iris and Her Friends* emphasizes Bayley's survival strategies as a caregiver. These survival strategies become more important after years of caring for an Alzheimer's patient. Retreating into one's memory and fantasy life becomes not only a pleasurable form of escape but also essential for the caregiver's physical and mental health. "The comfort I give Iris depends on my ability to lead this inner private life, whose vividness ironically depends on Iris not being present in it. It is all pre-Iris; all done and gone long before our own life together" (59–60). He offers a psychological guide to caregiving, showing (rather than merely telling) us that the "caregiver finds himself becoming two people: one closely identified with the sufferer and her symptoms, as I was with Iris's downstairs; the other in a state of almost enjoyable detachment, much aware of any treat he can save for himself" (153). In effect, Bayley's memoirs are an *Upstairs, Downstairs* account of caregiving, in which he attends to Iris's here-and-now needs while escaping into his past life with her and, before that, his life as a single person. Though he admits that he doesn't "care for that word *caregiver*, just because it has become so unavoidable" (273), he writes authoritatively about his experiences, and according to the book jacket of *Iris and Her Friends*, he is an active supporter of Alzheimer's International.

Part of the value of reading Bayley's memoirs is that caregivers learn not to feel guilty for becoming angry at those for whom they care. Bayley writes about his love for Iris but also his hate for her at times. "Hardly a day goes by without my flying into a brief frenzy, shouting at Iris, or saying in level tones something like this: 'I don't know *what* to do with you—you exhaust me so much.' Or sometimes saying, with a reassuring smile, 'Have you any idea how much I hate you?'" (*Iris and Her Friends* 76–77). Sometimes he becomes so enraged at her that he can scarcely control his violence. "Once she put her hands over her head and whimpered, 'Don't hit me.' She knew better than I did what might happen" (77). On one level he is shocked by his behavior, but on another level he is not. He then asks a question that is not entirely theoretical: "Would a child, or a senile adult, prefer to be looked after by a parent or partner who loves her and knocks her about, rather than go into some sort of state care?" His answer is equivocal—"Depends on the degree of knocking about, I suppose" (77).

Midway through *Iris and Her Friends* Bayley postulates two complementary laws, existential in nature, which are survival strategies for everyone, not just caregivers and their patients. "There is certainly a law of the conservation of trouble, the troubles we must all undergo in this vale of tears. If some are taken away, by God or the government or scientific discovery, we can be sure not only that the ones which remain will seem more burdensome than before but that quite new and unexpected ones will appear" (128). Phrased differently, there will always be suffering, though the causes and symptoms may change. There is certainly nothing new about this law, however much we may deny it. The second law is less obvious but no less important. "Fortunately, there is also a law of the conservation of pleasure. In bed in the morning, waiting for the day to begin, I comfort myself with this knowledge. Thank goodness for it. As troubles get worse, small satisfactions increase, both in intensity and in expectation" (128) Thus he looks forward to putting Iris to bed, pouring himself a drink, and reading a page or two of a book. "I cling to this pleasure grimly, as if I were holding on to the side of a lifeboat" (129).

Many biographers worry about the possibility of exploiting their subjects, a fear that must be heightened in memoirists who write about deceased spouses. The fear is probably greater when the memoirist's spouse is still alive. Biographer Peter Conradi acknowledges that while the vast majority of the hundreds of letters Bayley received after writing *Elegy for Iris* were positive, some were negative: some people "felt Iris was cast in this very public role of quixotic benefactress without her consent. Like the gentleman witnessing Lear's madness, it was a 'sight most pitiful in the meanest wretch<th>/<th>Past speaking of in a king!'" (591). Bayley never mentions this concern in *Elegy for Iris*, but he does in *Iris and Her Friends*. *Elegy for Iris* became a best seller in the UK and the United States, and it was soon made into a film. Suddenly Bayley himself was an international celebrity, more famous, perhaps, than Iris Murdoch during the height of her career. Did he know that the two memoirs would become a media event and that he would soon become a celebrity? There is a moment in *Iris and Her Friends* when he meditates on the solitary nature of writing, lamenting the fact that Iris will not be able to read his present book. "I am playing to an audience of one—myself. Iris is indifferent to my performance, and presumably unaware of it. I have to be my own audience; and giving a benefit for an audience of one is part of the solitude of this unchosen profession of caregiver" (154). Writing is also a kind of caregiving. It's true that Bayley is playing to an audience of one as Iris's caregiver, but he is playing to a much wider audience as a writer about caregiving. And so even when he states that he must be his own audience, it is hard to imagine that he was unaware of the tens or hundreds of thousands of readers who would read his story. Writing—in this case, a memoir about one's disabled or deceased spouse—is also a form of self-caring.

We learn less about Iris in the second memoir but more about Bayley's motives for writing. We discover, for example, that a major reason he wrote the books is to prevent Murdoch from becoming an empty character, a "she" devoid of consciousness. "Did I write about Iris last year to stop her becoming such a She? It didn't feel like that, but the urge may have been there. And when the book came out, she loved to see it, and the picture on the cover. She once would never have believed such a thing would be done, and have known that I couldn't do it, or have done it. Nor would I once. But it comforted me to see her smile in a pleased, proprietary way, far away from it all as she now was" (*Iris and Her Friends* 243–44). Did Iris intuit what Sandra Gilbert calls in *Death's Door* "textual resurrection," when an author like Walt Whitman implies that "through a weird process of transubstantiation, his flesh and blood will metamorphose into paper and ink, offering his devoutest readers a chance at communion with 'the origin of all poems' incarnated on his pages?" (72). Writing brought both Bayley and Murdoch satisfaction, even pleasure—not surprising given the fact that they were both prolific authors who had devoted their lives to the craft of writing. And writing was for both of them a way to express their feelings about each other. Bayley does not analyze the reasons for his wife's happiness when seeing *Elegy for Iris*, but he does describe the look on her face as she glanced at the book. "I saw a glimmer of pride, almost of a fond and motherly pride, in the smile she turned on me. I had actually written a book about her!"(244). He tells us in the same paragraph that his brother, Michael, who was fond of Iris, also approved of the book, believing that it "helped the Alzheimer's cause." Bayley concludes the chapter by telling us that his wife's and brother's approval—or disapproval—was the only thing that mattered to him about the book. "That was all the approval I needed, and disapproval there—from Michael or from Iris herself (and I know she would have expressed it somehow had she felt it)—would have been the only kind that I feared" (243–44).

Does Bayley disclose too much in *Iris and Her Friends*? He indirectly raises this issue when he refers to an interview with an American physician-journalist who in Iris's presence began raising personal questions about how her illness has changed their relationship. "Naturally, we were talking about her, like two doctors discussing a patient, and the journalist gave me a slightly anxious, questioning look. (She had already said, 'Don't answer any questions you would rather not.') I think I have followed Iris's own example, now that Alzheimer's has removed her from the ordinary decorum of daily life, in ceasing to feel any embarrassment about this sort of thing. The journalist's queries were euphemistic ('Do you have to help her on the loo?'), but we both glanced appealingly at Iris from time to time, as if for reassurance" (202).

Bayley's appeal to "nature," and to Murdoch's lifelong belief in artistic truthfulness, leaves little doubt that he intended to write as honestly and openly as possible about their present lives. Iris herself, he adds, "at least gave the impression of knowing exactly what we were talking about: Her face had an expression of courteous but faintly amused interest" (*Iris and Her Friends* 202). Her "consent" here, however, is problematic, as Bayley knows. As the interview continues, interviewer and interviewee appear to exchange roles. "A question seemed to be imminent—'Do you still have, er, sexual relations?' I could not help feeling curious to see when it would come. Feeling like a prostitute with a nervous client, I gave the lady a look of invitation, but Iris was now getting frankly bored and her air of polite amusement had disappeared" (203).

The journalist never does raise the question, allowing Bayley to raise it himself in the memoir. "To be honest," he begins—an unnecessary verbal tic in that he never questions his honesty elsewhere in the narrative—"it wouldn't have been an entirely easy one to answer" (*Iris and Her Friends* 203). He then proceeds to answer the question as delicately as possible. Noting that sex can be more complicated than "Do you or don't you?" he admits that the "old indeterminacy in our own sexual relations seems to prolong itself naturally into the unending confusion of Iris's present days." Again he appeals to "nature" to suggest his acceptance of the present situation. If this is a circuitous way of answering "no" to the question of sexual relations, he implies that sex can still be "felicitous." Iris's "long periods of anxiety are followed by brief happiness, inconclusive moments of peace and close embrace" (203).

Bayley is not yet finished with the question, however, for he then reflects on the importance of the caregiver's fantasy sex life. This was not something he was prepared to disclose to a journalist, largely because a newspaper article could not record the ambiguities and nuances of such a discussion. A rich fantasy life is one of the great "friends" of Alzheimer's disease, he acknowledges. "My fantasies accommodate persons both real and imaginary, the real ones mostly from the past" (*Iris and Her Friends* 204). Nor are characters in novels exempt from being either the fantasizer or fantasied object: he gives the example of Holden Caulfield in *The Catcher in the Rye* fantasizing over Eustacia Vye in Thomas Hardy's *The Return of the Native*. "I still have a recurrent tendresse," Bayley confesses, sounding like Humbert Humbert in Nabokov's *Lolita*, "for one or two of Barbara Pym's female characters" (204). He concludes his discussion of his fantasy life with a paradox: "I am not exactly lonely—how could I be when so close to Iris, every hour of the day and night? And yet that closeness without communication, however loving it may be, is also its own kind of loneliness" (205). This observation—loneliness amid constant companionship, closeness without communication—is less startling than his next: "If Iris were to have to go from me, into a hospital or home, all these solitary and friendly pleasures, fantasies, too, would vanish like a puff of smoke" (205). He would not merely be lonely, then; he would also be bereft. This knowledge makes the present situation, however wrenching it may be for him, more desirable—or at least less undesirable—than the future, however much relief he may feel from no longer being a caregiver. "The solitariness of a close relationship—and how much closer could we get now?—is, for me, the fertile ground for fantasy, as it is for memories, the ones that go far, far back" (205).

The memoirist makes other piquant observations about the role of sexual fantasy for the caregiver—and noncaregiver. "Fantasy and enactment are separate, and their cohabitation, to use a word slightly ridiculous in this context, is part of the charm of each" (*Iris and Her Friends* 206). He then relates an "absurd story" about a sleepy wife telling her husband, "Oh, do get on with it, George," to which her husband responds, "Sorry, dear, I can't think of anyone at the moment" (206). In his pragmatic words of wisdom and ironic wit, he sounds like a cross between an erudite Ann Landers and Dr. Ruth, spicing his lively insights with countless literary examples. Unable to imagine Jane Austen sexually fantasizing over her characters—"Fantasy shrinks from the sharp edge of her intelligence"—he nevertheless points out that Anna Karenina would have been delighted with her husband's large ears if she were in love with him. "The sight of them would have fed both love and amusement together" (206).

Bayley does not hesitate to describe the caregiver's most difficult challenges, including caring for one's incontinent spouse. "I don't know how it is with three-year olds, but Iris's toilet habits, if you can call them that, have become unpredictable. Sometimes she will go to the right place, even though she makes a mess of it. More often, she will do it on the carpet outside, or in another room. Then she lays the results, as if with care, on a neighbouring chair or bookshelf. I don't mind a bit cleaning up, an operation which seems mildly to amuse her. I can make a joke of it, too, and we can laugh about it together. A small domestic challenge I can easily meet, and Iris seems to enjoy seeing me do it" (*Iris and Her Friends* 185–86). His description of cleaning Iris after one of her bowel movements could not be more different from Philip Roth's graphic account in his memoir *Patrimony* of cleaning his incontinent father, suffering from a massive brain tumor. Roth's horror contrasts Bayley's cheerful acceptance. It is the difference between a tragic and comic vision of life. "Love accepts the comic," Bayley writes with philosophical wisdom (207). For Roth, and for writers such as Janet Malcolm, art rests on betrayal. Roth promised his humiliated father that he would not tell anyone about his incontinence but then disregarded the dying man's wishes. For Bayley, art involves no such betrayal, since he believed Iris would not have objected to readers knowing about her life as an Alzheimer's patient. His statement about Henry James and Dostoevsky—"True art never exploits" (247)—applies to his own writings as well.

Bayley and Murdoch were both devoted to writing about the truth, and they admired writers who were themselves truthful. Bayley quotes with approval Auden's statement that "insofar as poetry, or any of the arts, can be said to have an ulterior purpose, it is by telling the truth, to disenchant and disintoxicate." He believes that Auden was not only the most inclusive and technically skilled poet of the twentieth century but also the "most truthful" (*Selected Essays* 82). So, too, does Bayley tell the truth about Iris's illness. By refusing to romanticize Alzheimer's disease, he shows us how illness can disenchant and disintoxicate life. He captures both the horror and the beauty of life, and in doing so, he remains true to experience. His view of art is consistent with his wife's. "I think art consoles," Murdoch said to Christopher Bigsby in an interview. "The thing is to console without telling lies. . . . I think to be consoled by art is absolutely OK. In a way it is the highest consolation, good art is the highest consolation." She then makes a revealing qualification of the preceding sentence. "Well it is not the highest, I think things to do with human love are the highest consolations—but it can be so high, that good consolation" (118–19). We can infer from these comments that the highest consolation for her is art that affirms human love—and nowhere is that better seen than in her husband's three memoirs of their life together. In an interview with John Haffenden, she gives the example of *King Lear* affirming truth and happiness. "Works of art make you happy. Even *King Lear* makes you happy, and yet it comes near to the edge of the impossible—that you could be made happy by a work of art which is about something terrible" (135). So, too, does *Iris and Her Friends*, like *Elegy for Iris*, make us happy.

"Sex may be the ever-interesting topic," Bayley states when writing about his past infatuations, "but love is interesting only to oneself" (*Iris and Her Friends* 178). This is one of the few statements in *Iris and Her Friends* with which I disagree. Throughout the memoir he makes statements about love that hit home, at least to me. "The habit of memory has become a real solace now," he declares at the beginning of *Iris and Her Friends* (11), but memory is a solace only when one's memories are positive. Only a masochist would wish to find solace in dark memories—or someone who wishes to remember the grim past in a more hopeful way. Memory is a "feast" (59) to Bailey because he has so many happy, fulfilling memories, enough to dine on every night for the rest of his life. If he feels existential guilt because he can still enjoy what his wife can't, he does not need to torture himself over the past. There is *nothing* about his marriage that he regrets, except that he did not have more time with Iris before she fell ill. He recognizes this when he asks rhetorically, "Have I been given, as a kind of bonus or legacy, the memories that in her brain have been wiped away?" (72).

Iris Murdoch remains Bayley's muse in health and in illness—an "elusive muse, a muse who has to be coaxed, cosseted, rescued from herself" (*Iris and Her Friends* 190). This helps to explain his reluctance to place her in a nursing home. "Were she to be in a home, however 'happy' they would try to make her, the sense of apartness would soon destroy us both. Perhaps me before her, perhaps her before me? At the moment, she keeps me sane. The final egoism, is it? What would happen to me if she weren't here? Is that my real fear?" (187–88). His worst moments in the memoir occur toward the end when he fears he has lost his muse. "I can do nothing without her. Without her, I shall have nothing to write, and nothing to do" (265). While the context of this fear is a literal loss—Iris jumps out of their moving car and then disappears for several minutes—he cannot help dreading the time when she will no longer be alive.

And yet Iris can still express her love, in language, even if her words no longer make sense. "The other day in the car, she laid a hand on my knee and said with emphasis, '*Susten poujin drom love poujin? Poujin susten?*' I hastened to agree, and one word was clear. As soon as I could stop the car, we kissed each other. She knew what she meant even when there was no meaning, and there *was* in that word" (*Iris and Her Friends* 233). This is one of the many loving and lovely moments in the memoir when their heartfelt intimacy comes through. Bayley can speak for her when she can no longer speak for herself, at least not in recognizable language. *Iris and Her Friends* leaves us with love, loss, and a hint of recovery, not for the Alzheimer's patient, for whom recovery is impossible, but for the caregiver, even when he fears that recovery is all but impossible.

No matter how fatigued, stressed, or despondent Bayley becomes in *Iris and Her Friends*, no matter how close he approaches his own breaking point—he refers in the last chapter to having a breakdown, though he gives us no specifics—the reader never senses that he would not live his life all over again even if he knew how it would end, for him and for his wife. He recites lines from *Macbeth*: "Canst thou not minister to a mind diseas'd, / Pluck from the memory a rooted sorrow" (188). He might also have cited Malcolm's words in the same play: "Give sorrow words: the grief that does not speak / Whispers the o'er-fraught heart, and bids it break." As Iris's long, dark journey comes to an end, we wonder whether Bayley's sorrow will be too much for him to bear. Earlier he has presented, with little commentary, examples of friends, teachers, and acquaintances who have been unable to survive the deaths of beloved spouses. He tells us in *Elegy for Iris* that one of Iris's favorite Oxford professors, Eduard Frankel, was "devoted to his wife, and he had told a close friend that when she died, he would follow. He did, taking an overdose the same night" (61). Nor did their friend Janet Stone get over the sudden death of her husband, the painter Reynolds Stone. "Widowhood did not suit her at all," Bayley remarks sadly in *Elegy for Iris* (197), a statement he repeats in *Iris and Her Friends*: "She had tried to make a new life for herself in her Salisbury cottage, devoted like a museum to her husband's paintings and engravings, but she missed him and their life together too much for recovery" (249).

Too much for recovery: the words resonate within the reader. How will Bayley do in widowhood? He observes at the beginning of *Iris and Her Friends* that he does not regard suicide or euthanasia as one of Iris's friends (13), repeating this a few pages later when he thinks of Dr. Kevorkian, "death's angel," who is the opposite of a friend (17). "Sweet are the uses of adversity," he exclaims, the "commonest, sanest Shakespearean wisdom" (17). He might have recited a line from *The Aeneid*, which biographer Peter Conradi quotes: "The day may dawn when this plight will be sweet to remember" (402). And yet Bayley admits that he "longed for death, like Anna Karenina abandoned, as she thought—no, as she knew—by a lover who had become a stranger to her. The person beside me seemed a stranger, too" (255). Bayley's darkest moments in *Iris and Her Friends* occur when he contemplates homicide and suicide. Sometimes he says to Iris, "Don't worry, darling, we shall soon be dead" (13), which is always met with disturbing silence. He admits that he "had frequent thoughts of doing ourselves in together, if there were a nice, safe reliable way" (13). He mentions that in 1983 the writer Arthur Koestler and his wife did precisely that. "He was ailing and had cancer. She was young and in good health, but she wanted to go with him. Hard to understand, and yet there it is" (13). He then reveals that when Alzheimer's disease began to ravage Iris's mother, her companion began to amass on her behalf a large quantity of sleeping pills. "After her death, I found and appropriated them, thinking they might come in handy one day—if they worked" (14). His house is so cluttered that he can't find the pills—a wry end to what may be the most unsettling moment in the memoir.

Bayley never returns to this subject again in *Iris and Her Friends*, and one senses that he never seriously considered ending Iris's life or his own. Her illness, paradoxically, shored up his strength. He affirms this paradox by using an uncharacteristic Christian rebirth image: "For by needing me now, Iris also sheltered me, nourished me simply by having nothing to give of which she could be conscious. In losing her own, Iris had given me a new life. How could I live without her now, and without her friends, the friends of Dr. A.? I wondered" (263).

Widower's House

Life without Iris becomes the subject of the final volume of Bayley's trilogy, *Widower's House*. With its lengthy and curious subtitle—"A Study in Bereavement, or How Margot and Mella Forced Me to Flee My Home"—*Widower's House* alternates between a farcical and melancholy tone, strikingly different from the earlier memoirs. *Widower's House* fills in some of the gaps of the story of Bayley's caregiving experiences and explores for the first time his motivation in writing about his wife. The memoir also reveals, at the end, that Bayley has found a new companion—an old friend who, like him, has lost a beloved spouse—with whom he can begin a new life.

Widower's House opens with Bayley's assertion that Iris's death has irrevocably changed his life. He is, quite simply, not the same person he used to be. "I could not escape back into my old self, because my old self no longer existed. In widowhood you lose not only your loved one but much of yourself. And there was no new one to take its place" (3–4). The only recognizable trait from his earlier personality is self-pity, which, he suspects, is true for all widows and widowers. Iris was the center of his life when she was alive, the source of his faith and belief in life. She was the sun around which he revolved, and her extinction has resulted in his own darkness.

Bayley's insistence that his old identity is irretrievably gone is misleading, however, for if style is the man, he is still the same person, at least in many fundamental ways. Notwithstanding his self-pity, he is still an ironist and paradoxicalist. He delights in surprising his readers with statements like "How much I had suffered lately from [friends'] kindness, and from goodness" (*Widower's House* 18). He is even more self-effacing than in the earlier memoirs, preferring to focus on his weaknesses—his cluelessness, haplessness, and unworldliness—rather than his strengths—his devotion to Iris, active support of Alzheimer's International, and commitment to educating the public about bereavement. His characterization of Murdoch in *Widower's House* is identical to that in *Elegy for Iris* and *Iris and Her Friends*. "Who could ever have been cross with Iris? It would have been undignified. My own occasional tantrums, of course, had no dignity, but they were part of our private language and understanding and always ended in laughter, almost before they got going" (10–11).

For the first time in the trilogy, Bayley raises the question of whether he exaggerates Iris's strengths: an unnamed "shrink" asserts "blandly" that "bereaved persons have a tendency to idealise the dead loved one" (*Widower's House* 167). I don't know who this unnamed shrink is, but Colin Murray Parkes makes this statement in *Bereavement*: one aspect of the work of grieving is the "re-evaluation of the dead person, an activity sometimes termed 'idealization,' since it is the happy memories and valued aspects of the relationship that we treasure and wish to perpetuate" (71). "Did I do that?" Bayley asks and then rules out the possibility. "I wouldn't have thought so. True, I found myself thinking the other day, in the context of our mutual acquaintance, that I had never heard Iris speak ill of anyone, or say anything sharp about any of our friends. But that wasn't idealising her. It was no more than the truth. And that quality of hers sometimes irritated me when I would have liked a good malicious gossip about some tiresome acquaintance recently endured. Iris had her own brand of wholly private political correctness. She didn't disapprove of gossip and backbiting: She just never indulged in them herself" (167–68).

The memoirist may not idealize Iris, but he presents her as a human saint, aiding him even when she is ill. "While Iris was alive, even in the grip of Alzheimer's, she had protected me just because she was being looked after by me. A firm bulwark, she had stood between me and the people who wanted to help us. Now that I was alone in the world, it was more difficult by far to resist encroachment" (*Widower's House* 28). Another interpreter might locate agency—the cause of this "protection"—within the caregiver rather than the patient, but throughout the trilogy Bayley endows Iris with the power to protect him even when illness has destroyed her volition. She stopped eating and drinking about a month before her death, but she retained her enigmatic benevolence. In death she appears as approving as she was in life. Thus he perceives her smiling at him whenever he does something that enables him to continue his life without her.

Even during the final stages of Alzheimer's she was "never difficult or ungentle with me" (*Widower's House* 110). At Vale House,the Alzheimer's nursing home in Oxford, where she died, "Iris was happy. Her face lit up like an angel's when I appeared every morning, but this seemed not because of me but because she was so happy that she displayed her happiness like a child" (209). Bayley's description of her death intimates that their union can never be shattered, not even by the cessation of life. He states in one of his books that for Shakespearean tragedy, "death is very much a part of life . . . to be lived through and endured as life itself" (*Shakespeare and Tragedy* 51). He presents Iris's death just as naturally, to be lived through and endured. Like most Alzheimer's patients, she died without uttering final words, but her sibylline silence only adds to her mystery.

Garrett Stewart points out that death is the only event in life that novelists can only imagine rather than know. Iris's death scene is extraordinary in many ways. The death scene is Victorian in spirit, not so much in the belief that the deceased spouse has gone to a better world, but in its aura of radiance, innocence, and spirituality. There is a startlingly playful quality about the way in which Bayley opens and closes his wife's eyes, almost as if she were a doll. He does not fantasize reunion with his deceased wife, but there is a sense of communication with the dead: their love seems to survive her passing. In contrast to the ravages brought on by Alzheimer's disease, Bayley portrays Iris's death as an example of *ars moriendi*—the art of dying well. We see, in short, a beautiful death, world's apart from the long process of depersonalization and dehumanization that preceded it. Unlike Nietzsche, who believed that we have art in order not to perish from the truth, Bayley portrays art here in the service of truth.

Geoffrey Gorer has observed that just as sex was the great unmentionable subject in the nineteenth century, so is death the great unmentionable subject in the twentieth—and now, we may add, the twenty-first—century. Other researchers, such as Howard Spiro, have reached similar conclusions. "Once, when grandparents, parents, and sometimes children—too often children—died at home, everyone knew death first-hand. Death is as common as birth, but it went into hiding in our twentieth century" (xv). Bayley's description not only removes death from its fearful hiding place, exposing it to full view, but it also destigmatizes Alzheimer's disease, showing us how he continues to love and honor Iris. She seems mysteriously aware of his devotion even at the moment of death.

In an example of art mysteriously anticipating life, Bayley believes that the final page of Iris's last novel, *Jackson's Dilemma*, uncannily foreshadows her smiling death. He is fascinated by the eponymous character who reminds him of the novelist who created him. "Jackson was a haunting character, and also a strangely successful one. The reader believed in his powers, his benevolence, his capacity to help others without, apparently, needing to do more to help himself" (*Widower's House* 119). Bayley suggests to an Irish monk that Jackson "might be Iris's own inner self of what was happening to her . . . 'the end of what is necessary,' death, which cannot but be good" (119). Bayley rejects the monk's more orthodox Christian interpretation and continues to believe that Jackson embodies Iris's spirit. Although by the end of the novel Jackson has lost his powers, he rescues a spider, as his creator would have done. "In the last sentence, he smiled, as Iris smiled on the day she died" (119).

Midway through *Widower's House* Bayley begins a discussion of why he wrote about Iris. Unlike John Milton, who believed that "thoughts wander through eternity," Bayley believes that "eternity is not in the afterlife, but, rather, in our minds"—from which he concludes that "communing with the dead in this way must be one of the oldest of all human indulgences. And the most comforting?" (107). Despite the question mark, there is little doubt that Bayley found comfort in writing about his deceased beloved. Noting, ironically, that the "dead expect the attentions the living bestow on them, and almost unconsciously, the living assume this must be so" (107), Bayley declares that in Thomas Hardy's late poetry, "the dead continue to converse with the living, quarrel with them, patronise them for still being above ground, become satirical at their expense. They can be downright nasty sometimes, too" (108). Bayley then reveals, in one of his most suggestive statements, that writing about the dead "is a way not only of continuing to feel in touch with them but of expiating guilt" (108), a statement that clearly applies to Hardy, who was nasty to his wife, Emma, throughout their long and grim marriage but wrote hundreds of love poems about her immediately following her death. "Hardy's poetry flourished alike on his lack of belief and on his devotion to the uses of poetic survival" (108–9).

So, too, has Bayley flourished in his devotion to the uses of artistic survival, his wife's artistic immortality and his own. Brooding over such issues "cheered one up"; now he could understand why Hardy wrote those love poems. "Not only was she still very much there for him but she carried him back . . . to the days and the places where he had first met her, when their 'days were a joy.'" But, Bayley continues, there is a major difference between the two writers. "I could write about Iris again, as I used to before she died. But I was writing about her the other way round. Hardy kept Emma alive, at least for a while, by writing about her. I had felt that Iris was alive with me until this morning. Now I felt, quite suddenly, that she really had ceased to exist; and that is why I could write about her as if she were still alive" (*Widower's House* 109). He doesn't elaborate on why it was only when his wife ceased to exist that he could write about her for the third time. His diary entries in *Iris and Her Friends* indicate that he was writing about her throughout much or most of her protracted illness. As with Hardy, writing was a way for him to feel in touch with his deceased wife, but there seems to have been little if any guilt, existential or otherwise, toward her that required expiation—unless we assume he felt a degree of guilt over his "occasional tantrums." One cannot imagine the dead Iris quarreling with Bayley, as Hardy imagined his dead wife doing with him. Bayley does not idealize Iris, as Hardy idealized Emma, but he acknowledges the obsessional intensity with which he wrote about Iris, implying that this was something he *needed* to do. Writing was for him nothing less than rescue work, an essential part of his life support system during and immediately following his wife's death. "I clung to writing as a form of belief. I didn't believe anything else, but I believed in Iris, and believing in her was a belief in her survival, both for me in my own way and for everyone who read her work. How could I not believe that?" (134).

Bayley does not cite the extensive research that has been published on bereavement, but many of his observations support the major clinical findings. As I report in *Dying to Teach*, one characteristic of widows and widowers is obsessional review, which Ira Glick, Robert Weiss, and Colin Murray Parkes define in their book *The First Year of Bereavement* as "going over and over the same scenes," which is an integral part of the mourning process. "It was distressing to the widows that they were so absorbed by the review and could not simply recognize their loss and be done with it. But they seemed unable to stop" (126). Nor could Bayley stop. "For the bereft, memory grows into obsession: It grows and grows. I threw away everything I could, but I did not throw away the diaries I had kept when Iris was ill. I studied each detail of the record again and again, everyday. It was not just 'remembrance of things past.' It was remembering the time that still seemed present" (*Widower's House* 136). After her death, he read all of her books—a daunting task. Unable to speak to her, he communicated in the way he knew best: "writing to her—with her, as it seemed—was the only way of communicating I still had" (136).

And then something peculiar happened. Bayley could not remember that he had started the present book about Iris. His short-term memory was so impaired—he doesn't use the word *traumatized* but that seems to be what happened—that he had forgotten he had lain in bed in the early mornings after Iris's death and written about her illness and their life together. When he does remember, he searched the drawers and folders of his house, looking through old papers on the floor, to no avail. Mystified not only by what he had written but also by where he had misplaced the post-Iris writings, he continued the search. He describes his state of mind immediately following her death as like being in a "trance, when I seemed to live with the dead, and not with the living" (*Widower's House* 104). Then one day he found the writings, in a cardboard box stuffed with letters on the kitchen table. "I was still amazed, as I read, by the way I had forgotten all about it, as if memory had lost all function and purpose now that Iris was dead, and could refer only to the time she had been ill, and we had been together" (105).

Bayley attributes his memory loss to two unusual women who do their best to attend to his emotional, physical, and sexual needs. He calls them Margot and Mella—pseudonyms, we learn, in the author's disclaimer at the beginning of the book: "Some of the visitors to *Widower's House* are composites drawn from a wide array of people the author has known." Their comic and at times farcical pursuit of him forms the plot of the story. Bayley and Iris had known Margot and her husband for years. Overpowering and exhausting, Margot would invite them to spend a weekend at her house, an event Bayley never enjoyed. After her husband's death, Margot spends two years of "disconsolate grieving" (7), after which she seems to get over the loss. Bayley discourages her from visiting Iris when she is ill, but after her death, he finds himself and his house "under siege," a metaphor that he delights in developing. In one of the funniest moments in the narrative, he describes in chapter 2 how he is lying in bed, relieved that Margot's three-day visit is coming to an end, when suddenly she whispers in his ear "go to sleep" and then crawls in next to him. "Sleep was the last thing that seemed possible at such a moment. A bulky form nudged me tentatively, then settled down against me like a piece of soft cargo released by the derrick and bedding down into its position in a ship's hold" (50). He then changes metaphors to describe his feeling of entrapment: "I remained as immobile as a spider trapped in an empty bath, uncertain in which direction to run" (51). Unlike the spider that the eponymous protagonist in *Jackson's Dilemma* rescues, the spidery Bayley has no protector. To his relief, she is not interested in making love, despite her continued whispers in his ear, "her voice husky and penetrating" (51).

An even funnier moment occurs in the next chapter, appropriately titled "Comedie Francaise," when Margot invites herself to the widower's house and encounters Mella, who is wearing Bayley's old dressing gown. The two women unpredictably bond into "sisterhood" (*Widower's House* 72). Unlike Margot, Mella *is* interested in making love with Bayley. Though not formally one of her former Oxford tutors, he had agreed to instruct her for a few sessions on the Russian writers. She strikes him as a "nice person, full of enthusiasms but remarkably ignorant, even, so far as I could see, of the English authors she was supposed to be working on" (24). Unsure of her age, he speculates that she might be in her early thirties, less than half his own age. After Iris's death, Mella appears and disappears frequently and mysteriously from his life, ostensibly to clean and organize his chaotic house. He can't decide whether to welcome her companionship or resent the disruption of his quiet, solitary existence. During one of her cleaning expeditions, he enters his bedroom and sees her lying with her eyes closed on his bed, apparently not breathing. As he approaches the bed, she springs up, throws her arms round his neck, and begins kissing him. He portrays her, here and elsewhere, as sexually adventurous, if not seductive, and portrays himself as a reluctant and passive participant. After their lovemaking, he contemplates escaping from his house: "It was ridiculous to have been manhandled as I had been by a slip of a girl like Mella. But after all, I was an old gentleman who had never been particularly strong at the best of times" (68).

Bayley's narration of his unexpected and unpremeditated sexual relationship with Mella is fascinating for what it reveals and conceals. In describing himself as a widower under siege, he bears little responsibility for what happens. "The idea of making love to her had never occurred to me before. And if it had done so, I would have rejected it as quite unsuitable" (*Widower's House* 84). There is nothing illegal or immoral about their lovemaking—they are both consenting adults. Nevertheless, he remains troubled by their past academic relationship. "Mella was not exactly my pupil, but our relationship was still a formalised one: that of student and teacher" (84). He rules out the possibility he was sexually attracted to her—or to anyone, for that matter. Indeed, until the moment in which they make love, there is no hint in *Widower's House* of his sexual desire. Earlier in the story he refers to Margot's and Mella's behavior "as if they were dismasted ships in a gale, drifting on to a lee shore"—a phallic metaphor that seems more appropriate to his life than to theirs. Loneliness, not lust, compels Bayley to go to bed with Mella. Unlike Margot, who in his view "had only wanted to be kind" (*Widower's House* 53), Mella has "manhandled" him—a word almost suggesting sexual abuse. Thoughts of Mella elicit some of his most candid observations of Iris. Contemplating how he might politely end his relationship with Mella, he considers using the "fatal French phrase, '*Je t'aime Bien*'—fatal because it reveals with unforgiving French logic the difference between saying 'I'm really fond of you' and saying 'I love you'—'*Je t'aime*'" (94). He then reveals that he never said "I love you" to

Iris: "There was no need to, and it never occurred to me" (94). Later in the memoir he tells us that the "greatest source of pleasure and relaxation" that marriage afforded him was the "sense of her wholly separate being" (200). Marriage allowed both of them to devote themselves to their work and to each other. No friend of Freud, Bayley would nevertheless agree with the psychoanalyst's definition of health as the ability to love and work.

Iris's death has shattered Bayley's ability to love and work, and thus his health. The grief immediately following her death had kept alive some of his feelings—"frenzies of rage and despair" as well as "fits of love," but with the passing of grief came thoughts of death, to which he returns for the first time since the beginning of *Iris and Her Friends.* "I felt not only that I had not been living since grief, now so much missed, started to go away, but that I hadn't wanted to live. I preferred the other thing: just waiting to die" (*Widower's House* 198). Mella's arrival put this death wish on hold, yet he knows that she's not the right woman for him, though he can think of no one better at the time.

Bayley is never disturbed by the possibility that Iris would disapprove of his relationship with Mella. On the contrary: Iris seems to give her blessing. "I thought about Iris. She did not seem so very far off now—not so far off as the dinner parties of those distant days. And she seemed to be smiling at me in her old way" (*Widower's House* 69). Indeed, Iris seems to be smiling nearly every time he refers to her in *Widower's House*, her invisible presence hovering protectively in the background. I find it remarkable that Bayley does not seem burdened by guilt, sexual or existential, when he goes to bed with Mella. Nor is there what J. William Worden calls *recovery guilt*, which some people feel "when they move through their grief and want to get on with their lives" (155). Sharing his innermost thoughts on almost every other aspect of bereavement, Bayley nevertheless avoids elaborating on his feelings about making love with Mella. Did he feel a reawakening of sexual desire? Was he less lonely making love with Mella? More lonely? Did he think about Iris when he was Mella? Did he think about other women? How did he feel about their age difference? He raises none of these questions. Instead, he implies that he and Mella continued to make love on other occasions, not because of sexual attraction, but because of —habit. "We went to bed, certainly, as we had done the day before, but I think it was probably just because we had done it the day before that we now felt something like a mutual obligation to do it again. Politeness, really: Each felt the other must be expecting it" (76).

Politeness—and discretion—guide Bayley's narration of his sexual misadventures in *Widower's House*. "Sex is a subject about which the humorist is well advised to go carefully and to tread delicately—not usually a receipt for successful joke making" (144). He does indeed tread delicately. If he is reluctant to explore in great detail his sexual needs during his post-Iris life or to reveal his thoughts about the generational and cultural differences of making love with a much younger woman, the reader is not inclined to be overly critical—especially if that reader has also lost a spouse. Bayley does, after all, reveal a great deal about his sexual relationship with Iris, including the phenomenon that he wittily refers to as "barnacling": "The great whales, as I had read somewhere, and lesser cetaceans, too, as well as huge fishes like the whale shark, memorably encountered by Thor Heyerdahl during the voyage of the *Kon-Tiki*, have the habit of rubbing off the barnacles on their backs against some convenient large object: a ship, a pier, even another whale" (78). The "barnacling business," he adds, "was by nature a comedy" (79)—as much of sex is a comedy, he would no doubt agree. He intimates that he and Iris did a good deal of barnacling during their own marriage, and that such behavior was deeply gratifying to both.

Neither Margot nor Mella can supply Bayley with what he needs after Iris's death: mature companionship. Conflicted by the present situation in which his desire for a quiet, introspective life results in unbearable loneliness, he doesn't know where to turn or what to do. With Iris he had felt closer and closer apart; without her he feels bereft. Though he sees Mella once or twice a week for over a year, he admits he has never been interested in her. She remains only a diversion to him, and he excoriates himself for selfishness. After Margot and Mella exit his life, he feels relief, which he likens to the "principle of Sam and his brick wall": "If you spend some time, like the proverbial Sam, banging your head against the wall, you know that the ensuing period, before the cycle starts up again, will be agreeable. Margot and Mella had made a fine wall" (*Widower's House* 101). The women's departure entitles him to "unlimited wall remission" (101), but the relief soon fades, replaced by alcohol, television, a sleeping pill—and the question of what to do with the rest of his life.

It is at this point that Bayley comes across his post-Iris writings. Rereading them turns out to be a revelation, allowing him to discover how he thinks and feels about his present crisis. He makes several noteworthy observations that help to illuminate the nature of grief. "Bereavement has to be acted," he asserts. "This turns out to be one of life's little ironies, only discoverable after a death" (*Widower's House* 123). Playing the role of bereaved husband is Bayley's most formidable challenge, and with characteristic honesty he adds that it is not always possible to know the difference between acting and feeling bereft. Interestingly, he argues that none of the "acting business" applied to Iris when he was caring for her. "There was no one then before whom to play the part. Not even myself. For the first time in my life, I supposed, and it must have applied to all the rest of us 'carers,' too, I found myself in what seemed the truly natural state of man: doing not what I wanted to do but what had to be done; sinking into daily depression; flying into rages; knowing wild moments of the purest relief and elation, when I loved Iris more than I had ever done before, and felt closer to her than I had ever felt before" (124).

Without contradicting Bayley's heartfelt statement, I recall that when I was caring for Barbara, I was aware that I was being judged by another person. "You will be tested," a retired colleague said to me upon learning of Barbara's terminal illness. I did not know exactly whether I was passing or failing the test and who, in particular, was testing me, though it seems obvious now that I was judging myself. Even when I felt that I was dying with Barbara, seeking to exchange my life for hers, I could see myself as both a dying husband and a detached caregiver. I suspect this is true of many caregivers. I never felt like I was "acting" or playing the role of a caregiver when I was with Barbara, but I could observe myself as I struggled to attend to her needs. Just about the only time I lost control of myself, and also lost this self-awareness, was when I frequently burst into tears. My only recourse was to wait until the flood ended, which sometimes took a minute or two.

My experience crying was different from Bayley's. Like him, I compared my "explosion of tears" to a "sudden cloudburst or a flash flood," but whereas he described the sensation of weepy helplessness as "compellingly comforting and engrossing" (*Widower's House* 148), I experienced the explosion as wrenching and awful. Crying for me was what Bayley calls the principle of Sam and the brick wall—comfort came only when I stopped weeping. Bayley mentions that men weep as often as women, but this is untrue. Many researchers have analyzed the gendered nature of crying. Tom Lutz states that the "prohibition against male tears . . . takes center stage in the middle of the twentieth century" (237). Jeffrey Kottler argues that unlike women, men apologize for their tears. "Not having been rewarded very often for crying, since such behavior represented a humiliating loss of control, men are likely to feel remorse and shame after letting their tears show. Rather than feeling good about their authentic expressions of self, or even relieved at the release of tension, they more often feel some degree of regret and resolve to show more self-control in the future. The result of this self-restraint is that the average man cries only once per month, roughly one quarter as often as women" (151). Nor is it true that "both sexes are secretly indifferent to the tears of the other" (148), as Bayley claims, since many are moved by the tears of another.

Pondering the newly discovered pages, Bayley "decided it must have cheered me up to write them. I decided it would do me good now to go on writing." He realizes, "in an indifferent way," how "extremely self-centred" he has become (*Widower's House* 124). Has writing made him self-centered, or has he made this discovery through writing? He doesn't answer the question. It seems, however, that writing about his life is a healthy decision, one that centers his life after Margot's and Mella's departure. And so he continues writing where he had left off the morning after Iris's death. Writing about the "serious business of widowhood," he thinks about all the places he and Iris visited, including the Canary Isles, where their dear friend Audhild Villers (Audi, for short) lived. And it is with Audi that he begins his new life.

Bayley briefly mentions the Norwegian Audi in the earlier memoirs. She and her "Russian-Jewish-Polish" husband lived in a "charming little house" in the interior of the Canary Island of Lanzarote, where the pure and dry volcanic air was helpful to her severe asthma (*Elegy for Iris* 197). Murdoch had dedicated one of her novels to these close friends. Bayley and Iris often visited Italy with Audi and her husband, and while swimming with her in a small harbor, Bayley describes how he lost his lower denture, which occasions the following wry, self-mocking description: "Even a mild Canary onion was too much for me. It was like trying to cut with one half of a pair of scissors" (198). After her husband's death, Audi "missed him terribly" (200), and Bayley and Iris would visit her in Lanzarote, where she continued to live. Near the end of *Elegy for Iris* Bayley makes an observation whose significance does not become fully apparent until the end of *Widower's House*: while being bathed by Audi, Iris says, "I see an angel. I think it's you"(257), an image Bayley has often used to describe Iris. That's all we learn about her in *Elegy for Iris*. The hygienically challenged Bayley recalls a funny story about Audi in *Iris and Her Friends* during a brief visit with them in Oxford. Soon after her arrival, he sees Audi cleaning the bath. "'Audi,' I said, 'please don't bother. There's no need'"—to which she exclaims, "'Oh, yes there is,' she said. "I want to take a bath"' (253). The two burst out laughing, and we learn no more about her in the memoir.

Audi appears prominently in *Widower's House*, not only as the book's dedicatee but also as Bayley's new companion. "During Iris's illness, Audi was immensely helpful when she visited. And Iris loved her. In the days when Iris was well, they had a very special relationship. Friends used to say, what do they talk about all the time?" (159). Audi's closeness with Iris bodes well for her later relationship with Bayley, as does her experience with bereavement. "At that time, Audi had been nearly eight years a widow, a veteran in the trade. Although she said nothing about it, I knew how much and how continually she missed her husband" (159). During Bayley's visits to Audi, she is often playing solitaire, which seems to characterize her life as a widow. Unlike Margot and Mella, she maintains her distance from him. In fact, she appears to drop out of the story from the first reference to her, on page 158, until near the end, when Bayley decides to flee from Widower's House to escape the ubiquitous Mella and begin a new life elsewhere. And so he flies to Lanzarote, where Audi listens to his tale of leaving home "with patient indulgence" (243). More of a listener than a speaker, she is "one of nature's true scholars" (244), helping him track down with her annotated copy of Milton an obscure allusion to *Paradise Lost* that appeared to him in a recent dream. Audi discreetly refuses to offer an opinion of Margot and Mella, stating that she has too little knowledge on which to form a judgment. In her presence all of Bayley's anxieties magically disappear. A week later they walk hand in hand in Audi's garden after supper, marveling at the night-flowering cactus. As she expertly guides him through the darkness, we suspect that they will help each other complete their journeys through life. "The flowers were like a dance of the blessed spirits. I didn't believe in blessed spirits, but I believed that Iris was with me once more, joining us in the warm breath of the night" (245–46).

Bayley ends *Widower's House* by observing that although the initial grief following Iris's death was difficult to live with, "much worse had been its aftermath, and all the new problems and difficulties it had brought" (246). Audi also realized this, for she had been living in grief's aftermath far longer than he. He feels no conflict of loyalty between his devotion to Iris's memory, on the one hand, and his new union with Audi, on the other. Quite the opposite. "Iris came always closer to both of us" (246). He does not tell us that he marries Audi—that information we learn from the brief author's biography following the close of the story.

Iris has been one of those angelic spirits to Bayley, and presumably Audi will be one, too. He remains discreetly silent about her life and character, respectful of her privacy. Had she been romantically interested in him during Iris's illness? Did she hope to have a relationship with him after Iris's death? Was Bayley thinking about her when he exclaims at the beginning of *Widower's House* that "*all old friends were now threats*" (11; emphasis in original)? Was she intimidated by Iris's worldwide fame as a novelist? Bayley leaves these questions unanswered.

We learn more about Bayley's new marriage in 2000, a year after Iris's death, in a March 18, 2001, interview he gave to the *Observer*. He and Audi, his junior by seventeen years, have a great deal in common, including their love for Iris. "Audi and I talk incessantly about Iris; never stop, really. It's our favourite subject, if you like." Iris remains an absent presence to him—and to his new wife—blessing both of them. Theirs is a companionship not of grief but of joy, a love affair between one man and two women. Asked by the interviewer whether the "ghost of Iris might get in the way of the relationship," he responds: "'Oh, no no no. Certainly not,' he says, gently and resolutely. 'Iris and Audi are completely different, for a start. We talk the whole time, even more than Iris and I talked. I mean, Audi is a natural talker, though she's somewhat dyslexic when it comes to writing. I adored Iris's silence, and I like very much that Audi is a talker; I find it equally relaxing.'" He also indicates that Iris would have endorsed his books. "'We really were secretive,' he says, 'but as you get older you anyway sort of cast shame aside.' Though he knows that some of Iris's friends felt he should not have written about her, he has no worries at all that she would have approved. 'She always encouraged me to do what I thought best,' he says. 'So I have no doubts about that. None at all'" (Adams). He might also have quoted one of Iris's statements in *Acastos: Two Platonic Dialogues* in which, speaking through Socrates, she affirms the importance of storytelling. "We are all artists, we are all story-tellers. We all have to live by art, it's our daily bread—by what our language gives us, by what we invent for ourselves, by what we steal from others. And we should thank the gods for great artists who draw away the veil of anxiety and selfishness and show us, even for a moment, another world, a real world, and tell us a little bit of truth. And we should not be too hard on ourselves for being comforted by art" (63).

THREE
DONALD HALL AND JANE KENYON
"Art Is Created against Death"

Donald Hall's relationship with Jane Kenyon began in 1969, when she enrolled in his large undergraduate course An Introduction to Poetry for Non-English Majors at the University of Michigan. He never met her individually in the class of 140 students, but the following summer she was accepted into his small poetry workshop. He recognized her talent as soon as he read her poem "The Needle," which she had written at the age of nineteen. Their friendship began in January 1971. They were at first wary of each other, partly because of the failure of recent relationships—two years earlier Hall had divorced his wife, to whom he had been married for fifteen years, and Kenyon was also ending a painful relationship. Did they want to begin a new relationship so quickly after the end of failed relationships? Then there was the age factor—he was nineteen years older than she. As he reveals in *The Best Day the Worst Day*, misgivings about a new marriage assailed him. He did not know for certain whether he loved her, nor did he know whether he wished to spend the rest of his life with her. Other doubts plagued him. Would she be sympathetic to the time he needed to continue his life as a creative writer? Would her desire to become a poet last? Would the inequality of the teacher-student relationship lead to the equality necessary in a good marriage? They found themselves drawn toward each other despite these doubts, and they decided on Christmas Day of 1971 to marry the following year. He was forty-three, she twenty-four. Four years later they moved to his ancestral farmhouse, Eagle Pond Farm, built by his great-grandfather at the foot of Mount Kearsarge in Wilmot, New Hampshire, where they lived until her death in 1995 at the age of forty-seven.

Hall and Kenyon had a close and loving marriage, each nurturing the other's creativity. Intimate marriages such as theirs are rare, especially when husband and wife are both poets who seek to craft their own unique voices without attempting to dominate, compete with, subvert, or silence the other's. Unlike most couples, Hall and Kenyon lived in the same house in which they worked, which made it difficult to separate their personal and professional lives. That they were able to do so makes their marriage more remarkable. Rarely were they separated from each other for more than a few days. It was at Eagle Pond Farm that Kenyon emerged as an important American poet, creating short lyrical poems that gained the admiration of the literary community. Long before he met Kenyon, Hall was a prolific and successful writer, the recipient of many honors and awards, including poet laureate of New Hampshire—a title that was bestowed on Kenyon at the end of her life—but as a result of their marriage, he became a love poet, able to imagine a husband's devotion to and intimacy with his wife. As he writes in *The Old Life*, "We learned how to love each other/by loving together/good things wholly outside each other" (82). In 2006, eleven years after his wife's death, he was appointed U.S. poet laureate. Hall and Kenyon were the subject of Bill Moyers's documentary *A Life Together*, broadcast on PBS in 1993, and Moyers included interviews with both poets in his 1995 book *The Language of Life*. Both wrote about depression, cancer, marital love, and the fear of losing each other. Devoted to each other in sickness and in health, they both developed serious forms of cancer that tested their faith in themselves and in each other. Each became the other's caregiver, writing poems and, in Hall's case, several essays and a stunning memoir, about the other.

Long before Kenyon's illness, Hall was keenly aware of the theme of loss in his life. "I've come to think that the sense of being abandoned is central to my spirit," he observes in an interview published in his 1978 book *Goatfoot Milktongue Twinbird* (8). Elaborating, he points out that many poems are elegiac—"not just over death, but over the loss of youth, or the loss of friends" (8). The theme of loss, he suggests, may arise from the memory of birth and thus is universal. "Being born is a kind of abandonment and loss—loss of that comfort of the fluid and warmth inside the womb, out into the hostile air that makes you cry" (8). Later losses may trigger memories of the primeval loss of security, expulsion from the mother's womb. This is, admittedly, highly speculative, and Hall feels uncomfortable with such theorizings. Yet he conjectures that there is something in his temperament that compels him to return repeatedly to this subject, a psychic force that he links to the decision he made in the middle of his career, when he was teaching at the University of Michigan, to give up his tenured professorship and move back to New Hampshire, a state that he associates with loss. His heightened awareness of the inevitability of loss drew him to art, which he describes as a "bulwark" against extinction. "Art is created against death," he states boldly (16), a belief that has comforted him amid the many losses in his life. Hall would agree with William Empson's observation in his poem "Ignorance of Death" that "Because we have neither hereditary nor direct knowledge of death/It is the trigger of the literary man's biggest gun" (79).

Many of Hall's poems and essays celebrate art as a bulwark against death. "I take art in—like many people—in order to keep myself sane and whole and reasonably happy," he declares in his 1995 collection of essays *Principal Products of Portugal* (75–76). "When someone dear to me dies, I go back to the seventeenth-century poets for consolation" (79). He makes a similar observation in his interview with Bill Moyers: "When I make poems I'm consoling myself by making the poem out of loss, but I also have some notion that I'm talking to somebody else at any time now or in the future" (Moyers 148). Kenyon echoes this belief in *A Hundred White Daffodils*: one of the tasks of the poet is "to console in the face of the inevitable disintegration of loss and death, all of the tough things we have to face as humans. We have the consolation of beauty, of one soul extending to another soul and saying, 'I've been there too'" (183–84).

Far from being escapist, art enables Hall to confront and work through his fears. "When I grieve I go to poems that grieve," adding the qualification that art is not primarily funereal, "but mostly we read poetry for the love of it, not in search of consolation" (*Principal Products of Portugal* 86). Providing pleasure and comfort, the poem "exists to say the unsayable" (85), expressing the coexistence of opposites, such as love and hate, joy and sorrow, life and death. Few twentieth-century writers have been more devoted to art, or more prolific, than Donald Hall, and few have been more eloquent in writing about love and loss.

"Reading and writing have filled the days of my life, good times and bad ones, reflecting passages of love, despair, anger, and joy. Reading and writing take their places even in mourning or in fear of death. By words I remember my first consciousness of mortality" (146). In *The Best Day the Worst Day* Hall offers his most memorable pronouncement on the therapeutic nature of art. "Poetry gives the griever not release from grief but companionship in grief. Poetry embodies the complexity of feelings at their most intense and entangled, and therefore offers (over centuries, or over no time at all) the company of tears" (118).

It is easy for a healthy person to extol the value of art as an antidote to death. It is harder for a dying person to do so. Only when artists are in a life-threatening situation can they test whether they are able to transmute their terror into a poem or story. Hall has had two close encounters with death, his own and his wife's. He has written extensively about his experience with cancer—he was diagnosed with colon cancer in 1989, when he was sixty-one, and following surgery, the cancer metastasized to his liver in 1992, requiring chemotherapy and another operation, a lobectomy, in which two-thirds of his liver was surgically removed. He made an excellent recovery, despite the fact that his physicians gave him a one-in-three chance of survival over the next five years. Jane Kenyon battled cancer twice. The first time occurred in 1985, when she discovered a lump on her neck that turned out to be a mucoepidermoid carcinoma. It was surgically removed and never reappeared. The second time was in 1994, when she was diagnosed with leukemia. She went into remission as a result of chemotherapy. When the cancer returned, they flew to the Fred Hutchinson Cancer Research Center in Seattle, where, as a result of a bone marrow transplant, the cancer again went into remission, only to reappear. She died eleven days after being told that her disease was terminal. The story of their life together before and after her diagnosis appears in Hall's 2005 memoir, *The Best Day the Worst Day*.

Life Work

Hall's account of his own cancer appears in his 1993 autobiography *Life Work*. The epigraph contains five quotations praising the life-saving nature of work, including one by the nineteenth-century Spanish philosopher Miguel de Unamuno: "Work is the only practical consolation for having been born." This is not the first time Hall has rhapsodized over work: in his 1988 poem *The One Day*, his speaker cites three different artists on work: "Matisse said, 'Work is paradise'; Rodin, 'To work is to live without dying'; Flaubert, 'It passes the time'" (46). Hall might also have cited John Ruskin's Victorian credo, "Life without work is guilt, and work without art is brutality."

Throughout *Life Work* Hall offers his own memorable formulations of the importance of work. Writing, his life's work, produces for him what he calls a state of "absorbedness" that allows him to forget about the fears and worries that might otherwise paralyze him. This absorbedness resembles what the psychologist Mihaly Csikszentmihalyi calls "flow," in which we lose all sense of time and self-consciousness. Hall's absorbedness enables him to write about cancer while simultaneously being released from the terror of worrying about cancer. "This morning, as I write this medical report for *Life Work*, I find that work remains the matter, not only in defiance of death but in plain sight of it. It absorbs me to write these pages; it absorbs me more nearly than anything else has done for the past week or ten days. Writing about cancer allows me to transcend my cancer by the syntax or rhetoric of dread and suffering" (67–68). Hall would agree with Isak Dinesen's observation that "all sorrows can be borne, if you put them into a story or tell a story about them" (qtd. in Arendt, *The Human Condition* 175). After quoting a quatrain written by fellow poet Stanley Kunitz about the need to scribble fast when one is close to death, Hall states that "if work is no antidote to death, nor a denial of it, death is a powerful stimulus to work. *Get done what you can*" (68; emphasis in original). Earlier in the book he speculates on why work is essential to his life. "Surely it is an ecstasy of transport, of loss of ego; but it is also something less transcendent: To work is to please the powerful masters who are parents—who are family, who are church, who are custom or culture. Not to work is to violate the contract or to disobey the injunction, and to displease the dispensers of supper and love, of praise's reward. Not working becomes conviction of unworthiness. We prove ourselves worthy by the numbers of work" (25–26). In his elegiac memoir *Eagle Pond*, Hall once again champions work, remarking that "it's a trick, doing a sixteen-hour day, seven days a week, without becoming a workaholic" (172).

Life Work is the perfect title for Hall's book, for he cannot think of life without work, which is the center of his life. His admiration for those who have devoted themselves to work is boundless. One of his role models, not necessarily for his theories but for his heroic work ethic, is the creator of psychoanalysis. "Freud loved work. At the prime of his life in Vienna, he was said to live by the clock. Compulsiveness? Anyone who loves accomplishment lives by the clock and the list" (92). Freud remained committed to work even when he was dying of cancer, an illness Hall realizes may end his own life before he completes *Life Work*. He quotes two of Freud's statements from his book *Civilization and Its Discontents*, including the observation that "one gains the most if one can sufficiently heighten the pleasure from the sources of psychical and intellectual work" (qtd. in *Life Work* 93). For Hall, no less than for Freud, a "major palliative is work" (93). In *The Best Day the Worst Day* Hall returns to the subject of work, telling us that immediately before Kenyon's bone marrow transplant he made a detailed list of all the medications he gave his wife and the questions he needed to ask her doctors and nurses. "My life was never so occupied; I lived for my work" (177). On the day of her funeral he "kept busy, too distraught for sorrow" (9–10).

Life Work touches on many of Hall's most significant autobiographical events, including the failure of his first marriage and his psychotherapy in Ann Arbor from the middle sixties into the seventies, in which, during his sessions two or three times a week, he learned to be "unguarded enough to allow slips of the tongue, always grist for the mill" (5). He also recalls his years of depression and self-medication with alcohol between marriages, his decision to move to New Hampshire with Jane Kenyon to begin the life of a freelance writer, and the joy of his second marriage, when for the first time in his life he was able to love and work. But even as *Life Work* recounts Hall's past, it dramatizes his present, for while working on the book, he discovers that his cancer has returned. Instead of suspending the book, he decides to continue recording his unfolding story. The book is written in "real time," with neither the author nor the reader knowing how the story will end.

Kenyon wrote "Otherwise" in 1992, after Hall's first bout with cancer but before they learned it had spread to his liver. It is one of her best poems and the title of a posthumously published volume. Only twenty-six lines long, the poem reveals the speaker's fear of her lover's impending death. Kenyon repeats the word "otherwise" five times, each time reinforcing the certainty of loss. The poem opens with the speaker telling us that she "got out of bed / on two strong legs," knowing that "It might have been / otherwise" (*Collected Poems* 266). After spending the day with her lover, she ends the poem lying in bed, happy in love and work, but with the knowledge that one day she knows it will be "otherwise." As Kenyon biographer John Timmerman points out, the "precariousness of one's life emerges as the underlying pattern of the poem. It might have been otherwise—precisely because life so often is. That understanding, in and of itself, grants the day, with all its routine activities, its precariousness" (208). Neither Kenyon nor Hall could know that the predicted death in the poem would come true in three years, carrying away not the husband but the wife. Hall notes in *The Best Day the Worst Day* that both "Otherwise" and Kenyon's other poem about his anticipated death, "Pharaoh," brought him pleasure despite the subject matter. He recalls lying in bed, fatigued from surgery and chemotherapy, when he heard "Pharaoh" for the first time. "Jane brought me 'Pharaoh" and asked me, with real concern, if I minded . . . I did not mind, nor the anticipation of my death in 'Otherwise.' I loved these poems" (144–45; ellipsis in original).

Part of Hall's strength as a writer lies in his ability to speak authentically about vulnerability, his own and others'. Vulnerability is different from sentimentality, he tells us in *Goatfoot Milktongue Twinbird*: "Sentimentality is the opposite of true vulnerability; sentimentality is emotional dishonesty used to protect oneself from the harshness of the truth perceived. And on the other hand, to be vulnerable is to be open to that wounding perception. The sentimental man is the man closed to wounding" (155). To write authentically about vulnerability, then, one must acknowledge being wounded—an acknowledgment that lends itself to further wounding. The writer must not only disclose pain but also be prepared to be pained by the self-disclosure. "As a commitment or an engagement, vulnerability would be the attempt to walk through the woods without weapon or armor. The attempt *really* to do this. That would be a good thing" (155). To write nonsentimentally about vulnerability, in other words, is to write sincerely—a key word for Hall, one that he explores in his best-selling textbook *Writing Well*. "The worst liars sincerely say—to themselves and to the world—that they are the most honest" (5). And yet Hall is not willing to banish this word from the writer's (or reader's) lexicon. In a demonstration of writerly intertextuality, he then quotes Peter Elbow quoting from Ken Macrorie's book *Uptaught*: "*Sincerity is the absence of 'noise' or static—the ability or courage not to hide the real message*" (4; emphasis in original).

There is little noise or static in Hall's books. He exposes his vulnerability in ways that few writers dare. He never glorifies sickness or death, and he writes with compassion and wry humor. Witness, for example, how he writes in his 1982 book *The Weather for Poetry* about the depression and suicidal thinking that characterized life in his early forties. First he tells us that he had a daydream of suicide, a fantasy to which he would return whenever existence became unbearable. He admits that he could not commit suicide because of its devastating impact on his children. But the self-destructive wish persisted, and he began to imagine ambiguous forms of suicide. "One way was driving. But I was too *moral* to drive into another car" (19). He then began looking for massive objects into which he could crash. "One day I was checking out bridge abutments on highways, finding ones that looked as if they would work; I must have been coming to the end of my despair, because I allowed myself to see that I was driving ten miles under the speed limit, as I was daydreaming suicide by fast driving. I realized, at that moment, that I did not want to. I laughed aloud in the car, and I felt at the same time a sadness, or a pain, that I had to give up this dream" (19).

This story reveals Hall's nonsentimental vulnerability. One can imagine his anguish and confusion, his conflicted intentions, his desire to end his life without unduly hurting his children, and his realization, finally, that his determination to live is greater than his wish to die. He knows what many people lost in depression forget, namely, that suicide is both a personal and an interpersonal act that devastates loved ones for the rest of their lives. He is neither proud nor ashamed of feeling suicidal; he tells us, following this account, that despair affected his writing, as did excessive alcohol. In writing about his life in his forties, he walks through the woods without weapon or armor.

So, too, is *Life Work* a dark journey with an uncertain destination. Part of the book reads like an extended diary entry about the ominous reappearance of cancer. Hall writes like an oncologist, clinically recording each detail and explaining its significance; like a journalist, getting all the facts straight; like a psychologist, probing the affective and cognitive aspects of illness; like a poet and literature teacher, using figurative language and avoiding dead metaphors. He writes from the position of both patient and doctor, describing the emerging facts from subjective and objective viewpoints.

Hall is one of our most stylish writers. In his 1968 book *The Modern Stylists*, he tells us that style is the man: "Style is ethics and psychology; clarity is a psychological sort of ethic, since it involves not general moral laws, but truth to the individual self. The scrutiny of style is a moral and psychological study" (6). The scrutiny of style is also an artistic study. Hall's style, in *Life Work* and elsewhere, is that of a man unafraid to write about any subject, including the one that might kill him, and willing to educate himself to educate his readers. He is a writer's writer, at home with the greatest and most difficult poets and writers, be they seventeenth-century metaphysical poets or novelists like Henry James. But he is also a freelance writer, a popular and populist writer who writes and edits textbooks, literary studies, children's books, poetry anthologies, plays, memoirs, and baseball books. He is one of a handful of academics who gave up teaching to devote himself full time to writing, a decision that proved to be spectacularly successful.

Of all his literary forebears, Hall most resembles, stylistically and thematically, if not temperamentally, Hemingway, for he writes about grace under pressure, prefers understatement to overstatement, combines high culture and low culture, insists upon concrete details in his writings, and has little patience for fools and imposters. Both loved sports, Hemingway prize fighting and big game hunting, Hall baseball. (In *Fathers Playing Catch with Sons* he writes hilariously about the time in 1973 when, forty-four years old and grossly overweight, with a full beard and hair hanging to his shoulders, he tried out for the Pittsburgh Pirates.) Like Hemingway, he keeps returning to the subject of death, in part to exorcise his fears of it. Both battled many of the same demons, including depression and suicide. No less than Hemingway, Hall is committed to self-discipline and a fierce work ethic. And yet Hall has little of Hemingway's misogyny, cruelty, and intolerance. Hall is Hemingway who decided not to kill himself, not to destroy his creativity through womanizing and drinking, not to pretend to more courage than he had, not to turn against the men and women who befriended him, not to walk away from the woman he loved, not to become an unconscious self-parody.

Hall could not have known this at the time, but writing about cancer in *Life Work* proved to be a rehearsal for *The Best Day the Worst Day*. "A scan Tuesday morning, read on Wednesday, showed something in the liver; it is the liver to which colon cancer metastasizes. Wednesday morning I watched the screen during ultrasound and saw the barbell shaped darkness on the liver's right lobe. No one *knows* what it is until pathology puts dyed cells under a microscope; but of course it is a metastatic lesion" (66). Later he discovers that the barbell shape is a characteristic form of liver cancer. "The ultrasound technician describes it not as a barbell but as an hourglass. Ah, metaphor; do the sands run out?" (66). Waking up from the anesthesia after the liver biopsy, he looks carefully into his wife's eyes for news of what the surgeon has found: "She will not lie to me" (67).

The news is cautiously hopeful, but as Hall contemplates the future, when the cancer may begin to multiply again, causing another deathwatch, he cannot avoid thinking melodramatically. "The nature of this book alters. Shall I change the title from *Life Work* to *Work and Death*? Box office, he said sneering. Oh, let me return to my theme: I have worked all this preoperation week but not on *Life Work*: I finished the graveyard (!) essay and the review of Tom Williams that I had almost finished" (67). Committing himself to absorbedness, he finds a way to escape from paralyzing fears. One senses that, as with Hemingway, writing provides Hall with a feeling of invulnerability, even when writing about his impending death.

Hall records in *Life Work* that he plans to resume his writing following liver surgery. He is determined to get his affairs in order. "Arrangements include a long note to Jane, in case I die on the table, about money and manuscripts, possible posthumous essay-collections or collections of poetry. I could die on the table; I could live twenty years" (69). He writes matter-of-factly about the prognosis, refusing to be paralyzed by the odds against recovery. But a few pages later he admits that the probability of the cancer returning, quickly overwhelming his body, produces distressing thoughts that may further weaken his immune system. "When I panic, panic confounds itself with guilt and rage—because Bernie Siegel, Chopra, and other visualizers tell me that I kill myself by negative imagining, the victim guilty as ever" (113). While recovering from liver surgery, he recalls Jane telling him that in his mother's house she kept seeing a man out of the corner of her eye whom she had never seen before, a figure who vanished quickly. It was Hall's father, who had died of cancer when Jane was eight years old. The disclosure depresses him, for they both know that the room in which they sleep is the same room in which his father had died. A break in the narration occurs, followed by a return to the importance of work. "When I am not working I brood and hold close to Jane. It is a dreadful absorbedness, yet I can still work much of the time, and when I work I am absorbed in work" (114).

Life Work ends where it begins, but Hall's life has changed irrevocably in the three months it has taken him to complete the manuscript. In addition to writing many poems, two or three short essays, a book review, and dictating hundreds of letters, he has gained two more grandchildren, helped his mother recover from a heart attack, lost most of his liver and "nine-tenths" of his complacency. The medical crisis has also strengthened his marriage. "I have come so close to Jane that I feel as if I had crawled into her body through her pores—and, although the occasion of this penetration has been melancholy, the comfort is luminous and redemptive" (123). Hall generally does not use religious words like "redemptive"—on the previous page he admits that his Christianity and deaconhood at the South Danbury Church embarrass most of his friends. He acknowledges feeling a conflict between his temperamental skepticism, on the one hand, which compels him always to search for a material explanation, and his spirituality, on the other, which shines more like a "strobe" than a "flashlight." What he does believe in fully, unequivocally, passionately is his devotion to work and to Jane, a faith that sustains him in sickness and in health.

The Museum of Clear Ideas

Published the same year as *Life Work*, *The Museum of Clear Ideas*, dedicated to "Jane," reveals the same elegiac tone and thematic preoccupation with death. The volume begins with a poem called "Another Elegy" for a fictional contemporary poet named William Trout who, struggling with mental illness, alcoholism, and instability, becomes a metaphor of the mad artist who dies prematurely, a fate to which Hall could imagine himself succumbing. The next section, "Baseball," consists of nine poems (each corresponding to an inning in a baseball game), each containing nine stanzas of nine lines, with nine syllables per line. In the next section, "The Museum of Clear Ideas," a series of mistranslations from the first book of Horace's Odes, Hall adopts the voice of Horace Horsecollar, a "minor character," as he tells us in the notes at the end of the book, "in Walt Disney's comics," who offers us his (and Hall's) despairing vision of modern poetry. The last section, "Extra Innings," consists of three poems—"The Tenth Inning," "The Eleventh Inning," and "The Twelfth Inning"—which contain ten, eleven, and twelve stanzas, respectively. As with *Life Work*, *The Museum of Clear Ideas* reveals not only Hall's prodigious commitment to work but also his belief that death is his muse. "The truest/aphrodisiac is our certain knowledge that we will die" (50).

In "The Tenth Inning" Hall abruptly writes about a woman named "Jennifer" who is recovering from cancer surgery. That woman is Jane, as he admits in *The Old Life* (15). Protective of her privacy, he nevertheless describes the surgical removal of the tumor on her neck in the same way that he does twelve years later in *The Best Day the Worst Day*. Afterward they drove home in silence and waited anxiously for news of the biopsy. He recalls telling her that the growth is malignant and that they must wait an additional six days for the pathologist's report about the likelihood of metastasis and the probability of recurrence. As he has done in *Life Work*, only from the opposite spouse's point of view, Hall imagines the cancer leading to death. "In self-pity I watched the widower/weep by her grave: lamenting, lamented" (*The Museum of Clear Ideas* 105). Finally they receive the long-awaited report: a "'muco-epidermoid carcinoma,/the size of a grape, intermediate/in virulence, encapsulated in/the membrane of the salivary gland'/—with no likelihood of metastasis/and little for recurrence" (105–6). In "The Eleventh Inning" he discloses his colon cancer diagnosis in 1989 (without mentioning the 1992 metastasis to the liver), and then he turns to his father's death from lung cancer at age fifty-two. In "The Twelfth Inning" he discloses that Jennifer is taking five drugs for depression. "The Twelfth Inning" ends with the defeat in September of his beloved Boston Red Sox, but he and his wife happily return to their daily routine, suggesting that they can live with cancer.

Without

But Jane Kenyon couldn't, and Donald Hall eulogizes her in his haunting 1998 volume of poems aptly called *Without.* Dedicated to her memory, *Without* is his most powerful collection of poems, many of them penned as she lay dying. As he observes in *The Best Day the Worst Day*, "It took me half my life, more than half, to discover with Jane's guidance that two people could live together and remain kind" (111). Until the poems that describe his life without her, he often writes about himself in third person, perhaps because it gives him more distance and, therefore, more objectivity. Beginning with "Her Long Illness," which continues at intervals throughout the volume, he recalls sitting by her side at the hospital while "chemotherapy dripped/through the catheter into her heart" (*Without* 1). Both as a poet and husband, he reveals the need to memorialize and immortalize her even as he cares for her. These twin roles, artist and caregiver, never seem to clash with each other: indeed, they fulfill complementary needs within him. As with his earlier poetry collections, he is unafraid to expose his—and now her—vulnerability, but this time he captures the terror of their situation. "Overcome with dread, / they wept and affirmed / their love for each other, witlessly, / over and over again" (1).

In the next poem, "A Beard for a Blue Pantry," Hall recalls the early years of his marriage to Jane, when she "made bread so honest / it once went blue in the pantry" during a heat wave (*Without* 2). He then describes how each morning they "worked together / apart" on their own poems, a paradoxical image of connection-amid-separation that recalls John Bayley's observation in *Elegy for Iris* that early in their marriage he and his wife moved "closer and closer apart." Hall elaborates on this theme in *The Best Day the Worst Day*, stating the need for a "third thing" in marriage (an idea he first suggested in the last poem in *The One Day*): "Third things are essential to marriages, objects or practices or habits or arts or institutions or games or human beings that provide a site of joint rapture or contentment. Each member of a couple is separate; the two come together in double attention. Lovemaking is not a third thing but two-in-one." Their third thing includes their "cats and dog to fuss and exclaim over—and later five grandchildren" (109). Poetry and Christianity were also third things.

Shortly after Jane's leukemia diagnosis, Hall's mother fell ill and died, and in "Song for Lucy" he relates how she cared for him in his childhood when he was ill. "She nursed so well, I loved/being sick." He quotes Freud's observation that "a man thrives his whole life/if he received as a child/his mother's entire devotion" (*Without* 6). He writes lovingly about his mother who, while never an alcoholic, sometimes found herself "drinking Scotch and vomiting/to drink more Scotch, behaving as good companion/to my depressed father" (7). She was able to nurse her husband when he was hospitalized for a bleeding ulcer ten years before his death. Physically healthy until weakened by congestive heart failure at the age of eighty, she lived another ten years, dedicating herself to the "enterprise" of love.

In one of the few poems in which she is well enough to speak, Jane names the ring he places on her finger, on the occasion of their twenty-second anniversary, "Please Don't Die." She also whispers a line from the fifteenth-century Scottish poet William Dunbar's "Lament for the Makers": "Timor mortis conturbat me"—The fear of death confounds me (*Without* 9). The fear of death doesn't prevent Hall from driving to his mother's home in Connecticut, where he describes in "The Porcelain Couple" wrapping up her cherished family heirlooms. Returning home exhausted, he gazes at the many treasured possessions he and Jane have acquired in the last twenty years. Each object is meaningful to him, representing a different moment of their marriage.

The most poignant stanzas in "Her Long Illness" capture the caregiver's helplessness as he witnesses a loved one's suffering. The poem shows how, in Eric J. Cassell's words, suffering is "an affliction of the *person*, not the body" (xii; emphasis in original). Husband and wife suffer individually and collectively. They are so close to each other, literally and figuratively, that they seem to share their loneliness with each other. Suffering creates an "ardent merging" that enables them to recall passionate connections in the past. The knowledge that she is worried for *him* only intensifies his grief. "It must have been unbearable/while she suffered her private hurts/to see his worried face/looming above her, always anxious to *do/something* when there was/exactly nothing to do" (*Without* 13). The early poems in *Without* offer a glimmer of hope that

Jane will recover, hope that her massive infusions and bone marrow transplant will succeed. The "Total Body Irradiation" evokes the specter of Chernobyl. With her immune system now destroyed, she is forced to live in an "antibiotic cube," and he must don a surgical gown and sterile latex gloves to visit her, occasioning one of the few comic moments in the volume, when Jane tells him that he looks like a "huge condom."

Some of Hall's observations in *Without* are developed in greater detail in *The Best Day the Worst Day*, such as the disclosure that he momentarily imagined throwing himself in front of a bus while walking to Jane's hospital. He recalls ruefully a social worker's alarm upon hearing this. Hall recounts in both the poem and the memoir an incident in Seattle in which Jane expressed anger toward him: "I wish you could feel what I feel." The statement piqued my interest, and when I mailed Hall an early draft of this chapter, asking him to elaborate on her words, he responded: "I think it was the only time that she ever showed anger during those fifteen months" (February 13, 2008). The incident was so upsetting to him that he dreams of her "crouched in terror at the bottom / of the cellar stairs while he / crept down, his hands clutched to choke her" (*Without* 27). But this suicidal and homicidal fantasy is atypical, and I suspect that he includes this material to show he is human. A brief description of Jane thrashing in the hospital while being intubated, turning blue because she had stopped breathing, appears in the memoir.

The poems in *Without* convey the intimacy of two lovers who are losing each other. As Jane begins to recover from the harrowing bone marrow transplant, Hall confesses that "He felt shame / to understand he would miss / the months of sickness and taking care" (*Without* 34). That moment of shame is, ironically, short-lived; on the next page Jane's hematologist tells them, in the presence of an assistant, that she has terrible news—"'The leukemia is back. / There's nothing to do.' / The four of them wept. He asked how long, / why did it happen now? / Jane asked only: 'Can I die at home?'" (35).

Significantly, they use the little time left to choose the poems for Jane's posthumous collection, *Otherwise*. Hall is the driving force here, even though she is the one who insists, when he asks her if they should delay until she feels stronger, "'Now,' she said. / 'We have to finish it now'" (*Without* 37). We never learn how she feels about her artistic legacy, whether she is comforted by the knowledge that her poems will survive her death. Clearly her artistic reputation comforts *him*. "Art was dependable, something / to live for," he tells us during her illness (31). Unlike Sylvia Plath and Anne Sexton, who both associated creativity with martyrdom, Hall believes that the creation of art strengthens the artist: poetry arises from absence and brings forth new presence. Poetry has brought him Jane Kenyon, first in his poetry classes at the University of Michigan, and then in marriage. They spend their final days together working on what will be her posthumous collection of verse. By helping her choose the poems for *Otherwise*, Hall becomes not only her editor but also her artistic caregiver, nursing both the poet and her poetry. Afterward, they decide on her burial clothes, she agreeing to his suggestion that she wear the white salwar kameez she had bought when they were recently in India. He does not tell her that, a year earlier, "dreaming awake, / he had seen her / in the coffin in her white salwar kameez" (38).

Hall suggests in *The Best Day the Worst Day* that Jane was more religious than he, more devout, more mystical, but this is not evident in *Without*. There is little religious consolation or comfort for either of them. Nor is there, tellingly, any hint that they may be together in the future. After her death he refers only passingly—and ambiguously—to their religious beliefs. "You know now / whether the soul survives death. / Or you don't," adding that they never dared to speak of Paradise (*Without* 50). In one of her most religious poems, "Notes from the Other Side," Kenyon affirms life after death. The poet divests herself of despair when she imagines her lover's casket being lowered into the ground, and her heart is calm: "God, as promised, proves / to be mercy clothed in light" (*Collected Poems* 267). But as Hall states in *The Best Day the Worst Day*, she could not be certain about an afterlife as she lay dying.

Instead, husband and wife concentrate on this world, not the next, talking about their adventures together, the richness and beauty of their lives, and their happiness as a couple. But these joyous memories only deepen her anguish over death. She cries inconsolably, "No more fucking. No more fucking!" (*Without* 40). In revealing the sexual side to their marriage, Hall portrays her here, as he later does in his memoir, as a woman who celebrates the fullness of life, body, mind, and soul. Later in the poem he wonders how Jane would have fulfilled her sexual needs had he predeceased her. "You would have found / a lover, but not right away." He then invokes Yeats's statement in old age about his early lover,

Maud Gonne, slightly misquoting him on purpose: "The sexual/intercourse of angels . . . is a conflagration/of the whole being" (72). Hall's heaven appears little different from earth, and he has no reluctance to state that "I want to fuck you/in Paradise" (72). Without implying either that he is Yeats or that Jane is Maud Gonne, Hall suggests, in language worthy of Yeats, that their marriage has been a conflagration of the whole being—an image of marital fullness that recalls Lewis's "feasting on love" in *A Grief Observed*. One can only assume, since there is no evidence to contradict this, that Jane would have felt comfortable with these sexual disclosures. Nowhere does Hall question how she would have felt reading his poems and memoir about her.

Kenyon is now close to the end, barely able to speak or walk. Terrified that she will fall at home, Hall calls an ambulance to take her to the hospital, but she resists, imploring him to "be with me when I die" (*Without* 41). Her penultimate statement is perhaps the most heartrending in the entire poem: "'Dying is simple,' she said./'What's worst is . . . *the separation*'" (42; ellipsis and italics in original). As her friends visit her for the final time, she repeats their names, weeps, touches them, and smiles, but on the last day she "stared silent goodbyes/with her hands curled and her eyes stuck open" (43). She utters her last word, "O.K.," in response to his statement that he is going to mail his letters. He kisses her when he returns and, with her "brain-stem breathing," her cool lips answer his kiss. For twelve hours he watches her, and when her chest finally goes still, "with his thumb he closed her round brown eyes" (45).

The deathbed scene in *Without* is peaceful and serene, as it is in John Bayley's memoir *Iris and Her Friends*. There is no pain or discomfort in the imperceptible transition from life to death, nothing fearful or unsettling. Both writers "humanize" death, to use Philippe Ariès's word from the last page of his magisterial book *The Hour of Our Death*: "Death must simply become the discreet but dignified exit of a peaceful person from a helpful society that is not torn, not even overtly upset by the idea of a biological transition without significance, without pain or suffering, and ultimately without fear" (614). Her passing affirms *ars moriendi*: a peaceful death. In her final hours she resembles a work of art: "In the last hours, she kept/her forearms raised with pale fingers clenched/at cheek level, like/the goddess figurine over the bathroom sink" (*Without* 45).

Deathbed scenes abound in literature, and Hall's reaction to his wife's death is the opposite of Frederic Henry's emotionally numb response to seeing Catherine's lifeless body at the end of Hemingway's *A Farewell to Arms*: "It was like saying good-by to a statue" (322). Hall, like Bayley, is fortunate to be with his wife at the moment of expiration. Only by watching her chest go still does he discern the end of her life. The peacefulness of his wife's death has a calming effect on him, as does the peacefulness of Iris Murdoch's death on John Bayley. There is no weeping, wailing, keening, or tearing of hair, no *conclamatio mortis*, the death shout that occurs in some cultures. There is only a quiet acceptance. Hall instinctively closes Jane's eyes, perhaps less for her sake than for his own: it seems that one can gaze upon the dead only if the dead do not return the gaze. Why? Perhaps because of a superstitious fear of the dead, or because of the wish to avoid violating the dead's privacy. Perhaps closing Jane's eyes suggests that the dead can no longer see. Or perhaps it is simply a kind gesture to allow the deceased to rest in peace. Interestingly, in *The Old Life* Hall recalls the time when he met Edwin and Willa Muir, Kafka's translators, both of whom were in their sixties. "I asked Willa / how it was to be old, / and she said it was 'surprisingly / good . . . except that one / will need to close the eyes of the other'" (62; ellipsis in original).

The second half of *Without* focuses on Hall's life after Jane Kenyon's death. In making a photo gallery of her, writing poems to and about her, visiting the cemetery where she is buried (as often as three times a day), answering hundreds of letters about her, even looking at her collection of slips from fortune cookies, he engages in "obsessional review," an essential part of the mourning process. It is the same bereavement ritual we saw John Bayley engage in immediately following Iris Murdoch's death, when he studies in detail everything she wrote. Both men are so absorbed in obsessional review, in rereading their wives' writings and reflecting on their final moments together, that they almost forget their grief. Hall replays over and over again their last days together, partly because he cannot stop thinking about her, and partly because he knows he will write about her in order to bear witness and re-create her life in loving words. After his wife's death, Hall reads *Beyond the Pleasure Principle*, in which Freud theorizes the repetition-compulsion principle, the need to repeat traumatic experiences for the purpose of mastering them. Hall is sympathetic to Freud's thesis; writing has long been his treatment of choice to work through grief and loss. It is not closure he seeks or moving on with his life but learning to live with the dead, to maintain his relational bond with her, to find a way to internalize his wife so that he can remain connected with her and overcome the dreadful separation.

Without chronicles the first year of Hall's bereavement, and we can see the subtle changes wrought by time. Jane dies in April, but he avoids citing T. S. Eliot's overquoted opening line from *The Waste Land*: "April is the cruellest month." On the Fourth of July he is still watching her die: it is a grim Independence Day for him, and thoughts of her death prevent him from reading with understanding *The Man without Qualities* in bed. In "Midsummer Letter," written four months after her death, he is momentarily happy while walking to his car under the summer night, but he still cannot play her CDs or tapes. In "Letter in Autumn," six months after her death, he hears her ask plaintively, "Perkins [her nickname for him],/am I going to live?" (*Without* 60). He is still in a state of denial if not shock over her death. He is still crying, though he tries to "wave it off" by telling himself, "I just/did that" (60). He is not yet ready to discard his wife's clothes. In "Letter at Christmas" he describes the spasms of grief that still overcome him, as when, enjoying dinner with friends, he suddenly needs to drive home. In "Postcard: January 22nd," he imagines himself growing heavy, "now bear[ing] your death" (73)—an image that may evoke the poem's gestation. In "Midwinter Letter" he reveals that his health remains surprisingly good, with no return of cancer and his diabetes under control. It is still too early to recall with pleasure their joyful years together: "Remembered happiness is agony;/so is remembered agony" (76). He still has flashes of homicidal and suicidal rage, but they do not alarm him. In the final poem, "Weeds and Peonies," nature is in the process of tentative rebirth and renewal. "Your peonies lean their vast heads westward/as if they might topple. Some topple" (81). It is not an affirmative word on which to end the volume, but it is too soon to expect full recovery.

No less than John Bayley, Donald Hall does everything he can to remain attached to his wife's memory while he continues to live his life as best he can. Both writers are striking examples of the continuing bonds approach to bereavement. Hall never attempts to "let go" of his deceased wife or to disengage from grief. Nor is he interested in "closure," for good clinical reasons. As Charles A. Corr and Donna M. Corr point out, "Linear, fixed stages in mourning are not favored by contemporary scholars, nor is language such as 'recovery,' 'completion,' or 'resolution' that may imply a misunderstanding of bereavement and grief or a fixed end point for mourning" (132). Jane Kenyon remains a living presence, a palpable presence that is never absent from his life, not even after her death. Death has ended her life but not her presence, and her husband begins the task of forging a new relationship with her that will sustain him for the rest of his life. He does not seek to end his caregiving: he now turns his attention to her poems, editing them with the same loving care with which he nursed the poet. From the old Freudian decathexis approach to bereavement, his grief seems excessive, but from the new continuing bonds approach, it seems perfectly normal.

I read *Without* during Barbara's illness and then again after her death. There were times when Hall's experiences were so uncannily close to my own that I felt like the boundary between poet and reader had dissolved. No less than Hall and Jane Kenyon, Barbara and I were overcome by dread when we learned of her diagnosis—pancreatic cancer has a 99 percent mortality rate, even higher than that of adult leukemia. Like them, we affirmed our love for each other, witlessly, over and over again. The fear of death confounded Barbara and me, as it did Jane. Barbara and I often felt merged during her illness, as did Hall and Jane. Each of us found it unbearable to see the worry on the other's face. Like Hall, I was always anxious to do something, even when there was nothing to do. No less than Jane, Barbara suffered from depression and panic attacks after her diagnosis, taking some of the drugs she did, including Haldol and Klonopin. Barbara too wanted to die at home, not in a hospital, and she often remained dry-eyed, silent, trying to let go, while I wailed. Barbara would have agreed with Jane that separation is worse than death. Hall and I were both full-time caregivers for the duration of our wives' illnesses, he for fifteen months, I for twenty months. We never lied to our wives about the severity of their illnesses, and while we were both cheerleaders, realizing the importance of maintaining hope, we never conveyed false hope; as Hall states in *The Best Day the Worst Day*, "In mortal circumstances, nothing is so repulsive as mendacious optimism" (191).

Both Jane Kenyon and Barbara worried incessantly over their husbands, fearing they would not do well without them. They were protective of their husbands, preferring to confide their fears of dying and death to nurses: "Speaking to a tender and compassionate woman, speaking to someone not her potential widower, Jane let her despair show forth more than she did when she talked with me" (*The Best Day the Worst Day* 189). Unlike Jane, Barbara was not a poet and had no desire to help me write her obituary or listen to my eulogy of her; but she recorded daily entries in her diary until she could no longer write. The last entries were only her pain level, which was intense. Both women drew comfort from their dogs, whom they loved unconditionally. Barbara wanted to be buried with her beloved dog Ebony's cremated ashes, which we kept in an urn in the garage. Jane's dog Gus was still alive at her death, but after he died, Hall scattered his ashes on Jane's grave. Both Hall and I howled and wailed during our wives' illnesses, but we were prepared to let them go, not wishing to prolong their suffering. No less than Hall, I have learned after my wife's death that "Remembered happiness is agony, / so is remembered agony." Finally, both Hall and I have written memoirs about our wives—writing was our major form of grief-work.

Jane Kenyon wrote only two poems after her leukemia diagnosis, "Eating the Cookies," about cleaning out Hall's mother's hospital room after her death, and "The Sick Wife," uncompleted at her death. Exhausted by the debilitating bone marrow transplant, she spent the last year completing some of her earlier poems and choosing, with her husband, poems for her posthumous new-and-selected poems. Before the leukemia diagnosis, however, she wrote several poems about her husband's cancer and her own experience with mental illness. It is instructive to compare her poem "Chrysanthemums" with Hall's poem in *Without* called "The Porcelain Couple," which describes his response to his lobectomy in 1992. Both poems convey their love for each other during the medical crisis, but they focus on different aspects of the experience. Hall's poem, only sixteen lines long, affirms his wife's caregiving: Jane pushes the morphine bolus, drives him home from the hospital, and rubs his body "back to life with her hands" (12). She seems to be the agent behind his recovery. Together they rock on the hospital bed in horror. Their "ardent merging" recalls passionate memories when they made love, followed by a feeling of calmness. Hall's poem is a liebestod, celebrating love and death.

Kenyon's poem, sixty-five lines long, is more introspective, fraught with dread. Neither the cancer diagnosis, surgery, nor recovery is an occasion for recollections of past sexual experiences. Whereas "The Porcelain Couple" emphasizes husband and wife's connection with each other, "Chrysanthemums" depicts their separateness. Significantly, Hall brings to the hospital his mini tape recorder and a stack of letters, prepared to work whenever possible. Unlike Hall, who could work during his illness, Kenyon could not work during her own illness: she seems too depressed to do anything but read. She lacks, in short, his absorbedness. The speaker lies on her husband's hospital bed, eyes closed, waiting for the surgery to end. The attendants ask her to leave when they move him back into the room, and she feels further distanced from him. He remains sleeping hours later, well into the evening. She tries to read, pausing repeatedly to look around her, sensitive to every change in the room. Because he is unable to press the bolus for pain medication, she pushes it for him every eight minutes so that he can sleep without pain. The reader can feel her anguish and helplessness, but her poem is much more restrained than Hall's. As her husband recovers, they both resume their daily lives: "The most ordinary gestures seemed / cause for celebration" ("Chrysanthemums," Jane Kenyon: *Collected Poems* 238–39). Only at the end, when she drives him home, do they begin to cry, "he first, and then I."

"Having It Out with Melancholy"

"Having It Out with Melancholy," perhaps Kenyon's best-known poem, describes not only her long history of mental illness but also the various treatments that were prescribed for it. She begins the poem with an apt quotation from Chekhov's *The Cherry Orchard*: "If many remedies are prescribed for an illness, you may be certain that the illness has no cure" (*Collected Poems* 231). Kenyon never does find a treatment that cures her illness, but she learns to live with it—until she develops leukemia, when she confronts a distinctly different medical illness that is not only incurable, like manic depression, but also fatal. Many twentieth-century American poets have written about their experience with mood disorders, including Robert Lowell, Sylvia Plath, and Anne

Sexton, and others have written memoirs about their experiences, such as William Styron's *Darkness Visible*, Kay Redfield Jamison's *An Unquiet Mind*, and Andrew Solomon's *The Noonday Demon*. I suspect that both Hall and Kenyon would agree with Solomon's conclusion that "the unexamined life is unavailable to the depressed": "That is, perhaps, the greatest revelation I have had: not that depression is compelling but that the people who suffer from it may become compelling because of it" (438). Keats—Kenyon's favorite poet—wrote about this subject in "Ode to Melancholy."

Kenyon's contribution to the literature of melancholy lies in her refusal to glamorize mental illness or allow the fear of cultural stigma to silence her. In her interview with Bill Moyers, she jokingly refers to her psychiatrist as her "mixologist" (Moyers 229), and unlike so many others afflicted with mental illness, she publicly expresses gratitude toward those mental health professionals who have done their best to help her. She describes how mental illness affects every aspect of her life, including her relationship with husband, friends, and God. Mysterious in its comings and goings, melancholy can never be permanently cast out because it is an essential part of the self. The best one can do, she implies, is learn to live with it. The poem reaches no epiphanic conclusions about the origins, meaning, and treatment of mental illness, but it offers realistic reassurance to those who suffer from mood disorders.

"Having It Out with Melancholy" is divided into nine sections, beginning with "From the Nursery" and ending with "Wood Thrush." Kenyon personifies melancholy as a sly antagonist who patiently waits for the opportunity to strike. The adversary first appears in her nursery, when he "lay down/on top of me, pressing/the bile of desolation into every pore" (*Collected Poems* 231). Melancholy teaches her to exist without gratitude, undermining her belief in God. "We're here simply to wait for death," he tells her, adding, "the pleasures of earth are overrated" (231). Described as the "anti-urge," the "mutilator of souls," melancholy appears to be winning the fight. He goes into hiding in the second section, "Bottles," only when the poet is willing to try one powerful antidepressant after another, so many, in fact, as to suggest that none are effective. This section of the poem reads almost like a pharmaceutical textbook, listing eleven different drugs for the treatment of anxiety and depression.

Perhaps the most despairing moment in the poem occurs in the third section, "Suggestions from a Friend," when someone insinuates that "You wouldn't be so depressed / if you really believed in God" (232)—an accusation that is bound to add religious guilt to her psychological misery. She describes in "Often" how she tries to flee from her self-tormentor by going to bed immediately after dinner. The fifth section, "Once There Was Light," is the most mystical. She recalls how in her early thirties she saw a "speck of light in the great / river of light that undulates through time" (232). She found herself "floating with the whole / human family" (233), magically released from the burden of consciousness, only to be reluctantly brought back to human existence by her enemy. Section six, "In and Out," describes the relief she experiences when she hears her dog's reassuring breathing—a therapy almost as effective as the monoamine oxidase inhibitors that abruptly end her pain in section seven, "Pardon."

The penultimate section, "Credo," conveys Kenyon's belief that although her new antidepressant appears to be working, she knows her "Unholy ghost" is certain to reappear. Melancholy turns her into someone who cannot speak, read, or even "call for an appointment for help" (234). In the final section, she is "high on Nardil and June light," waking at four in the morning to hear a wood thrush. Overcome by its "wild, complex song," she mercifully cannot remember "What hurt me so terribly / all my life until this moment" (235). The final line conjures up the image of the bird's "bright, unequivocal eye," suggesting clarity and joy. The poem ends with the poet's identification with the thrush, as psychiatrist Peter Kramer notes. "Like her wood thrush, Kenyon does not equivocate. She speaks with a straightforwardness that serves to reclaim the dignity of stigmatized sufferers from depression. She bears an affliction, one she does not flinch from naming and depicting, and one she cannot help embodying" ("Unequivocal Eye" 255).

"Having It Out with Melancholy" was painful for Kenyon to write and to read aloud, Hall observes in "Ghost in the House," mainly because it was so personal. "It pained her to expose herself. But writing the poem also helped her to set depression out, as she knew it, depression and its joyful tentative departure. She wanted the poem to help others who were afflicted" ("Ghost in the House" 88). Kenyon's poems on depression have been compared with Plath's, but as Laban Hill points out, there are differences. "While Plath's poems can be overwrought, self-absorbed, and self-dramatizing, Kenyon's work contains a New England reserve that makes her poems much quieter and absent of histrionics. Also, Plath was obviously consumed by her depression. In contrast, Kenyon never gives up the fight" ("Jane Kenyon"135). One can only speculate on Plath's life and art had she married a man who could understand and appreciate her creativity and who would not compete with or give up on her even as she gave up on herself. Hall was such a man, and he never allowed Kenyon to give up the fight.

In her interview with Bill Moyers, Kenyon reveals that she has suffered from depression her entire life. "I'm manic-depressive, actually, and I was not properly diagnosed until I was thirty-eight years old. In my case it's more like a unipolar depression. Manic-depression usually involves both poles of feeling. That is, when you're happy you're too happy, when you're sad you get too sad. Mine behaves almost like a serious depression only and I rarely become manic" (225). Agreeing with Moyers that depression "is really the land of the living dead"—he, too, has suffered from the mood disorder—she admits it is difficult reading poems about depression in public. But, she adds, people are moved when they hear these poems read aloud, in part because many of them know people who are depressed. She endorses Moyers's observation that reading or hearing poems on depression can help those who suffer from the illness. Acknowledging a genetic component to depression that runs in her family, she states that it has taken her a long time to realize she is not to blame for her mental illness. "It's like having heart disease or diabetes. I've decided that I want to increase people's understanding about this disease. I want to ease people's burdens" (229). Unlike Hall, who seems to be able to write no matter what his psychological mood may be, Kenyon admits that she cannot write when depressed. "I have been able to revise when I'm depressed, but I don't initiate things when I'm depressed. I can't call the plumber to come and fix the drain. I can't initiate anything. I can't move" (231).

Hall has also written about bipolarity, not only in relation to Kenyon but also as a phenomenon affecting many artists, especially poets. "All humans are bipolar and writers are extreme," he asserts in *Principal Products of Portugal*: "Most writers suffer from bipolar mood disorder, or manic-depressive disease, largely without delusion but with painful depression and the elated energy of mania. My own bipolarity is subclinical; I tend toward mild mania, a cheerful fellow interrupted by long mild depressions" (269–70). In *Breakfast Served Any Time All Day*, published in 2003, eight years after his wife's death, he elaborates on the relationship between creativity and manic-depressive illness, speaking now with greater clinical precision. "The incidence of bi-polar mood disorder in artists, especially in writers, rises high in proportion to the rest of the population. Bi-polarity implies gross swings of mood, but not necessarily the madness of delusion or suicide" (217–18). He does not romanticize manic depression, but he realizes that in its milder forms mania can inspire great art. "The confidence and energy of a limited manic state is the divine afflatus, the sense of possession or transport, inspiration, the vatic voice that speaks unbidden" (218).

In affirming the creative and adaptive implications of manic depression, Hall champions Jane Kenyon's creativity as well. He also reveals his deep empathic understanding of her. He was the perfect companion for her during her periods of health as well as illness. His ability to intuit his own "subclinical" bipolarity allowed him to understand and empathize with his wife's clinical bipolarity. Rather than being alarmed by her mood swings, he was able to provide her with the love, support, understanding, and security she needed, as did Leonard Woolf when Virginia Woolf suffered from psychotic breakdowns. Hall did not judge, criticize, or condemn Jane during these bouts of illness. Nor did he dismiss her suffering or explain it away, as did one of her "friends," as a symptom of religious despair. He made sure she did not harm herself when she was severely ill, and he reminded her of her creativity when she was feeling better, motivating her to "give birth" through the creation of art. "Manic depressives may kill themselves when they are down," he writes in *Breakfast Served Any Time All Day*, "but when they are up they give birth" (218).

Hall came to realize that he had a limited ability to help her when she was severely depressed. "When she was low I might attempt to comfort her, as she did me in my bad times, and sometimes comfort or loving helped, but there were times I could not reach her, times she was beyond my help. At these times I learned not to fuss at her; I did not ask, 'Was it something I said?' (During years of psychotherapy, before I knew Jane, I learned that I was not responsible for everything around me)" (*The Best*

Day the Worst Day 134). Sometimes Hall's boundless energy and enthusiasm had the opposite effect on her, paradoxically worsening her depression. They did not always tell each other when they were upset. Nor did they expect each to be the other's therapist, especially for problems that existed before their marriage.

Kenyon's collapse in 1982, a few months after the death of her father, resulted in the most serious depression of her life. This was the time when she was diagnosed as bipolar, and she went on permanent medication. Some of her drugs were more effective than others, and even those that helped, such as doxepin, prescribed for severe depression, had to be given in increasingly larger doses. Kenyon told Moyers in the 1993 interview about the disastrous consequences of ending medication only to discover that she could not live without it. Hall writes sensitively not only about Kenyon's manic and depressive stages but also about their impact on his own moods. "At first when Jane turned manic, I became depressed, which allowed me to understand that her depression had for years provided me with secondary gain: I could flatter myself that I was a rock, the reliable one who kept things going" (*The Best Day the Worst Day* 140).

In "Ghost in the House," Hall returns to the relationship between mood disorders and creativity, citing psychiatrist Kay Redfield Jamison's observation in *Touched with Fire* that while manic depressive illness appears in only about 1 percent of the general population, studies indicate that it affects 38 percent of artists. He recalls how, six months after her father's death from cancer, "Jane sank under a torment and torrent of wild crying. At home she curled on the sofa in the fetal position and wept for three days. I wanted to hold and comfort her, as I had done earlier when she was low, but now I could not touch her. If I touched her, she would want to scream" ("Ghost in the House" 85). This must have been a terrifying time for Hall: many if not most people in his situation would find themselves infected by their spouses' anxiety or depression, unable to cope with the situation. But he remained emotionally controlled. Writing with both clinical precision and heartfelt love, he lists her many medications and their effect on her physical and psychological health, including the various side effects each produced. He also describes the need to accommodate the different sides of her personality that emerged during her manic periods.

Hall is no less sensitive to his wife's spiritual needs. As she notes in her interview with Bill Moyers, her religious faith helped her cope with her psychological problems. She is far more explicit in the interview about her Christian beliefs than she is in any of her poems or prose essays. "My belief in God, such as it is, especially the idea that a believer is part of the body of Christ, has kept me from harming myself" (Moyers 230). Her faith in a loving, forgiving God gives her hope, she adds, that her depression will lift. So, too, does writing give her hope. As Moyers observes, "We now know that grief can be a consolation if you work through it therapeutically, and a poem can help us do that, though not be sugar-coated optimism or denial" (235–36).

Hall and Kenyon worked hard to prevent competition from destroying their marriage. Sylvia Plath and Ted Hughes are a cautionary tale of what happens when a female poet, forced to live in the shadow of her more famous poet-husband, finds the situation unbearable, resulting in murderous rage that turns against the self, ending in suicide. Hall and Kenyon did everything they could to avoid a similar fate. Complicating their artistic relationship was the initial inequality between them: they began as teacher and student, one a well-known poet, the other a novice. Marian Blue's 1993 interview with Hall and Kenyon reveals the accommodations that each made for the other. "The first couple of years after we married," Hall observes, addressing his comments to his wife, "you wouldn't write anything except when I left for poetry readings, so there was something—I don't know if 'intimidated' is the right word—but there was some pressure. But consider this: I was nineteen years older than Jane—and still am—and I had published four or five books. I also work sixteen hours a day, which means I'm a living reproach. Finally Jane just said to hell with that, and did her own work. I have always thought it was brave of Jane to put her head down and keep writing" (Kenyon, *A Hundred White Daffodils* 189). They developed ground rules to ensure their personal and professional well-being. They never rushed the other's work, never showed poems to the other unless they were finished, never allowed other poets or critics to make invidious comparisons, never offered false praise or harsh criticism.

Given their personal and professional closeness, it is not surprising that each was devastated by the other's illness. In the Moyers interview, Kenyon speaks about her shock upon learning of her husband's cancer diagnosis. Citing Elisabeth Kübler-Ross's stage theory of dying, Kenyon first experienced disbelief, followed by "howling." We don't hear howling in her last poem, "The Sick Wife," when she was almost too sick to write; instead, we sense her quiet desperation that she has come to the end of her life. Unable to leave the car while her husband buys a few groceries, she "had learned what it's like/not to be able to button a button" (Jane Kenyon: *Collected Poems* 297). The poet contrasts the freedom of the healthy mother with small children and the retired couple moving through the parking lot with the sick wife, immobilized in the car. Scarcely able to move, though not yet fifty, she can only sit in the car, noticing the windows steaming. The poem ends lamentingly as the "cars on either side of her/pulled away so briskly/that it made her sick at heart" (297). The biographer John Timmerman observes that "The Sick Wife" is a poem "without self-pity": "Kenyon's final poem[is a] powerful engagement of reality to the last" (223). There is a poignant detail about "The Sick Wife" upon which Hall comments in *The Best Day the Worst Day*. She had dictated the poem—her last, unfinished poem—to a friend, and when Hall asked her the next day if she had not dictated it to him because of the fear "it was terrible" (214), she agreed. He convinced her that it was powerful and worthy of inclusion in her posthumous volume.

The Best Day the Worst Day

The Best Day the Worst Day pays tribute both to its subject, Jane Kenyon, and to its author, Donald Hall. It is inconceivable that he could have written such a profound meditation had he not experienced love and loss in his own life. In his textbook *Writing Well*, Hall might object to my statement, offering the following warning to those who write on literature: "If you love an author's work, it is fascinating to know something about his life, and nothing is wrong with this knowledge. But when you are writing about the work, write about the work" (272). I agree with this observation, but the reader nevertheless assumes that the memoirist's life and story are closely related. With a few changes, *The Best Day the Worst Day* would continue to move us as a work of fiction, but it would not have the same impact that it does as a story about a real-life relationship. One of Hall's most striking revelations in the memoir is his conscientiousness in responding to the outpouring of letters he received in response to his wife's illness and death. "All attentions to Jane were gratifying, even distracting. The mail in the first weeks was prodigious, more than a thousand letters in the first month. Every night I dictated answers. I didn't answer for the sake of politeness; answering gave me comfort. I wrote everyone, even strangers, about her last days and hours, about her brain-stem breathing, about pulling her eyelids down. It helped, to spread my sorrow and outrage onto the world. I know—I think I even *knew*—that I wrote as if this misery had never happened before, an old husband closing the eyes of his much younger wife" (6).

Hall respects his readers and letter-writers. As lonely as he is after his wife's death, he knows that he is not simply talking to himself. He is as attached to his readers as they are to him. Few activities require more introspection and solitude than writing—I can think of *none*—but the knowledge that one is being read creates a relational bond that enables the writer to keep working in the face of adversity. Whether it is companionship in grief or companionship in joy, the writer-reader relationship counterbalances the loneliness and sadness arising from loss.

Hall also stays in touch with relatives and friends by telephone. During the five months he and his wife are in Seattle for the bone marrow transplant, he telephones his children nearly every day. He also telephones his mother whenever he can. These telephone calls, like his letters, allow him to convey the latest news about Jane's medical condition and to express his fears and hopes about their future. No doubt he would have felt far more lonely, isolated, and disconnected during this period had he not been in constant contact with others. His desire to communicate with everyone interested in Jane's condition extends to the mourners who wish to send condolences at her death. "Everyone was invited" to her funeral, he tells us early in the memoir (11), and he takes every opportunity to thank those who express their sympathy. But while she was still alive, his gregariousness and openness do not distract him from his main role as caregiver. He is always attentive to his wife's needs, especially when she requires rest and quiet. "I was guard dog," he admits when friends would telephone Jane in the hospital; "'three minutes,' I would bark" (131). A loving son, father, and grandfather, he uses canine imagery to describe his instinctual protectiveness of wife and mother, both of whom were seriously ill. The guard dog metaphor captures both sides of Hall's personality, his fierce loyalty and vigilant wariness.

Jane Kenyon's death is the main loss in *The Best Day the Worst Day*, but both Hall's mother and mother-in-law died around the same time as his wife. There were times when he simply could not attend to all of his dying relatives, but he makes every attempt to be with them. The reader marvels at Hall's ability to devote himself to his dying wife *and* to his dying mother and mother-in-law. Not once does he express an unkind word to any of the three women or bemoan his fate—especially since he was functioning with only a third of his liver and living with the knowledge that it was unlikely he would be around for many more years.

What kept Hall functioning? As with John Bayley, humor helped him survive crises that might have undone those without this resource. Since the humor is mainly directed at himself, we laugh at him and with him—compassionate humor, sometimes black humor, never cruel or cynical humor. "For six months Gus [the dog] remained in depression," he tells us at the beginning of *The Best Day the Worst Day*, after announcing Jane's death. "He lay in the parlor day and night, a room Jane and I seldom entered, with his face on his paws, hardly looking up when spoken to. Finally he decided that I was *it*—and spent day and night as close to me as he could get" (5). Here is his response to a well-wisher whom another writer might dismiss as clueless: "One man addressed a letter to Jane, praising my work and hers, commiserating with her on the death of Donald Hall. I wrote him that he had two surprises coming" (6). Worried that she will not be able to discharge her responsibilities as poet laureate of New Hampshire, Jane is reassured when her husband reminds her that "the laureate's duties—I had done time in that office—could be accomplished by Gus the dog" (191). After Jane returns home from several months in Seattle, their dog sniffs her cautiously. "I had expected him to leap over the roof, but it was clear that he required nasal certainty. He could scarcely believe his olfactory equipment. Could it be fraud? Could this woman possibly be the winner of a Jane Kenyon smell-alike contest? Gradually he believed, and he began cautiously to sing, little high-pitched notes" (198).

Like Bayley, Hall enjoys poking fun at himself, as we can see when he describes a medical problem that arises early in their marriage. "Thirty percent of males with adult-onset diabetes become impotent. (The word is used for different conditions. I was orgasmic but could not sustain an erection.) At first I was intermittent and then I was no longer intermittent. We made alternative love, and Jane was kind, but she was not content with our curtailment—a monogamous woman in her thirties for whom lovemaking was primary" (*The Best Day the Worst Day* 235). Shame and vanity compel him to conceal this problem from his physician. The problem persists, and he visits first a psychotherapist and then a urologist, who informs him about penile implants. Hall arranges for an operation to insert a "bionic erection—general anesthesia, incision, insertion of stainless steel surrounded by plastic" (236). The surgery was painful, and for two weeks he was jittery: "A permanent hard-on is nerve-racking; it feels like a permanent hard-on." Soon he feels like a new man, and for the rest of her life Jane thanks him: "'Perkins, what you did for me!' In vain did I insist that I did not do it only for her." Noting that for the "impotent period of middle life" he had lived in a "steady gray mild . . . depression," one in which his "poems turned passive," he now observes that "prosthetic manliness brought vigor back to my poems" (236).

Hall's manliness enables him to transcend narrow gender stereotypes. The fear of "unmasculine" grief never worries him. Throughout *The Best Day the Worst Day* he cries more than his wife—not only cries but also howls, weeps, wails. He never hesitates to express his emotions—despite the fact, as he points out, that "women are better than men at acknowledging dread and fear. Eighty percent of women are more clear or open than men in expressing grief or dread" (42). He rarely attempts to conceal his grief, as when he admits that in the hospital "I walked the corridors weeping. Nurses and doctors and a social worker stopped to hug me" (71). His emotionality, however, never prevents him from fulfilling his many caregiving responsibilities. There is never a moment when he expresses doubt or fear that he will be unable to care for his dying wife. As grief-stricken as he is, he cares for her with exemplary skill and patience.

In his efforts to help understand his wife's dark moods and his own, Hall becomes a student of psychology, reading everything he can on the subject. To this extent he resembles William Styron. "Throughout much of my life," Styron admits in *Darkness Visible*, his "memoir of madness," "I have been compelled, perhaps unwisely, to become an autodidact in medicine, and have accumulated a better-than-average amateur's knowledge about medical matters (to which many of my friends, surely unwisely, have often deferred)" (9). Like Styron, Hall is an autodidact in medicine, familiar with Freud's writings. Speaking positively about his own and Jane's therapy, he is one of the few major American poets who has written repeatedly and unambiguously about the value of psychotherapy and medication for mood disorders. He tells us in *The Best Day the Worst Day* that Jane "spoke of needing psychotherapy" when they first started seeing each other in 1970. "Through friends in the field, I helped her find a smart Freudian, whom she visited two or three times a week, cheap enough because he was still a student. Therapy did not cure her depression but helped her identify feelings (telling love from rage, for instance) so that she could attempt the deliberate life" (52). During the 1960s Hall had experience with his own smart Freudian: in *The Old Life* he describes his six years of psychotherapy in which he learned to understand and express his repressed feelings. Perhaps the most important moment in therapy occurred when his analyst correctly predicted that "one day . . . you will be able to love someone" (78).

Writing about Jane's psychological breakdown in 1982, which initiated a new phase of her bipolarity, Hall refers to Freud's "Mourning and Melancholia." "The distinguishing mental features of melancholia," Freud writes, "are a profoundly painful dejection, cessation of interest in the outside world, loss of the capacity to love, inhibition of all activity, and a lowering of the self-regarding feelings to a degree that finds utterance in self-reproaches and self-revilings, and culminates in a delusional expectation of punishment. This picture becomes a little more intelligible when we consider that, with one exception, the same traits are met with in mourning" (*S.E.* 14:244). Perhaps the worst symptom of depression is lowered self-esteem, as Styron suggests from his own experience. "Of the many dreadful manifestations of the disease, both physical and psychological, a sense of self-hatred—or, put less categorically, a failure of self-esteem—is one of the most universally experienced symptoms" (*Darkness Visible* 5).

However relevant Freud's "Mourning and Melancholia" may be to Styron's suicidal breakdown in 1985 and to Jane Kenyon's breakdown in 1982 , it has limited relevance to Hall's mourning during her illness and following her death. The following sentence from "Mourning and Melancholia," densely packed with meaning, does not appear to correspond to Hall's situation while his wife is alive: "Profound mourning, the reaction to the loss of someone who is loved, contains the same painful frame of mind, the same loss of interest in the outside world—in so far as it does not recall him—the same loss of capacity to adopt any new object of love (which would mean replacing him) and the same turning away from any activity that is not connected with thoughts of him" (*S.E.* 14:244). *The Best Day the Worst Day* never reveals a loss of interest in the outside world or turning away from reality. As a caregiver Hall is never inhibited in any of his activities or engaged in the self-accusations symptomatic of clinical depression.

There is little doubt that however grief-stricken Hall is during *The Best Day the Worst Day*, he experiences "normal grief." This becomes more evident in light of Erich Lindemann's classic 1944 article "The Symptomatology and Management of Acute Grief." He lists five main symptoms of the "pathognomonic characteristics of normal or acute grief": "somatic distress," "preoccupation with the image of the deceased," "guilt," "hostile reactions," and "loss of patterns of conduct." Sometimes a sixth symptom occurs: "the appearance of traits of the deceased in the behavior of the bereaved" (42). Apart from Hall's preoccupation with Jane Kenyon—how could he write a book about her if he were not preoccupied?—his grief appears well within the normal range. There is nothing to indicate what clinicians call pathological or "complicated" grief, which arises from unresolved ambivalence toward the deceased. Pathological grief, according to Mardi Horowitz and her colleagues, is the "intensification of grief to the level where the person is overwhelmed, resorts to maladaptive behavior, or remains interminably in the state of grief without progression of the mourning process towards completion" (1157). What seems pathological, Horowitz adds, is not the "emotional or ideational content of a state but its intensity or prolongation" (1159).

It is not Freud but John Bowlby whose work on mourning helps to explain Hall's companionship in grief. Bowlby's comprehensive three-volume work, *Attachment* (1969), *Separation* (1973), and *Loss* (1980)—records how children respond to the experience of being separated from and later reunited with their mothers. M. D. S. Ainsworth noted in her obituary on Bowlby in 1992 that attachment theory "has had a stronger impact on American psychology than any other theory of personality development since Sigmund Freud" (668). Bowlby holds an ambiguous place in psychoanalysis, at times agreeing with the orthodox Freudian view that mourners need to detach themselves from the deceased while at other times implying the opposite. Attachment theory generally lends itself to maintaining affectional bonds with both the living and the deceased. Children who are separated from their mothers demonstrate a predictable sequence of behavior that can be classified into three phases: protest, despair, and detachment. Each of these three phases, Bowlby suggests, corresponds to a different aspect of psychoanalytic theory: protest involves separation anxiety; despair implies grief and mourning; and detachment suggests a defense mechanism.

Far from ending with childhood, attachment behavior persists into adulthood. Bowlby draws attention to four pathological variants of adult mourning, including unconscious yearning for the lost person; unconscious reproach against the lost person, combined with conscious and often unremitting self-reproach; compulsive caring for other people; and persistent disbelief that the loss is permanent (*Loss* 15–16). In Bowlby's view, these pathological variants of adult mourning are only exaggerations of normal processes. "Loss of a loved person gives rise not only to an intense desire for reunion but to anger at his departure and, later, usually to some degree of detachment; it gives rise not only to a cry for help, but sometimes also to a rejection of those who respond" (*Loss* 31). Just as children's behavior may be classified by three major types of attachments, secure attachment, avoidant attachment, and anxious/ambivalent attachment, so may adult's behavior reveal the same types. Contemporary attachment theorists Cindy Hazan and Phillip Shaver have extended Bowlby's theory to romantic relationships, demonstrating that the "best predictors of adult attachment type were respondents' perceptions of the quality of their relationship with each parent and the parents' relationship with each other" (516). Hazan and Shaver conclude that the love experience of secure adults is characterized by "trust, friendship, and positive emotions"; moreover, secure adults believe in "enduring love, generally find others trustworthy, and have confidence that the self is likeable" (513).

Viewed from the perspective of attachment theory, the mourning we see in *The Best Day the Worst Day* does not strike us as pathological or avoidant. Like nearly all people who lose a loved one, Hall yearns for his wife immediately after her death—"I kept reaching to touch her" (*The Best Day the Worst Day* 4)—but this yearning, or what British thanatologists call pining, is not only conscious but understandable. We never see unconscious reproaches against the lost person or compulsive caring for others. There can be little doubt that Hall demonstrates "secure attachment" to Jane Kenyon, and she toward him. Their marriage had been characterized by trust, friendship, and love, and both believed in the romantic idea of "till death do us part." Each trusted and was trusted by the other—and each was a secure, dependable caregiver for the other.

Hall's grief during his wife's illness was well within the range of normal, and only rarely does he engage in the magical thinking Joan Didion describes in her memoir. A stanza in *The Museum of Clear Ideas* reveals his awareness of different kinds of magic: "It was Sigmund Freud, I believe, who inquired: / 'What is it that poets want?' We understand / that magic thinking is fundamental, / but what does poetic magic ask for?" (89). Through the writing of poems and his memoir, as well as the passing of time, Hall is able to think about his deceased wife without feeling disabling guilt, grief, or remorse. This is one of the tasks of mourning—successfully accomplished, in his case. "One benchmark of a completed grief reaction," J. William Worden suggests, "is when the person is able to think of the deceased without pain. There is always a sense of sadness when you think of someone that you have loved and lost, but it is a different kind of sadness—it lacks the wrenching quality it previously had" (46). Hall's psychological health depended on his *refusal* to withdraw his libido from its attachments to his deceased wife. Contrary to Freud's advice, he could not and would not give up his relationship to the lost object. The result was not, in Freud's words, the shadow of the object falling upon the writer's ego but a private mourning that also became—in the form of *The Best Day the Worst Day*—a literary triumph.

Grief does not incapacitate Hall, but he does reveal on the opening page of the memoir that it took him two years before he could gather together his wife's letters, manuscripts, and unpublished poems. This revelation surprised me: I would have expected him to start *immediately* on this project, as I did when I began collecting Barbara's writings immediately after her death. I was also surprised that he does not tell us when he decided to write a memoir about their life together. Nor does he tell us whether he wondered how Jane would have reacted to reading *The Best Day the Worst Day*. There is only one moment in the memoir when he suggests that his wife might be displeased with one of his revelations about her. Amid a discussion of cooking for Jane during her illness, he mentions removing old bottles of spaghetti sauce and stew from a big freezer in the shed. He comes across "bicentennial stew, neatly dated 1976"—eighteen years old! "Jane laughed until she wept—but asked me never to tell" (101). She would hardly have become upset over this amusing detail, yet he never wonders about how she might react to his many disclosures about their life together—perhaps because he knows all of his revelations affirm their love for each other. Throughout *The Best Day the Worst Day* Hall implies that as close as he and Jane were before their respective illnesses, they become closer afterward. Referring to his colon cancer surgeries, he observes that his "approaches to death had brought us closer than we had ever been, a closeness that came to seem like identity" (38). The day of her diagnosis marked a new stage of their marriage. "We spoke of love as we did every day for fifteen months" (33). Unlike Hall, who accepted the probability of death after his cancer metastasized to the liver, Jane could not easily accept her own death from leukemia. "I worried for Jane, who was not stoical"(76). I suspect that until the last days of Jane's life, the psychological dimension of cancer—the anxiety and panic attacks and deep depression—was more difficult for her to cope with than the physical dimension of cancer. This was certainly true of Barbara, who also was not stoical. And yet both women struggled valiantly to stay alive. Hall conveys this passion for life in two heartfelt sentences: "This depressive woman who had often wanted to be dead, who had always feared and suffered from pain more than most—struggled and strained in the hope of survival. Her desire to live, her persistence in the face of agony, astonished her" (157).

As the end approaches, Hall "studied her breathing," attentive to every change. She is long past the power of speech and nonverbal communication, yet he seems to intuit her feelings. "I touched her and kissed her, but not so often as I wanted, because with whatever consciousness she maintained, she was concentrated on letting go" (1). One can only speculate on the dying person's consciousness, if any, during the moments preceding death, as Robert Kastenbaum observes in *The Psychology of Death*: "Often we have no way of knowing whether or not an unresponsive person is still experiencing life at some level. It is virtually impossible to rule out the null hypothesis: Lack of responsiveness does not prove lack of phenomenological experience" (15). Hall's willingness to let her go is perhaps the ultimate act of love, for he wants what is best for her, not what is best for himself. She had begun the process of letting go a few days earlier. The woman who had loved flowers and who spent so much of her life gardening now could no longer look at the bouquets of lavish and gorgeous flowers that relatives and friends sent her. Nor did she want her husband to play her favorite classical music CDs. "These things tied her to what she had to part from" (244).

One of Hall's rare moments of magical thinking occurs when he talks to his wife as if she were still alive. "I have no memory of speaking," he admits in the first chapter of *The Best Day the Worst Day*, immediately after the funeral, "but I am told that I said, 'We have to go, dear,' and walked to the car" (12). This is one of the few times that he cannot recall a statement or event. The chapter ends two pages later with his comment that "Jane reminded me to take my insulin." Though fatigue overcomes him, he drives back to the graveyard in the moonlight and "said goodnight to the fresh dirt over Jane in her Vermont hardwood box." A few days before her death they both work on her posthumous book and the details of her funeral—"the planner inside me still needed to plan" (246)—and he remarks that he "dwelt on the dying present to avoid the dead future" (247). Anguish almost incapacitates him, but he remains in control: "Now and then I howled, but I did not beg her to stay alive" (247). He still yearns for her after her death, but he knows she is gone.

The only evidence that Hall's grief may not be entirely normal lies in "Postscript 2005" at the end of the memoir. As curious as it is brief—it is only three pages long—"Postscript 2005" begins uneventfully. He visits the cemetery the morning after the funeral and later drives to his daughter's house, where he gives her Jane's ring, "Please Don't Die." After telling us he should have waited before he gave her the ring, he declares that he was not in his "right mind," and he then proceeds to make several puzzling remarks upon which he uncharacteristically refuses to elaborate. Observing that "everything I did, those first weeks and months, I did deliberately with lunatic clarity and without judgment," he felt "intense, overwhelming, permeating shame." He cannot locate the origin or significance of this emotion. "What did I feel shame for? For letting her die?" These are real, not rhetorical, questions for him, and he cannot answer them. He then admits that the shame reminded him of the time twenty-five years earlier when he was in Michigan, "desolate between marriages" (257). In *The Old Life* he describes himself during this time, in the late 1960s, when he was nearly forty-one, as "Hopeless, divorced, / abandoned, without love or my children"—a time when he realized that all of his losses "were my own contrivance" (76).

In the remaining three paragraphs of "Postscript 2005" Hall refers summarily to living a "scattery and hectic life, filled with misadventure." Ten years after her death, he continues to live at Eagle Pond Farm, and he weeps only "when I introduce her to a visitor." He also announces—and surely this must startle the reader—that "I love a woman who lives an hour away, with whom I spend a day and night each week" (258)—a woman who is presumably the memoir's dedicatee, "L. K." She is also the dedicatee of his next book, published in 2006, *White Apples and the Taste of Stone*—only now he reveals her full name: Linda Kunhardt, a New Hampshire resident who resigned from the rural Community School in 2006 after sixteen years of teaching.

What do we make of this curious postscript? Hall does not prepare us for this new love relationship in *The Best Day the Worst Day*, as John Bayley does about the new woman in his life in *Widower's House*. Hall could have omitted the postscript and ended with the chapter "Eleven Days," with its appropriate last sentence, "With my thumbs I pulled down the lids of her brown eyes" (255). This ending is aesthetically and psychologically pleasing, and it does not raise important questions that are left unresolved. It is odd that he transitions so quickly from

Jane Kenyon's death to falling in love with another woman, one with whom he has an ongoing relationship. This transition may have been slow in *actual time*—he doesn't tell us whether he fell in love again a month after his wife's death or eight years later—but it is only three pages after Jane's death, and thus in *memoir time* it seems abrupt and jarring.

The most perplexing question of "Postscript 2005" is the reference to shame—"I drowned under shame's ocean" (257). Why does he emphasize overwhelming shame rather than sadness or loneliness? What has he done—or not done—to cause this massive shame? What does he mean when he refers to his "scattery" life after his wife's death? In an interview published in Marjorie Ryerson's 2005 book *Companions for the Passage*, Hall includes several details about his life after his wife's death that do not appear in "Postscript 2005," though he makes no mention of feeling shame. "Postscript 2005" implies that work still seems to ground him, and in the years between Kenyon's death in 1995 and the publication of *The Best Day the Worst Day* in 2005 he produced three volumes of poetry, *The Old Life* (1996), *Without* (1998), and *The Painted Bed* (2002); three volumes of children's stories, *Old Home Day* (1996), *When Willard Met Babe Ruth* (1996), and *The Milkman's Boy* (1997); and the short story collection *Willow Temple* (2003). This is in addition to editing Jane Kenyon's *Collected Poems* (2005), writing many essays, and serving as a tireless advocate for his wife's poetry. How did he have time to live a "scattery" life?

The only time Hall felt "content" during these years, he states, is when he wrote Jane "grieving letter-poems" (*The Best Day the Worst Day* 257). Does this imply guilt, or shame, that he has unexpectedly, perhaps undeservedly, outlived her? If so, is this earned—or unearned—shame? That is, is this different from the "normal" existential guilt that nearly every survivor feels? I'm not sure. Nor am I sure whether his shame derives from the conflict, if there was one, between his devotion to his dying wife, on the one hand, and his commitment to his life work, writing, on the other. Recall his statement in *The Best Day the Worst Day* about immersing himself in the details of caregiving immediately before her bone marrow transplant: "My life was never so occupied; I lived for my work" (177). He implies here that he felt no difficulty suspending his writing for the exhausting work of caregiving. But others confronted with the same situation have felt conflict—often excruciating guilt. In his memoir *Grace and Grit*, the American transpersonal psychologist Ken Wilber acknowledges the anger and guilt he felt when, in an effort to care for his wife during her five-year losing struggle with breast cancer, he gave up his writing, which was essential for his psychic health. Feeling increasingly suicidal, he admits that the central problem for him was that "in my desire to do anything to help Treya, I had for over a year completely submerged my own interests, my own work, my own needs, my own life. I voluntarily chose to do this, and I would do it again unhesitatingly under the same circumstances. But I would do it differently, with more of a support system for myself in place, and with a clearer understanding of the devastating toll that being a full-time support person can take" (141). Hall never implies that he felt a conflict between love and work, perhaps because he did not abandon his work the way Wilber did.

Hall's poems published after Jane Kenyon's death cast new light on his shame. In "Kill the Day" he diagnoses himself, using Freud's 1917 essay, as suffering from depression: "Mourning resembles melancholia precisely except, / that melancholy adds self-loathing to stuporous sorrow, / and turns away from the dead its exclusive attention" (*White Apples and the Taste of Stone* 386). Some of the poems, such as "Wool Squares," reveal not only self-loathing but rage, as when he identifies with Dylan Thomas's widow: "'Leftover life to kill.' / Young Caitlin said / With Dylan dead, / Yet lived with an ill will / Forty posthumous years / Of rage, fucking, and tears" (*White Apples and the Taste of Stone* 376). Anger, self-pity, and the longing for release appear frequently in these poems, as well as a recognition, in "Distressed Haiku," that others—including perhaps himself—are tired of hearing and reading about his feelings: "Will Hall ever write / lines that do anything / but whine and complain?" (*White Apples and the Taste of Stone* 380). Even Jane may be growing tired of his suffering, as he suggests in "The Wish," in which she longs for him to release her so that she may rest in peace: "*Oh, let me go*" (*White Apples and the Taste of Stone* 377; emphasis in original). And yet amid this depression there are signs that he is learning to accept Jane's death and form new love attachments, as he intimates in "Charity and Dominion": "'I almost want to say that / I love—' You shook your head / fiercely and burst out: / '*But it would be a lie!*'" (*White Apples and the Taste of Stone* 393; emphasis in original). Surely it is not a lie to *want* to fall in love again—and to feel love and desire awakening again.

In "Grief's House," the penultimate chapter of his 2008 memoir *Unpacking the Boxes*, Hall continues the story of his life after his wife's death. He tells us in the beginning of the twenty-five page chapter that he originally conceived of *The Best Day the Worst Day* as the middle of a long memoir, but he was then persuaded by his editor to publish it separately. "Grief's House" repeats part of the earlier memoir. The tone of much of the chapter is tragicomic, as when he tells us about his obsession with the time of her death. "Saturdays I regularly burst into tears at 7:57 A.M., the moment of death," adding, parenthetically, "Twice, after I had wiped my eyes, I discovered that I was an hour early, and I would have to cry again" (151). As in *The Best Day the Worst Day*, he observes that the only time he was happy after Jane's death was when he wrote about her: "Writing to Jane and about her kept me going: the poetry habit that had been our first and continued connection" (157). He returns to this idea when he quotes from an article he wrote for the *Hartford Courant*: "As a poet ages, subject to inevitable losses, it becomes appropriate to write out of grief, appropriate, necessary, therapeutic. Over the fifteen months of Jane's illness, I loved caring for her, tucking her up in a tender quilt. My principal comfort was to comfort her—but I took comfort as well in continuing to write, even as she lay beside me, poems derived directly from her suffering"(161). Elsewhere in "Grief's House" he likens himself to Coleridge's Ancient Mariner, "required to repeat, over and over," the same story.

What is new and significant in "Grief's House" are the detailed disclosures about the period of his life immediately after his wife's death. He suffered repeatedly from dreams in which she abandoned him: "Always she left me because she preferred someone else, and because I was unkind or uncaring." He tells us that during Jane's illness he began to fantasize about being with other women. "The fantasies were adolescent, of naive abundant sexual adventure, and they interrupted my anxiety with a leering insistence, as if to offer compensation for Jane's possible death. But I was not about to betray her: I came on to nobody, undertook nothing" (154). The most significant revelation is that thirteen months after his wife's death, he went "manic" (164). It's not clear whether this mania was clinical or, to use his word from *Principal Products of Portugal*, "subclinical"; what is clear is that he felt out of control for several months. He admits to acting out sexually, compelled by a "monumental" neediness; losing three old friends because of errors of judgment; and experiencing rapidly cycling mood swings, "euphoria to dysphoria, rage to self-pity to rage" (167). Scared by his fantasies of homicide, he consulted Jane's psychiatrist, who prescribed psychotropic medication that eliminated the murderous rage but did nothing to lift the feelings of hopelessness. In time the bipolarity subsided, and he ends "Grief's House" mentioning the new woman in his life whom he sees once or twice a week. "Gradually over the years, I left grief's house and middle age for the thin air of antiquity's planet" (174). In *Unpacking the Boxes* Hall implies, like Bayley, that his relationship with a new woman does not threaten his relationship with his deceased wife.

"Postscript 2005" in *The Best Day the Worst Day* and "Grief's House" in *Unpacking the Boxes* dramatize the confusing life of a widower who, by dint of the age difference between himself and his wife, never expected she would predecease him. Life is mysterious and unpredictable, actuarial charts notwithstanding. Readers of *The Best Day the Worst Day* will be grateful for his remarkable memoir. His devotion to Jane Kenyon—first as her teacher and mentor, then as her husband, and finally as her caregiver and tireless supporter of her art—remains unique in American literature. They were each other's soul mate and muse, and the story of their life together, in sickness and in health, in sorrow and in joy, remains inspirational. So, too, is his devotion to literature inspirational. Indeed, this devotion has been his lifelong passion, as he indicates in *The Old Life* when he recalls asking the great sculptor Henry Moore "what is the secret of life?" The octogenarian Moore, about whom Hall had written a book decades earlier, responds without hesitation: "The secret is to devote / your whole life to one ambition. / Concentrate everything / you know, everything you can summon, / to accomplish this / one desire. But remember: Choose something / you can't do!" (70). Now an octogenarian himself, Hall has taken seriously this paradoxical advice, devoting himself to the impossible quest to bring back to life a lost spouse. The epigraph to *The Painted Bed*, by the modern Urdu poet of Pakistan Faiz Ahmed Faiz—"the true subject of poetry is the death of the beloved"—affirms Hall's single-minded devotion to honoring the memory of his deceased wife. He has created, in his writings on Jane Kenyon, a companionship in grief that will give pleasure to countless readers.

FOUR
JOAN DIDION AND JOHN GREGORY DUNNE
"Life Changes in the Instant"

Joan Didion's best-selling memoir *The Year of Magical Thinking* was published in 2005, scarcely a year after the death of her husband, John Gregory Dunne, who was, like her, an acclaimed novelist, essayist, and screenwriter. They were married nearly forty years. His sudden death—they were eating dinner in their apartment in New York City on December 30, 2003, when he suffered a massive heart attack and died literally in the middle of a sentence—shocked his wife, despite his long history of cardiac problems. One moment he was alive, and the next moment he was dead, an ending strikingly different from the slow deaths arising from cancer or Alzheimer's disease. Dunne's death precipitated Didion's year of "magical thinking," a reference to Freud's apt expression for the ways in which people deny traumatic events. The death happened so fast, without warning or preparation, without an opportunity to say goodbye, without time to process it, that Didion still finds herself in a state of shock, disbelief, and denial while completing the book. As if this loss were not painful enough, five days before Dunne's death their thirty-eight-year-old daughter and only child, Quintana, who had married earlier in the year, became severely ill with flu symptoms that quickly developed into a massive infection and pneumonia. By the time Didion completed *The Year of Magical Thinking*, Quintana had made a slow and partial recovery, but she then suffered a devastating stroke and died a few months after the publication of the book. And so Didion chronicles a double blow, her husband's death and her daughter's grave illness, a yearlong nightmare that ended with the loss of her entire family.

I began reading *The Year of Magical Thinking* as soon as it was published, when I was finishing the first draft of *Dying to Teach*. I mention *The Year of Magical Thinking* only briefly in my book, observing that the obsession to hold onto my deceased spouse compelled me to write the memoir, a phenomenon Didion describes in her own memoir. I recall thinking that I found her book disturbing at the time, but I couldn't put my finger on the problem. It was apparent from a first reading that she engages in self-blame throughout the memoir; she cannot exonerate herself even when she acknowledges there was nothing she could have done to prevent her husband's death. Only when I reread the book did I realize that, unlike other memoirs about deceased spouses, we learn surprisingly little about Dunne and even less about their long marriage. This is also true of *A Grief Observed*, but Lewis's memoir is only about a quarter the length of *The Year of Magical Thinking.* Unlike John Bayley and Donald Hall, Didion makes little attempt to characterize her spouse. Whereas they *show* us their deceased spouses, she merely *tells* us about hers. Perhaps most surprising of all, most of what we learn about Didion's marriage suggests the opposite of a warm, intimate union.

To be sure, Didion never refers to a troubled marriage, nor does she imply that they needed to learn how to live with each other. There is no suggestion of a marriage that had to overcome a rocky start or of a time when temperamental or cultural differences threatened to shatter their relationship. She mentions no marital infidelities, no flirtations with others, no period when they contemplated separation. Quite the opposite: she takes pride in the intactness of their marriage, especially during an era of widespread divorce. Noting that they were both writers who worked at home, she gives what appears to be a balanced portrait of their relationship. "I did not always think he was right nor did he always think I was right but we were each the person the other trusted. There was no separation between our investments or interests in any given situation. Many people assumed that we must be, since sometimes one and sometimes the other would get the better review, the bigger advance, in some way 'competitive,' that our private life must be a minefield of professional envies and resentments. This was so far from the case that the general insistence on it came to suggest certain lacunae in the popular understanding of marriage" (*The Year of Magical Thinking* 16–17).

Nothing Didion later writes qualifies their unconditional trust in each other, but there are many more references to arguments and misunderstandings than to moments of love or intimacy. In the next description of their marriage, she mentions how after his death she finds herself lying in bed alone in the morning. "There was a leaden feeling. It was the same leaden feeling with which I woke on mornings after John and I had fought" (*The Year of Magical Thinking* 31). These fights may have been too trivial to elaborate upon—it is impossible to imagine a long marriage without serious disagreements—but she does tell us about an argument that occurred after their daughter's wedding in 2003,when Dunne had a new pacemaker installed to restore his cardiac rhythm. "During the course of the summer, buoyed by the pleasure of Quintana's wedding and by the apparent success of the pacemaker, his mood had seemed to lift. In the fall it dropped again. I recall a fight over the question whether we should go to Paris in November. I did not want to go. I said we had too much to do and too little money. He said he had a sense that if he did not go to Paris in November he would never again go to Paris. I interpreted this as blackmail. That settles it then, I said, we're going. He left the table. We did not speak in any meaningful way for two days" (79–80). Nor is this the only time Didion describes an argument leading to days of angry silence. Later she recalls returning from a party in which they had stopped talking to each other, wondering which one of them "had said the wrong thing? Or stopped speaking? Or imagined that the other had stopped speaking?" (132–33).

Didion later remembers another incident related to their Paris trip. The night before their departure, they had gone to Madison Square Garden to see the Knicks play the Lakers, and her husband had interpreted a particularly heavy rain as an omen of good luck. "He did not mean the good seats and he did not mean the Laker win and he did not mean the rain, he meant we were doing something we did not ordinarily do, which had become an issue with him. We were not having any fun, he had recently begun pointing out. I would take exception (didn't we do this, didn't we do that) but I had also known what he meant. He meant doing things not because we were expected to do them or had always done them or should do them but because we wanted to do them. He meant wanting. He meant living" (*The Year of Magical Thinking* 182).

Immediately following this event, Didion writes about a married couple she and her husband met in Indonesia in 1980. Joe and Gertrude Black were Americans in their fifties who had led an interesting and fulfilling life. "Over the years John mentioned Joe and Gertrude Black frequently, in each case as exemplary, what he thought of as the best kind of American. They represented something personal to him. They were models for the life he wanted us eventually to live" (*The Year of Magical Thinking* 186). Dunne referred to the Blacks again a few days before his death, which Didion interprets as another instance of the failure of their own marriage. "He had wanted to be Joe and Gertrude Black. So had I. We hadn't made it. 'Fritter away' was a definition in the crossword that morning. The word defined was five letters, 'waste.' Was that what we had done? Was that what he thought we had done? Why didn't I listen when he said we weren't having any fun? Why didn't I move to change our life?" (186).

How do we interpret these marital tensions—and how much emphasis should we attach to them? Should we conclude that the ability to acknowledge one's marital difficulties, openly and candidly, betokens a strong, healthy relationship, one that does not need repeated claims of love to validate? Or should we conclude, to the contrary, that their marriage was not always good enough? Significantly, one of the few times the word "love" appears in the memoir is when Didion quotes her husband's statement upon seeing Quintana lying deathly ill in a hospital, her face and fingers distended from fluid. "John had kissed her swollen face. 'More than one more day,' he had whispered, another part of our family shorthand. The reference was to a line from a movie, Richard Lester's *Robin and Marian*. 'I love you more than even one more day,' Audrey Hepburn as Maid Marian says to Sean Connery as Robin Hood after she has given them both the fatal potion. John had whispered this every time he left the ICU" (*The Year of Magical Thinking* 68). Only once does Dunne express his love for his wife, using the line, "one more day I love you more than," to which Didion responds, "*As you used to say to me*" (207; emphasis in original).

To understand how husband and wife felt about each other, we may turn to their earlier writings for clues. Didion rarely discusses their marriage except in *The Year of Magical Thinking*, but Dunne's extensive writings offer us fascinating glimpses into their relationship: how each viewed the other, how each coped with depression, how each characterized the other, how each portrayed death, and how each felt about using the other's material for a book. Before writing *The Year of Magical Thinking*, Didion reread many of her husband's and her own books in an effort to make sense of their life together, and if we follow her footsteps, we may reach a deeper understanding of her memoir, including some of its contradictions and inconsistencies. She also refers to several clinical studies of death and bereavement that she read while writing *The Year of Magical Thinking*—books I also read while writing *Dying to Teach*. These clinical studies enable us to understand the value of writing and reading about spousal love and loss.

John Gregory Dunne was a prolific novelist, memoirist, literary critic, and screenwriter, the author of thirteen books. He was born in West Hartford, Connecticut, in 1932, the son of a prominent Irish American surgeon. After graduating from Princeton in 1954, he served for two years in the army as an enlisted man, an experience he found more valuable than college. He worked for *Time* magazine from 1959 until 1964, the year he married Joan Didion. Together they cowrote several screenplays, including *Panic in Needle Park* (1971); *A Star Is Born* (1976); *True Confessions* (1981), based on his 1977 novel; and *Up Close and Personal* (1996). Both Dunne and Didion had a love-hate relationship with Hollywood, writing screenplays mainly so they could support themselves while writing novels and nonfiction. "By the time we wrote our first screenplay," he observes in a 1963 *Paris Review* interview, "we had written maybe five books between us, which was what we wanted to do because we were our own bosses: with a book you are the writer, director, editor, cameraman. But I can say without equivocation that the movies have supported us for the past twenty-six years. We've written twenty-three books between us, and movies have financed nineteen out of the twenty-three" (*Regards* 399).

I was not familiar with Dunne before *The Year of Magical Thinking*, and after reading his novels, I was struck by the consistency of his narrative voice and vision. Nor was I surprised to hear him make the same observation about his fiction. "I've always thought a novelist only has one character, and that is himself or herself. In my case, me. So at the risk of being glib, I am the priest in *True Confessions* and the criminal lawyer in *Dutch Shea, Jr.* I've certainly never been a cop or a priest or a pimp lawyer, but these protagonists are in a sense my mouthpieces. I like to learn about their professions, which is why I so much like doing nonfiction" (*Regards* 384). The priest and the criminal lawyer are self-tortured, guilt-ridden characters who exhibit Dunne's fascination for those who play life on the dark keys. The priest in *True Confessions* is an authorial mouthpiece in another sense: he suffers from a serious cardiac problem that reflects the novelist's lifelong fear he would suffer the same fate as his father, who died of a massive heart attack in his early fifties. (In *Crooning* (75) and *Monster* (62), Dunne states his father died at the age of fifty-one, while in *Harp* (113) he lists the age as fifty-two.) Dunne returns to this fear in nearly all his stories, each time giving us additional information about his own cardiac misfortunes.

The priest in *True Confessions* and the criminal lawyer in *Dutch Shea, Jr.* are authorial in still another way: they and Dunne's other major characters are usually Catholic. "I'm not a practicing Catholic, but one thing you never lose from a Catholic education is a sense of sin, and the conviction that the taint on the human condition is the natural order" (*Regards* 383).

Vegas

The tainted natural order unifies all of Dunne's writings, fiction and nonfiction, and extends to all relationships, including marriage. In 1982 Dunne calculated that their marriage had consisted of "15 years of good days and three years of bad days, . . . a terrific ratio" (qtd. in Winchell 8), yet despite this assessment, one never senses from either his or his wife's descriptions that their marriage was emotionally intimate. There is little about marriage in his first two books, *The Studio* (1969) and *Delano* (1971), but he begins his third book, *Vegas: A Memoir of a Dark Season* (1974), with a memorable quotation by W. H. Auden: "Like everything which is not the result of fleeting emotion but of time and will, any marriage, happy or unhappy, is infinitely more interesting and significant than any romance, however passionate." Dunne must have found Auden's observation striking, as I did when I encountered it years ago, yet *Vegas* tells us curiously little about his own marriage, which he is reluctant to explore or share in detail. He is no less evasive about the extent to which his dark memoir is autobiographically accurate, as he intimates in the author's note: "This is a fiction which recalls a time real and imagined. There are, for example, comics, prostitutes and private detectives in Las Vegas; there is no Jackie Kasey, no Artha Ging, no Buster Mano. I am more or less 'I,' he and she less than more he and she." Is there a misprint in the last sentence? Apparently not, only an equivocation. Dunne never calls his wife by name in the book, never spells out the problems between them, but the shadowy marriage he portrays in the memoir appears to be more or less his own.

Nor is marriage the only ambiguous subject in *Vegas*. The opening sentences raise questions that are never answered in the memoir. "In the summer of my nervous breakdown, I went to live in Las Vegas, Clark County, Nevada. It had been a bad spring, it had been a bad winter, it had been a bad year" (3). We never learn whether the "nervous breakdown" is a vague feeling of malaise or a severe clinical depression. A physician tells Dunne, during a routine physical exam taken when he was thirty-seven years old for a $100,000 insurance policy, that he has "soft shoulders," which seems to be, he wryly admits, a "perfect metaphor for my life that season," the softness symptomatic of the "renegade cells eating away at the tissues of my life" (5–6). The "metastasis" began a year earlier when he discovered the names of classmates appearing in the obituary notes of his college alumni magazine. "I began to note in my diary the date of my annual medical checkup. I examined myself for lumps and bumps. I heard with dark dread a doctor tell me that he was sending a piece of tissue 'down for a biopsy.' I became quite simply, for no real reason, terrified of dying" (6).

The Year of Magical Thinking makes no mention of Dunne's midlife crisis, which began around 1969, five years before the publication of *Vegas*. He lists the concrete ways in which his obsession with death manifested itself. He sees reminders of his mortality everywhere: he imagines crashing in an airplane, wonders whether his obituary will appear in *Time* magazine, and finds himself knocked out in a fight he provokes by calling a driver who sideswiped him one day on Sunset Boulevard a "motherfucker." Unable to conceive a child—they adopted Quintana—he has his semen checked and learns that his spermatozoa has "passed the test": "'They won't win any races,' the doctor said. 'But they get there'" (10). So, too, does his marriage pass the test—marginally. He describes his home life as the "familiar season of discontent" in which husband and wife have a marriage that may be, in Auden's terms, interesting and significant but not especially happy or close. "I sometimes had the feeling that we went from crisis to crisis like old repertory actors going from town to town, every crisis an opening night with new depths to plumb in the performance. I bought a jacknife; she said it was atavistic. I said that living with her was like living with one piranha fish. She said dealings with women aged people." That Dunne's wife is a wordsmith seems evident when she explains why reading a French cookbook gives her a headache: "The particular rhythm of the sentences. They upset my alpha waves" (11).

The marital tensions appear throughout *Vegas*. On one occasion, Dunne calls his wife from Los Angeles, and she tells him she is lonely and depressed. After describing the stress in her life and everything that has been going wrong, she asks him, "What's new with you?" which provokes the following dialogue:

> "Jackie's got me a date with a nineteen-year-old tonight. She's supposed to suck me and fuck me."
>
> "It's research," she said. "It's a type, the girl who's always available to fuck the comic's friend. You're missing the story if you don't meet her."
>
> "But I don't *want* to fuck her."
>
> There was a long silence at the other end of the telephone. "Well, that can be part of the story, too," she said.
>
> There seemed nothing more to say. I was the one who was supposed to be detached. (*Vegas* 175)

Perhaps only a wife who feels secure about her marriage can offer such advice to her husband—and only if both husband and wife can separate life and art. But the wife's words fail to cheer up Dunne. Toward the end of *Vegas* he calls home again and tells his wife he will return home as "soon as I get my life in order," a remark that elicits their most tense conversation in the book:

> "Why not try living it?" she said. "For a change."
>
> "Oh, it's that kind of day, is it?"
>
> It was the old argument. She claimed that I vandalized other people's lives instead of coming to grip with my own. It was an argument without a rebuttal, which is what made it particularly infuriating. I knew why I was in Vegas. I just did not like having it spelled out. There were times when I think we fought only because we were good at it. Betrayal never worked for us. We each had too highly developed a sense of guilt, a sense that nothing was free, that every action carried a price tag. So we fought. I won the battles, but she seemed to be winning the war. Hers was a war of attrition, of nuance and inflection and pregnant pauses, the Viet Cong against the tactical nukes. It was an uneven struggle. (269–70)

Marital tensions and a midlife crisis explain Dunne's decision to drive to Las Vegas to escape from the vicissitudes of life. His odyssey takes him to a city even more surreal than Hollywood, populated by gamblers, con artists, and prostitutes whose unreality eventually proves to be too much. *Vegas* ends with the author back home, apparently changed by his peripatetic experience. He implies that he is no longer an "emotional paraplegic, obsessed by death" (287). We never learn whether he has worked out his marital tensions, one of the reasons for his precipitous flight from home.

True Confessions

Didion notes in *The Year of Magical Thinking* that when she reread *True Confessions*, she found the novel "darker than I had remembered it" (154). She doesn't explain why. She may have been thinking of the appalling mutilation-death of a prostitute named the "Virgin Tramp," but I suspect it was the fatal heart attack of Monsignor Mickey Gagnon while being serviced by a prostitute that caught Didion's eye. "Come to think of it," exclaims Lt. Frank Crotty, a hardened police detective, "it's not a bad way to go, the heart-attack hump, you don't mind going in a state of mortal sin. I'd take my chances, I think" (97). Crotty himself, we learn at the end of the book, dies of coronary occlusion. Significantly, the same ending—a fatal heart attack occurring immediately after sex—occurs in Dunne's final novel, *Nothing Lost* (2004). Dunne does not romanticize the cardiac problems that beset the more important characters in *True Confessions*, especially that of the Right Reverend Desmond Spellecy, who dies prematurely of a heart attack. "The arteries leading to his pump were shot and it was only a matter of time" (337), declares Tom Spellecy, who despite a lifetime of fraternal rivalry grows to love his brother. Tom remains alive and well at the end—"As for me, I'm in the pink. I'll be seventy-two next week" (341). Notwithstanding Tom's health, the number of characters in *True Confessions* who worry about dying of a heart attack surely must have disturbed Didion.

Quintana and Friends

The Year of Magical Thinking never refers to Dunne's next book, *Quintana and Friends* (1978), a collection of nonfiction essays dedicated to Alice and Calvin Trillin, the latter of whom spoke at Dunne's memorial service. Dunne tells us in the introduction that the work's existence depends upon two people, one of whom is his wife. "We have been married for fifteen years. I do not guarantee that we will be married sixteen, yet we did not guarantee to each other at the end of the first week that we would still be married at the end of the second, at the end of the fifth year that we would make it through the sixth, at the end of the ninth through the tenth. I think it is sufficient to say that she is the center from which the rest of my life proceeds" (xix).

While writing *The Year of Magical Thinking*, Didion worried about her daughter's illness, and for this reason it is surprising that she doesn't mention the lead essay in *Quintana and Friends*, a moving account of the decision to adopt their daughter at birth. The essay discusses the growing number of adoptees who try to discover their roots despite formidable legal obstacles. "I am in general sympathetic to this quest," writes Dunne, "although not always to the dogged absolutism of the more militant seekers" (7). The essay is a valuable corrective to the mistaken belief that all adoptive parents fear their children's efforts to find their biological parents. "In point of fact we accept that our children might seek out their roots, even encourage it; we accept it as an adventure like life itself—perhaps painful, one hopes enriching. I know not one adoptive parent who does not feel this way. Yet in the literature there is the implicit assumption that we are threatened by the possibility of search, that we would consider it an act of disloyalty on the part of our children. The patronizing nature of this assumption is never noted in the literature" (7).

Dutch Shea, Jr.

Dunne's next novel, *Dutch Shea, Jr.* (1982), focuses on a tainted criminal lawyer, his embittered ex-wife, and their eighteen-year-old daughter Catherine (Cat), who is accidentally blown up by a group of IRA terrorists. Dutch Shea does not worry about cardiac problems, but he cannot stop thinking about death, which is part of his paternal inheritance. Years earlier, John Shea committed suicide in prison, and the son cannot banish from his mind the image of his father hanging from a wet sheet in his cell. Dutch Shea's identification with his father's suicide parallels Dunne's preoccupation with his own father's premature death. Like the novelist, Dutch Shea is preoccupied with sin: he attends Mass but equates it with taking on another Legal Aid case, something he is unenthusiastically obliged to do. An attorney for the Association of County Funeral Directors, Dutch Shea is obsessed with death, a trademark of Dunne's authorial characters. Many of Dutch Shea's statements reflect the novelist's point of view, such as the belief that it takes an extraordinary degree of hostility to be a good criminal lawyer. Dutch Shea is indeed filled with hostility, toward others and himself, and as the story progresses the rage turns inward. He cannot act on another of his beliefs, that defense is an exercise in learning and forgetting.

Didion makes a shrewd observation about the novel in *The Year of Magical Thinking*: "I see now what I had failed to see in 1982, the year *Dutch Shea, Jr.* was published: this was a novel about grief. The literature would have said that Dutch Shea was undergoing pathological bereavement" (51). Dutch Shea finds himself unable to stop thinking about the police report of the horrific explosion that killed his daughter, an action to which he returns again and again in an unsuccessful attempt to work through his anguish: "A section of the restaurant's plate-glass window blew in when the bomb went off and severed Cat's head from her shoulders directly above the frayed collar of her blue button-down Brooks Brothers shirt. Her head had landed in a cut-glass Waterford bowl full of lemon sorbet on the sweets trolley, her right arm on the hood of a limousine belonging to the Danish charge d'affaires, who happened to be passing the restaurant on Charlotte Street the moment of the explosion" (*Dutch Shea, Jr.* 17).

Grief-stricken over his beloved daughter's gruesome death, Dutch Shea commits suicide at the end of the novel. Tellingly, Catherine is an adopted daughter about the same age as Dunne's daughter, a detail upon which Didion does not comment. But she does disclose in *The Year of Magical Thinking* another compelling autobiographical detail from *Dutch Shea, Jr.* that connects Catherine with Quintana. Brooding over his daughter's childhood, Dutch Shea recalls a drawerful of mementoes he kept in his study on the third floor of his house on Asylum Avenue in West Hartford, where most of the story takes place. The secret drawer contains her memorable sayings, including one about a bogey man who terrifies her. "The Broken Man was in that drawer. The Broken Man was what Cat called fear and death and the unknown. I had a bad dream about the Broken Man, she would say. Don't let the Broken Man catch me. If the Broken Man comes, I'll hang onto the fence and won't let him take me" (*Dutch Shea, Jr.* 30). The bereaved father can't help wondering whether the Broken Man had time to frighten Catherine before her death. In the autobiographical *Harp* (1989), Dunne reveals that the Broken Man was his daughter's name for her fear of death, though he doesn't add that he had used this detail in his earlier novel. "When my daughter was a child, she would often have nightmares about death. In these terrifying dreams, death was not an abstraction, but a person she called 'the Broken Man.' If the Broken Man comes, she would sob, I'll hold on to the fence so that he cannot get me." Dunne thinks about the Broken Man as he writes about one of his aunts who is drifting toward death. "Life seemed to be the fence to which she clung in terror, trying to stave off the grasping fingers of the Broken Man" (*Harp* 222).

Didion emphasizes the importance of the traumatic grief suffered by the eponymous character. After listing the many diagnostic signs of pathological bereavement, she observes that the novel is also about faith, a subject that she cannot help thinking about in light of her husband's death. "When he began the novel he already knew what the last words would be, not only the last words of the novel but the last words thought by Dutch Shea before he shoots himself: "'I believe in Cat. I believe in God.' *Credo in Deum.* The first words of the Catholic catechism" (52). Didion then muses aloud about the relationship between faith and grief, wondering whether they are indeed the same. "Dutch Shea has less impact on us than what he sees has," writes George Stade in an otherwise sympathetic review in the *New York Times.* "We are not as moved by his grief, by his quirky integrity and hard-won lucidity as Mr. Dunne wants us to be" (March 28, 1982). Nevertheless, the novel remains powerful in its depiction of pathological bereavement, which may arise from a horrific death, such as a father's suicide or a daughter's ghastly accident, or from a cardiac event that is all too common.

The Red White and Blue

Dunne does not identify Jack Broderick, the screenwriter who appears in three of his novels, as one of his authorial mouthpieces, but he surely is. Dunne's next novel, *The Red White and Blue* (1987), is not primarily a Hollywood story, "although a fair amount of it takes place in the gilded venues where celebrity and political action make common cause," Jack admits. He not only speaks throughout the story with Dunne's mordant irony but he also shares his creator's belief that screenwriters enjoy no prestige in Hollywood. "Screenwriting is not an ignoble profession. It is just one that does not require a great deal of ego investment, and that suited me perfectly. The most to which a screenwriter can aspire is to be a co-pilot, and again I was a good fit" (15). Or as Jack Warner opines, screenwriters are "Schmucks with Underwoods" (*Crooning* 200).

Jack Broderick is authorial in other ways. To begin with, there are many surface similarities between narrator and author. Both are sons of wealthy fathers; both graduate Princeton "without distinction" and then serve for two years in the armed forces. Both become full-time writers: Jack's book *Grunts*, based on taped interviews of students, recalls Dunne's book *Vegas*, based on taped interviews of colorful Las Vegas characters. Jack's statement that he is "tempted by the pornography of violence" (*The Red White and Blue* 127) applies to many of the characters in Dunne's other fiction and nonfiction. Both Dunne and Jack share an absurdist vision of life. Jack is a "successful failure" who uses irony as a way to distance himself from the vain and pompous characters he encounters in and out of Hollywood. Irony is for him "the vehicle by which the essentially second rate arrive at some kind of superiority. Screenwriting is the profession for someone of this temperament. The pay is good, the responsibility is small, the emotional stake minimal" (34). Jack might also have added that irony is the mode by which we recognize the discrepancy between appearance and reality. He may be a second-rate screenwriter, but he is a first-rate observer of human foibles.

The world of *The Red White and Blue* is larger than that of *True Confessions* or *Dutch Shea, Jr.*, but it contains the familiar assortment of tainted Irish Catholics. Several of Dunne's statements about religion could appear in the earlier novels, as when Jack's flamboyant brother, a Catholic priest aptly called "Bro," states that "confession is essentially a form of plea bargaining with yourself. Most people, when they examine their consciences, will plead their mortal sins in Monte Rio last night down to venial. Then if they still have a bad conscience, they add lying to the list" (*The Red White and Blue* 173). Jack asserts that confession is "Catholic psychoanalysis" (298), and later, when he tells his father, from whom he is estranged, "let's be honest with each other," he immediately dismisses his own words as the "reflex rhetoric of psychoanalysis, a religion I had abandoned as I had Catholicism" (365). Jack may think he has abandoned his Catholicism, but it remains with him, and with Dunne's other characters, not as an article of faith but as an ingrained habit. Many of the characterizations he attributes to others are authorial, as when he describes President Fritz Finn, whose brother is married to Jack's sister Priscilla, as "more than a practitioner of don't get mad, get even. He liked to let people know that he had, and would use, the means to get even. I think there was a pleasure principle involved" (200).

Jack's pleasure lies in exposing the contradictions and pretensions of the rich and famous. He is sympathetic to oppressed workers and mistrustful of those who claim to befriend them. He satirizes mercilessly those on the political left as well as those on the right; no one escapes attack. There are many insider jokes in *The Red White and Blue* that the Episcopalian Didion must have found amusing, as when one person hostile to a workers' strike berates the Catholic priests who have instigated it, to which another responds: "I think they're Episcopalians in disguise" (250). Of all the institutions Jack ridicules, none is more absurd than marriage. There are no happy marriages in this novel or in *any* of Dunne's novels. One of Jack's wives, Anabel, was a "marriage addict, which of course meant that she was a divorce addict as well" (335). Contrary to Jack's statement that he makes a living "writing love scenes" (419), they are only sex scenes. Love and intimacy never appear in Jack's—or Dunne's—stories.

Death, however, is a familiar story in Dunne's world, as it is in Didion's. *The Red White and Blue* describes many kinds of deaths, ranging from a convicted murderer's execution at San Quentin, conveyed in graphic detail, including two pages of "instructions for operating and cleaning lethal gas chamber" (101), to political assassinations. The most autobiographically significant death occurs near the beginning of the story when Jack describes a funeral service he has orchestrated for a fellow screenwriter:

> Jimmy and I had often talked about death, the inordinate fear of which we both shared. He was always, in the years we were friends, making notes for his funeral, switching the hymns and psalms, typing up each new version of his leave-taking and inserting it into the old Episcopal prayer book which was the only thing he took with him when he left Lake Forest after his father shot himself. Callie Dana [Jimmy's ex-wife] was clutching this battered old prayer book when I arrived at Jimmy's house in Trancas after his heart attack. He had been in his kitchen making a cassoulet—Jimmy was a determined although not a very good cook; as with his work he needed to share the credit—and when he was stricken he fell against the stove and the pot tipped over and the cassoulet had horribly burned his face. There in his Book of Common Prayer were the latest instructions, neatly typed and dated just two weeks before. *This is what I would like for my funeral* . . . (43–44; emphasis in original).

Jimmy Dana's death foreshadows with startling accuracy John Gregory Dunne's death decades later. Both deaths occur without warning during dinner, though the former's detailed funeral instructions dated two weeks earlier indicate a premonition of death. He had "this lousy ticker he didn't tell anybody about but me," Jack reports, explaining the need for secrecy: "These studios, you see, they hear a heart murmur you can't pick up without a U.S. Air Force listening device, they don't give you insurance, and that's one of the things we're going to take up in the next negotiation with the producers" (*The Red White and Blue* 45). Nor is Jimmy Dana the only character in the novel who dies from a heart attack or stroke. Jack's sister Priscilla dies at the age of twenty-nine when a "vein burst in her skull" (22), the same type of death to which their mother has succumbed. The same death awaits Jack's father, who suffers an "intercranial thrombosis. In other words, a blood clot in an artery of the brain" (370). No wonder Jack talks often about death, an inordinate fear that many of Dunne's major and minor characters share.

Harp

The funeral service in *The Red White and Blue* prepares us for the funereal tone of Dunne's next book, *Harp*, his most sustained meditation on mortality. Rereading *Harp*, Didion recalls that she and her husband were attending a funeral service for an acquaintance killed in an accident when he informed her of the results of his recent medical examination:

> The service ended and the parking attendant brought my car. As we drove away, my wife said, "What did the doctor say?"
>
> There had not been an appropriate moment to mention my visit to the doctor in Santa Monica. "He scared the shit out of me, babe."
>
> "What did he say?"
>
> "He said I was a candidate for a catastrophic cardiac event." (*The Year of Magical Thinking* 155; in *Harp*, Dunne refers to a "catastrophic cardiovascular event," 113)

A few pages later in *Harp*, Dunne reports that he began to cry when he informed his wife that the medical report scared him—to which Didion observes in *The Year of Magical Thinking*, "Either I had not remembered this or I had determinedly chosen not to remember this. I had *not sufficiently appreciated it*" (155; emphasis in original). She then ponders the implications of his response to the medical results. "Was that what he experienced as he himself died? 'A moment of terror as he realized the inevitable outcome of the accident, then an instant later the eternal dark'? In the sense that it happens one night and not another, the mechanism of a typical cardiac arrest could be construed as essentially accidental: a sudden spasm ruptures a deposit of plaque in a coronary artery, ischemia follows, and the heart, deprived of oxygen, enters ventricular fibrillation. But how did he experience it?" (156).

Neither *Harp* nor *any* book can answer this question, but the memoir opens with an unusual statement that conveys Dunne's heightened awareness of mortality: "I was not given to personal reflection, had always looked unkindly, in fact, on introspection. Then in the seventh year of the Reagan kakistocracy, the medical dyes shooting through my arterial freeways were forced to make a detour around a major obstruction." The opening section of the book begins, however, not with an account of his impending catastrophic cardiovascular event but with a telephone call he received at 4:30 in the morning announcing the suicide of his forty-three-year-old brother Stephen one of the dedicatees of *Dutch Shea, Jr.* Dunne is so reluctant to reveal in the opening chapter his brother's suicide that he immediately apologizes to the reader in the next paragraph. "It is an imposition on the reader to write that paragraph, but there are those of us for whom words have no meaning until they are down on paper. Clarity only comes when pen is in hand, or at the typewriter or the word processor, clarity about what we feel and what we think, how we love and how we mourn; the words on the page constitute the benediction, the declaration, the confession of the emotionally inarticulate" (*Harp* 15–16). Didion does not comment on these words, but she must have understood immediately his urgent need to achieve clarity through writing. The need for clarity was one of the main reasons she wrote her memoir. Nancy K. Miller felt a similar sense of clarity when writing *Bequest and Betrayal*, a memoir about her mother's death: "Writing about despair and confusion, even jotting down telegraphic shards in my diary, always feels like a small gesture toward clarity and hope. Writing anything in those moments seems to arrest the free fall of anxiety" (27). Didion knew, like her husband and Miller, that writing heightens our feeling of self-control. Dunne's statement that the words on the page constitute a benediction, declaration, and confession of the emotionally inarticulate—and, we may add, the emotionally articulate—reveals one of the impulses behind *The Year of Magical Thinking* in particular and spousal loss memoirs in general.

Dunne was similar to his brother in many ways. They were the youngest of six children, as close to each other as "tree and bark" (*Harp* 16). The two brothers and the other members of their Irish Catholic family "carried a full cargo of ethnic and religious freight as it shifted in the long passage between immigration and deracination" (16–17). They shared a room together while growing up and after college; both were harshly punished by their father, a "quick man with a strap to enforce discipline"; both had a tendency to stammer and would often discuss with each other "stratagems to avoid the minefields of speech"; both had a "cold eye for the warts and wens of social nuance." And yet as close as they were—each was the best man at the other's wedding and godfather to the other's child—Dunne claims he was unaware of his brother's intermittent bouts of melancholy. "I was impatient with the emotional extortion of much of what passed for depression" (18), he confesses, apparently forgetting the opening of *Vegas*, when he refers to his own "nervous breakdown."

After writing about his brother's suicide, Dunne describes the significance of his book's title. "I am a harp, that is my history, Irish and Catholic, from steerage to suburbia in three generations. The Kennedys defined a certain kind of Irish: Don't get mad, get even, was the commandment to which they swore allegiance—Irish to be sure, but gentrified. I am cut from a rougher bolt of Irish cloth: Get mad *and* get even is the motto on the standard I fly" (26). Dunne has used the reference to "don't get mad, get even" in *The Red White and Blue*, but now he elaborates on his own Irish American heritage. "There were four different stages of the Irish-American experience—immigrant, outcast, assimilated, deracinated. I was in stage four, deracinated in the sense that I never thought my Irish background had anything to do with a place called Ireland. My being Irish was more a component of a parochial school education, of nuns and priests with a flair for discipline and a taste for corporal punishment" (*Harp* 184). Later in the book he describes telling a group of Indonesian intellectuals about the "therapeutic effect of holding a grudge" (90). Inheriting his volatile temper from his father, he became an expert practitioner of grudge therapy.

Dunne gives plenty of examples of his harpish nature. Raised in West Hartford, the "ne plus ultra of the immigrant Hartford Irish dream" (43), he grows up in a world of "Haviland china and private schools and a retinue of help," finding himself becoming a "cloned Yank, slightly ashamed of my origins, patronizing toward the Irish still on the make" (*Harp* 44–45). Intent on rejecting his family roots—"My idea of rebellion was to go to Princeton rather than to Yale" (46)—he cultivated the identity, his "true harp voice," of a man "with a chip on his shoulder the size of a California redwood" (49). It was not, he admits unapologetically, an attractive voice. "Let me emphasize that a writer's voice does not have to be nice, and if the voice belongs to someone of Irish extraction, it rarely is" (49). Unafraid of political correctness or the possibility that his sweeping generalizations may be half-truths, he associates the Irish with an "inbred hatred of the Brits" and by extension a mistrust of all Protestants. Given his view of the Irish, there is nothing uplifting or idealistic about being a writer, especially an Irish American writer. "Although it is not necessary for a writer to be a prick, neither does it hurt. A writer is an eternal outsider, his nose pressed against whatever window on the other side of which he sees his material. Resentment sharpens his eye, hostility hones his killer instinct" (49). Dunne elaborates on this theme in *Crooning*, referring to writing as an "aggressive act" (12).

What happens when a belligerent, intensely competitive Irish American writer marries an Episcopalian from California who is also a writer, more famous than her husband? *Harp* offers several clues to the Dunne-Didion marriage. Some of the clues cannot be taken seriously, as when he describes receiving letters from "wackos" who invite both husband and wife to writers' conferences. "'You still have not taken my advice and dumped that miserable piece of Jewish dreck you are married to,' one letter says. My wife is a WASP from Sacramento. 'I know, I know, you are going to tell me she is a WASP from Sacramento. B.S. She went to New York City anxious to break into publishing and came upon the idea that if she put on the Jewish Whining Act she could get published. Well, she succeeded all too well. Now her whole thing is permeated with the Jewish whine'" (72). Other clues are more reliable, as when he describes his wife's reaction to a nasty comment made at one of the many posh Californian parties they attend in which writers are made to feel like pariahs because of their lack of social status. "'I won't be condescended to by someone's second wife,' she once told me bitterly.'" Dunne dutifully records this statement in his writer's notebook for possible use in a later novel, hinting at the professional competition with her. "Into my notebook, except I made it a third wife, because everyone we know is on a second marriage. It was her material, she said. It belongs to whoever uses it first, I said. I steal scenes from old screenplays I wrote that were never produced; an unpublished novel I wrote when I was just a baby has been so cannibalized over the years that it is now just a pile of bleached bones" (83). In *The Year of Magical Thinking* Didion denies that there was competition between the two writers, but it would probably be more accurate to say that they never allowed competition to destroy their marriage.

In *Harp* Dunne writes about his marital tensions, as he has done in *Vegas*, only now he is less evasive. Again, there is never a feeling of intimacy between husband and wife. One argument occurred in June,1970 when he and Didion spent the month crisscrossing the Deep South for an article they never wrote. "On the way back to New Orleans, on the Lake Pontchartrain causeway, my wife and I had a fight, ugly words, then silence. We spent the night at an airport motel, not speaking to each other, then took the 9:15 National flight to San Francisco the next morning, not exchanging a word until we got to the Hertz counter. I do not remember what the fight was about" (*Harp* 140). This is the only marital argument to which he refers in *Harp*, but he never describes any moments of closeness apart from their "enormous" (189) telephone bills when they are on writing assignments in different parts of the country. He wonders aloud in one section of the novel titled "Notes Written in a Lousy Italian Restaurant in Frankfurt" about how he should refer to his wife in print. "How do I deal with J? Is it too coy to just call her 'J' or 'Joan' or 'my wife'? No other ID. I think so. She dislikes being considered as part of a couple as much as I do. Too much mileage on that construct" (161).

Dunne also wonders how much mileage he can get from writing about his "cardiac adventure." A lot, the answer turns out to be, for the most important section of *Harp* focuses on the medical emergency that arises during the waning summer days of 1987 when he receives the alarming news about his heart. Immediately after telling us he is a candidate for a catastrophic cardiovascular event, he engages in an "Internal Affairs Investigation" in which he self-consciously reflects on how to tell the story of his possible death. Using a question-and-answer format, he decides that the story he is about to narrate is "more or less" true: "A name changed. A certain dramatic restructuring" (113). We learn during this inner monologue that both his father and paternal uncle died at young ages. Dunne can't help thinking of Santayana's famous observation that those who do not remember the past are condemned to repeat it—a disturbing insight for the genetically challenged. He then records the physician's interest in the kind of writer he is, to which he answers silently, "A good writer, I always want to say, but never do" (114).

Wondering how he will present this dialogue, most of which is irrelevant to the story of his medical emergency but too interesting to dispense with, Dunne includes the lines that Didion later quotes after his death: "When I told my wife he scared the shit out of me, I started to cry" (114)—an emotional response that seems out of character for a writer with a tough-guy persona. He then admits that as a storyteller he cannot resist exploiting the grimly ironic coincidence of learning the results of his medical exam on the day he attended a memorial service for his friend Anton Siodmak. And that is why, he tells his internal interlocutor, he has spent so much time writing about his deceased friend. "Because it's a hell of a good story, and I'm a storyteller. Because the memorial service did correspond to the day the doctor scared the shit out of me. Because I like to play one thing off against another. Because I think nothing in life is ever discrete. . . . And finally because I suppose some son of a bitch will probably do the same thing to me the day of my memorial service, if I ever have one, and if anyone comes" (115).

There are more ironies here than even Dunne could imagine, beginning with the most striking one of all: fourteen years after the publication of *Harp*, Dunne suffered a fatal heart attack, and two years later, someone would write a book about his death, not a son of a bitch but his wife. She too would see that his death was a hell of a good story, for she was as much a storyteller as he was, and she shared his belief that nothing in life is discrete.

In writing about his health crisis two years after it occurred, Dunne appears as interested in the process of narrative construction as he is in the event itself. He would understandably insist that the two cannot be separated. How we understand and interpret an event is part of the event itself, for no matter how committed we may be to truth and transparency, our memories are always selective, remembering (and highlighting) certain details while forgetting (and downplaying) others. As Donald B. Spence observes, we often cannot separate narrative truth from historical truth. Thomas Larson makes a similar observation: "What we learn in memoir writing is that memory has far more of its own agency than we thought, that the very act of remembering may alter what did occur" (34). Dunne writes with a wry ironic humor about his heart condition, noting that "I am not exactly afraid of dying, although there are moments when I dream of becoming the first to beat the rap" (*Hark* 115). Throughout the story he sounds like one of the battle-hardened protagonists of *True Confessions*, *Dutch Shea, Jr.*, or *The Red White and Blue*, weary, cynical, tough, and jaded. Dunne then tells us about a letter he opens, "with a certain reticence," from an insurance company. The letter is simple enough: his insurance company is willing to increase the value of his policy by 50 percent, with no raise in his annual premium, if he allows a paramedic to visit him, take his blood pressure, perform other minor tests, and ask a few questions. Dunne agrees. The paramedic appears, completes the tests, and leaves. Another paramedic shows up about a month later to repeat the tests, and now Dunne begins to worry. The insurance company then requests him to perform a stress test, and the result of the EKG printout indicates a problem that requires a visit to a cardiologist, who determines the existence of a critical lesion in his left anterior descending artery—what another cardiologist calls, with sardonic humor, a potential "widowmaker." Using dark irony, he relates in the next dozen pages his medical odyssey, as he ingratiates himself with the doctors and nurses in the hope they will provide him with better care.

The possibility of a widowmaker terrifies Dunne the man but fascinates Dunne the writer. He has, in fact, a double vision, that of a patient and an author, and the story is too good to depress him as long as he is well enough to write. "Being a writer, I knew this was good material, and from the day of Anton Siodmak's memorial service, I began taking voluminous notes on every medical appointment and on all the wild thoughts that ran through my head, storing them in a file I called 'Cardiac' on my computer" (*Harp* 120). He goes home after every medical exam and reads the *Merck Manual* to check the meaning of his doctor's words, recording dutifully the feeling of guilt that he is responsible for his occluded coronary arteries: "It was my fault; I had put them at risk, in harm's way because of my own bad habits, my failure to pay attention to my genetic history" (120). He feels constant apprehension and sometimes dread, as if he is living on borrowed time. Life becomes an emotional roller coaster, dizzying him with hope and despair.

How does a writer represent these vertiginous emotions without indulging in verbal inflation? "'Milk it,' I wrote in the 'Cardiac' directory, 'but no excessive melodramatics.' I wrote, and then erased, an item about the logical procedures I wanted followed in the event the unmentionable happened—for example, who would tell my daughter at college in New York (Calvin Trillin was to be given that honor); it was as if my wife, whom I jauntily called 'the little widow,' could not manage on her own. The entry was cheap and demeaning because I meant it to be read after the fact and make everyone cry about my sense of foreboding.

Good sense prevailed. 'Alt F4, block. Delete Block? (Y/N) Yes.' It was all part of the distancing, an existential interlude" (*Harp* 121–22).

No less than Donald Hall, who resolves to put his cancer diagnosis to good effect in a book, so does Dunne leap at the opportunity to transmute his cardiac problems into the stuff of art. Only some of this fascinating cardiac material in *Harp*, however, appears in *The Year of Magical Thinking.* Why? One can only speculate. Perhaps Didion could not bear to quote the words "the little widow," which may have sounded too perky in a period of anguished bereavement. Perhaps she did not want to be overly influenced by the style and tone of her husband's story, which might unduly color her own. Perhaps his jaunty tone no longer seemed funny. Or perhaps she felt, understandably, that her book was less about her husband's work than her own psychic pain. Whatever the reasons, she does not comment on his premonition of death.

Dunne gives us in *Harp* the middle and provisional ending of his medical story. Asymptomatic, he knows he can perhaps change his lifestyle—he is overweight and has high cholesterol—but he cannot alter his family predisposition to early and fatal heart attacks. "I was following in the genetic footprints left by my father and his brother" (123). He accepts his doctors' recommendation to have an angiogram to determine the extent of his occluded coronary arteries. His mind steeped in literature, he cannot help thinking of Ken's Kesey's grimly comic novel *One Flew Over the Cuckoo's Nest.* "The admitting nurse at St. John's Hospital in Santa Monica, where the angiogram was to be given, had that Miss Ratched nurse-knows-best manner" (*Harp* 125). The angiogram confirms the doctors' worst fears: the left anterior descending artery is 90 percent occluded. The angioplasty takes place five days later; two days after the medical procedure a major earthquake rocks Los Angeles. As Dunne jokes in a letter to a friend, "I suspect I am the first person to have an angioplasty on Tuesday and have it tested by an earthquake on Thursday" (126). The results of the procedure were, according to a cardiologist, "spectacular," and follow-up medical tests confirm the success. "'You've bought yourself a new life,' my internist said. I did not tell him the question it raised: What the fuck do I do with it? The first thing I did was move" (129).

Dunne ends his medical story with another "Internal Affairs Investigation," this one supplying us with additional information that casts new light on his earlier books. We now learn that the "nervous breakdown" to which he refers in the opening sentence of *Vegas* was not caused mainly by the cardiac problem but by the depression following the completion of a writing project—presumably *Studio*. "I was terribly depressed afterward, the way you are depressed after finishing a book": it was "like the postpartum depression of finishing a book" (130). Nor is he the first writer to experience postartem depression. The next hundred pages of *Harp* focus on other aspects of his life, but he updates his cardiac status in the book's last three pages. Seventeen months after the angioplasty he collapsed while walking in Central Park in Manhattan, and he decided, reluctantly, to tell his wife and physician. The symptoms seem to indicate aortic stenosis, requiring immediate open heart surgery to replace the aortic valve. Once again the writer in him takes over:

> "I think I know how to end this book now," I said to my wife on the walk home from Tim's. I knew I did not have to spell it out to her.
>
> "Terrific," she said, the novelist in her taking precedence over the wife who knew her husband too well ever to express the concern she felt, the husband who was so volatile except in times of crisis.
>
> "It's a hell of an ending," I said, and what I meant was that a writer's life is his only real capital, his and his alone to invest, and to imagine, and to reimagine, even unto this. (233)

The open heart surgery is canceled because the angiogram shows no aortic stenosis but only a "coronary tree"—a benign condition. The existential dilemma of why he has passed out remains unresolved at the end of *Harp*, to be explored, perhaps, in a later book by the author or his wife.

Harp remains Dunne's most autobiographically revealing book, the one in which he discloses not only the most personal information about his life but also his worst fears of death. It also dramatizes more fully than any of his other books the inner workings of his writerly self. *Harp* demonstrates his ironic sensibility, though some of his statements are ironic only in retrospect—and only to his readers, not to himself. In writing about his sister Harriet, for example, who died of cancer one year after the death of their brother Stephen, Dunne recalls a time when, shortly after he was released from the army and living alone in New York City, he and his sister belonged to a theater club and would go together every month to a Broadway play: "This was when I thought the theater was smart; with age came wisdom, and an antipathy toward the stage and its practitioners I have long since stopped trying to hide" (*Harp* 103). One can only wonder how he would have reacted to the knowledge that four years after his death, theatergoers would flock to see Vanessa Redgrave star in the Broadway play *The Year of Magical Thinking.*

Crooning

Dunne's next book, *Crooning* (1990), consists of several essays, nine of which were first published in the *New York Review of Books*, to which he was a regular contributor. *Crooning* reveals not only the details of his father's premature death but also the origins of his own preoccupation with mortality. "My father's was the first dead body I ever saw. He died suddenly, of a ruptured aorta, three days after my fourteenth birthday. I kissed him goodbye in the morning, a healthy vigorous man of fifty-one, and when I came home from school that afternoon the oxygen tanks on the back porch were like a psychic barricade, Stygian signposts. I was not a stranger to the cryptograms of death. My father was a surgeon, and when he talked about his practice his words were often encoded in body English—a slight shrug, a raised eyebrow, an almost imperceptible shake of the head: the cannibal cells had taken the high ground" (*Crooning* 75). Dunne's challenge as a writer is to find the words that were encoded in his father's body language. After the wake had ended and the mourners had gone home, he would sneak downstairs in his pajamas and stare at his father's face. "I tried to will him to breathe. I tried to coax movement into fingers bound with rosary beads. I listened for a heartbeat, as years later I would bend over my infant daughter's crib and listen for her heartbeat. I wonder still if I told him that last morning that I loved him" (75).

What provoked these vivid memories of his father's death, Dunne explains, were two recent visits to the Los Angeles County Morgue, where with a couple of homicide detectives he looked at forensic photographs of victims of grisly murders. "It was a festival of death," he recounts. "On the walls were autopsy photographs of particular or bizarre interest" (*Crooning* 77). In *The Red White and Blue* Jack Broderick refers to the "festival" of grief" to describe the "minuet of mourning" (457), but the festival of death in *Crooning* is more personal. Not everyone would be interested in looking at these photos, and Dunne never analyzes the motivation behind his fascination with victims of horrific murders or with the perpetrators of these crimes. Drawn to these acts and people for personal and professional reasons, he litters his novels with dead bodies, victims of homicide or suicide. There may have been a counterphobic motive behind writing about violent and premature death: the hope that such writing would keep the demons away, the Broken Man away, like whistling in the dark—or crooning.

Perhaps the most unusual autobiographical disclosure in *Crooning* appears in the essay "To Live and Die in L.A," in which Dunne writes about reading an autopsy report in 1979 of a black woman, Eula Mae Love, who became verbally and then physically menacing to a gas company employee who was attempting to read her gas meter. We learn that her husband had died six months earlier—since then, she had not paid her gas bill. The police were called after she brandished an eleven-inch boning knife and began hacking at a tree. During a scuffle, she was shot twelve times by two officers. Outraged by the LAPD's attempt to justify the shooting, Dunne admits that he became obsessed by the case, to the point where he bought a similar eleven-inch knife and held it by the handle. He then makes the following free association. "I replayed an incident of twelve years before when my wife, with cause, once tried to kill me. She stood on the landing in our house in Hollywood with a pair of scissors in her hand, threatening to throw them at me, promising to throw them at me. I stayed out of range. I knew she had a bad arm. I knew she threw like a girl. And I knew the scissors had no balance. I talked. Quietly. Reasonably. And out of range. The moment passed. The fury died. We are still married, I like to think happily" (*Crooning* 72).

Playland

Nearly all the deaths that appear in Dunne's fiction and nonfiction are sudden and unexpected, like his father's death—and, years later—his own. Didion doesn't mention Dunne's next novel, *Playland* (1994), another darkly comic tale about mobsters, Hollywood celebrities, gambling casinos, hookers, and murders, in which he speculates on what might have happened if Lizzie, the wife of narrator Jack Broderick (and the former nurse of his father), had died of a lingering illness rather than in an automobile accident. Dunne's narrator is the same callous screenwriter who appeared seven years earlier in *The Red White and Blue*. He has little empathy for the terminally ill, who may be grateful for extra time, or who may be so wracked with pain that they cannot die quickly enough. Nor does he empathize with caregivers, who may be so worn out and despairing that the extra time feels like prolonged torture. Jack's cynicism and anger toward the wealthy evidently blind him to the pain of lingering deaths. And yet he is not entirely insensitive, for he knows that film deaths bear little resemblance to real deaths. "People dying in movies did not have catheters inserted into their urethras. Nor did they have dementia. And no drooling and no incontinence and no shit on the sheets, those crosses of the terminal illness" (*Playland* 26).

Playland has much in common with Dunne's earlier novels. It opens with the death of Chuckie O'Hara, who, like Jimmy Dana in *The Red White and Blue*, scripts his own funeral service. Tom Spellacy, the narrator of *True Confessions*, makes a brief appearance in *Playland*, and Jack dutifully informs us of his death: "I did a Nexis search of Lieutenant T. J. Spellacy on my computer and ultimately found a small obituary in the *Los Angeles Times*. He had died of coronary artery disease in 1984, at the age of seventy-eight" (428). Dunne was sixty-two when *Playland* was published, about a decade older than Jack, who cannot help reading the daily obituaries, "which were a new fascination since birthday number fifty. Five-oh, and the sense of days dwindling down, September, November. Most mornings I turned to the obituaries right after a cursory glance at the headlines. The obits were a relief. A first look to check the ages of the recently deceased. Fifty to sixty. Those hurt. Too close to home. Then cause of death" (53). After listing the most frequent causes of death—AIDS, respiratory illness, cancer, and automobile accidents, Jack then cites the kind of death he most fears. "The cardiac cases were the ones I really hated. Congestive heart failure, 52. Cardiac arrest, 50. Coronary artery disease, 57. Over sixty was a good time to check out. Closer to sixty-five, actually. Over seventy was even better. 'In his sleep. Had not been ill. Two sets of tennis that afternoon.' And maybe a great fuck afterward. Even a lousy fuck. Jerking off, if that's all that's available. 'Quietly, in his sleep.' That's the one I would like to reserve" (53).

Monster

Dunne returns to cardiac issues in his next book, *Monster* (1997), a study of his life as a Hollywood screenwriter. The book describes Dunne and Didion's darkly comic ordeal writing a screenplay about the tragic life of Jessica Savitch, the television anchorwoman who drowned when she lost control of her car and plunged into a creek. It took the husband-and-wife team eight years and twenty-seven drafts before the script was turned into the film *Up Close and Personal* starring Robert Redford and Michelle Pfeiffer. *Monster* chronicles Dunne's love-hate relationship to Hollywood screenwriting—more hate than love. Why, then, did he spend so much time as a screenwriter? He admits that despite his reluctance to continue his frustrating involvement with the Disney film, whose future success seemed doubtful, and his unwillingness to work with Disney's point man Jeffrey Katzenberg, there was one compelling reason to attend the studio meeting. "Joan was practical: she said my cardiac distress, however optimistic the prognosis, was still an unknown factor that might kick in at any moment; we needed the health insurance, and this was the only card on the table" (*Monster* 16). In the section of the book titled "Mirabile Dictu," he repeats much of the information about fainting in Central Park that he first disclosed eight years earlier in *Harp*, but he now implies for the first time that perhaps the main reason he spent so many years as a screenplay writer was for health insurance.

Monster also details the cardiac events that occurred after the publication of *Harp*. Dunne must have decided when writing *Harp* that he wanted to save some of the cardiac material for a future book—*Monster*. As it turns out, the open heart surgery that is called off at the end of *Harp* is indeed necessary, for two years after he fainted in Central Park, he again fainted at a Honolulu airport while racing to hail a cab. "The results of the echocardiogram and the angiogram indicated a congenital defect of the aortic valve, the same defect that had killed my father at age fifty-one. The examining physician said I had two options: You have open-heart surgery or you die. Not next week or next year or perhaps even the year after, he said, but I had a condition that was 100 percent fatal, and 95 percent correctable by the surgical procedure. The option chose itself; I was wheeled into an operating room one week later" (62).

It took eight weeks for Dunne to recover from the open heart surgery, and by May 1991 he was back working on his novel *Playland*, which took him five years to write. Two months after the surgery, however, he was bitten on the ankle by an insect, and within a couple of days the wound had become dangerously infected: "My left leg below the knee was swollen to almost twice its normal size" (*Monster* 64). He was immediately hospitalized and hooked up to an "industrial-strength IV drip" in the emergency room. "What I had was bacterial cellulitis, an infection that because of my plastic aortic valve would put me at particular risk; as a foreign agent in my body, the valve would act as a magnet for infection, and if the infection hit the valve it could possibly trigger a stroke" (65).

One of Dunne's most revealing observations in *Monster* occurs when he discusses his reluctance to add more romance to *Up Close and Personal.* Despite Disney's demand to accentuate the romantic and sexual attraction between the film's lead actors, Dunne refuses, stating in exasperation, "I don't do love," a comment that a Disney executive finds "hilarious" (105). Hilarious or not, it's true that despite the fact that Dunne and Didion were both novelists, they did not write love stories. Nor did they write stories about marital love.

Nothing Lost

Nothing Lost, Dunne's last novel, was published posthumously in 2004, one year after his death. Didion makes two poignant references to it in *The Year of Magical Thinking.* Reading the final proof for the novel in her daughter's hospital room, she spots what she thinks might be a grammatical error in a sentence describing the character J. J. McClure. She makes a startling admission, one we would never expect from one of the country's most distinguished writers. "I never actually learned the rules of grammar, relying instead only on what sounded right, but there was something here that I was not sure sounded right. The sentence in the last-pass galleys read: 'It was as close a declaration of love as J. J. was capable of making.' I would have added a preposition: 'It was as close *to* a declaration of love as J. J. was capable of making'" (140; emphasis in original). Repeating the sentence to herself as she watches the ice floes on the Hudson river outside her window, she then ponders his state of mind as he wrote it. "It was not the kind of sentence, if you had written it, you would want wrong, but neither was it the kind of sentence, if that was the way you had written it, you would want changed. How had he written it? What did he have in mind? How would he want it? The decision was left to me. Any choice I made could carry the potential for abandonment, even betrayal. That was one reason I was crying in Quintana's hospital room. When I got home that night I checked the previous galleys and manuscripts. The error, if it was an error, had been there from the beginning. I left it as it was." I can't imagine Dunne or any other writer regarding this editorial decision as momentous enough to justify the potential for "abandonment" or "betrayal," but Didion can't help blaming herself: "*Why do you always have to be right. Why do you always have to have the last word. For once in your life just let it go*" (141; emphasis in original).

Didion's other reference to *Nothing Lost* involves a revealing statement Dunne made to her about the novel shortly before his death. "A night or two before he died John asked me if I was aware how many characters died in the novel. . . . He had been sitting in his office making a list of them" (*The Year of Magical Thinking* 147). The list, to which she added a name he had overlooked, includes eight characters and an additional four who die in an automobile accident. Didion returns to the list months after his death, wondering why the pencil was so faint, why he would use a pencil that barely left a mark. "*When did he begin seeing himself as dead?*" she asks (147; emphasis in original). She then quotes a physician who tells her that the divide between life and death is "not black and white."

Nothing Lost, with its eerily ironic title, begins with a quotation from Robert Penn Warren's novel *All the King's Men*: "For nothing is lost, nothing is ever lost." Warren may have been thinking of Henry James's observation, "Try to be one of the people on whom nothing is lost," which Dunne uses as the epigraph to *Harp*. The context in *Nothing Lost* is forensic: there are always clues to a crime, no matter how seemingly perfect. The title also has an existential meaning: what, if anything, survives our deaths? *Nothing Lost* is, like most of Dunne's other novels, a murder mystery, in this case, a horrific racial crime in which a black man is literally skinned to death, but it is also the novelist's final rumination over death. "I'm sixty-two," intones screenwriter Jack Broderick, tapping the scar on his chest, "I have a prosthetic aortic valve, a plastic St. Jude model—the only reason I tell you that is because I suspect you have a lawyer's passion for specificity" (*Nothing Lost* 93). With a novelist's specificity, Dunne describes in minute detail Jack's death after having sex with Teresa Kean. It is the kind of death for which Jack has longed in *Playland*, though he doesn't anticipate the shock of discovering his body. "His eyes were closed," Teresa says, "his face peaceful but drained of color. Even before I said 'Jack,' I knew he was dead. I felt for a pulse in his neck, but there was none. On his wrist he wore a MedicAlert bracelet. I read the instructions: 'Aortic valve prosthesis—takes anticoagulants—allergic to penicillin.' Already there was evidence of postmortem lividity pooling at his thighs" (97).

Teresa resists the urge to panic when she realizes he is dead, and she remains fully in control. She gathers his possessions—his studs and cuff links, credit cards, driver's license, and money clip—and places them on a table. She has the presence of mind to fold his pleated dinner shirt and hang it along with his bow tie and dinner jacket in the closet. Few people would be so neat and methodical in the same situation. She then listens to Mozart for a few minutes on NPR while contemplating what to do next. "In my criminal practice I had read countless death certificates. I knew the words appropriate to the failure of an aortic prosthesis. Myocardial infarction. Pulmonary embolism. Rheumatic valvulitis with stenosis and/or insufficiency. Bacterial endocarditis. Stroke" (*Nothing Lost* 98).

In killing off his fictional character, is Dunne rehearsing his own death? It seems possible, perhaps even likely. This rehearsal does not involve the circumstances of his own death the novelist died while having a quiet dinner with his wife—but the *cause* of his death. Dunne attributes Teresa's sophisticated medical knowledge of Jack's cardiac failure to her extensive reading of death certificates, yet it seems more likely that this knowledge would come from a man who has a long history of heart disease—or from a wife who has dutifully researched her husband's medical condition. Ironically, Teresa's remarkable composure foreshadows Didion's no less remarkable self-control when discovering *her* husband's death. Not that the two deaths are identical. Jack Broderick's death is bizarre: though dead for many hours, he still has an erection, a result of an injection of two drops of a high-potency corticosteroid, Prostaglandin E-1, which he injects into his penis shortly before love-making for a rare condition known as Peyronie's disease. "His right leg hung out of the bed, but his cock stood up like a rocket on a launching pad. I was full of cock metaphors. Lacrosse stick last night, rocket this morning" (*Nothing Lost* 97). Nor is Teresa the only one who exploits the grotesque humor of the situation. "As I left the bedroom with the two policemen, I heard one paramedic whisper to the other that they would need a van with a sunroof if the deceased did not lose his wood. Humor on the EMS beat" (101). Dunne's ending, by contrast, lacks comic appeal or high drama, suggesting that real death, as opposed to fictional death, is natural, ordinary, undramatic, and imperceptible—a death that is at once terrifyingly swift and reassuringly painless.

The parallels between Teresa and Didion extend beyond their knowledge of fatal heart attacks. Witness Teresa's reactions to the paramedics' questions. "They asked the name of the deceased individual—'individual' was their word—and how long he had been on the premises and if I had been aware of any signs of cardiac arrest prior to his becoming deceased and when had I noticed that he had in fact expired. I thought credit cards and driver's licenses expire, not people, people die, but 'die' was not a word that seemed to figure in the paramedics' professional vocabulary" (*Nothing Lost* 99). Teresa's demand for linguistic precision identifies her not as a criminal lawyer, whose professional training does not include an appreciation for compression and simplicity of prose, but as a novelist and wordsmith, a professional writer who knows, as Mark Twain famously expressed, that the difference between the right word and the almost right word is the difference between lightning and the lightning bug.

Regards

Not all writers shared Dunne's mordant humor during funerals. In the 1981 essay "Hessians," reprinted in the posthumously published *Regards*, he writes about attending the funeral of a screenwriter held in Beverly

Hills. The church was crowded, and he describes the scene as if it were in one of his tragicomic novels. "Two of the deceased's ex-wives were up front, and in a rear pew, keening rather more loudly than necessary, was the sixteen-year-old he had been romancing the last few months of his life. 'He kept worrying,' whispered my companion at the funeral, a screenwriter and a cad of international repute, 'that his pubic hair was turning gray'" (*Regards* 43). This scene appears, in nearly identical language, in *The Red White and Blue* when Jack Broderick sits next to movie producer Marty Magnin during Jimmy Dana's funeral.

This is vintage Dunne, the hard-boiled writer who sees sexual dalliance everywhere. "Tumescence as the arbiter of national policy is the plot machinery of trash novels," he theorizes in an essay on the Kennedys in *Regards* (125), reprinted from *Crooning* (110). In a postscript to "Hessians," he admits that the real-life funeral on which he opens the essay later appears in his novel *The Red White and Blue*. He describes how he fictionalizes the funeral, and though he doesn't use the word "scavenging" that appears in *Harp*, this is precisely his method of gathering literary material. He recalls that during the funeral service Gore Vidal leaned over and asked him, "Are you working," which prompts the following thought: "in truth I had no intention of using the scene in a book, and indeed the novel I was working on at the time would not have accommodated it" (53). But writers are always working, whether they realize it or not, and they are always absorbing material they may later use in their stories. The most intimate details of one's sexual life are rich material for the writer's imagination, as Dunne suggests in *Quintana and Friends*. "A natural disaster, a domestic crisis—such are the secret yearnings of a writer with an idea he doubts will work. My house was burgled twice and the two resulting pieces netted me a lot more than the burglars got. I can recall one columnist who eked three columns out of his house burning down, one on the fire, a second on the unsung dignity of fire fighting, and a third on his insurance adjuster and a long view on the charred artifacts of a lifetime. So avid for material is your average columnist that once, when my daughter caught my wife and me in flagrante delicto, I seriously wondered if there was a column in it (As it turned out, only a column mention.)" (46). Didion, too, acknowledges the principle of artistic scavenging, the ways in which writers transmute life into art. Both Dunne and Didion would agree with T. S. Eliot that "immature poets borrow; mature poets steal." "So no," writes Dunne unapologetically in *Regards*, "I had not planned to use the scene in a novel, but of course yes, it was always there waiting to be retrieved. And the answer to Gore Vidal's question should have been 'Always'" (54).

Slouching towards Bethlehem

After immersing oneself in John Gregory Dunne's fictional and nonfictional world, one encounters a strikingly different universe in Joan Didion's books. Dunne is an ironist who rarely seems surprised by what he sees. His characters retain their exuberance and self-confidence even when encountering the most disturbing sights, and they seem at home in the most violent places. His characters not only play life on the dark keys but they are attuned to dissonance. The writer may break down temporarily when describing to his wife his impending cardiac catastrophe, the state of his potential "widowmaker," but he quickly regains his composure. No matter how tragic or absurd life may be, he is there to chronicle it, often in a voice that approaches manic intensity.

By contrast, Didion's world always threatens to implode, leaving her among the wreckage. She seems more vulnerable than her husband, more attuned to the nameless dread and foreboding that characterize so many of her fictional characters. In a review of the 1977 novel *A Book of Common Prayer*, Peter S. Prescott called Didion "our foremost practitioner of the literature of permanent nervous collapse" (81), a remark that foreshadows Christopher Caldwell's observation about the 1992 collection of essays *About Henry*: "Didion has the neurasthenic's gift for sensing impending disaster" (247). And yet Didion, no less than Dunne, stares unflinchingly at the abyss into which many of her characters plunge. As she reveals in a 1978 *Paris Review* interview by Linda Kuehl, as a child she was interested in the "dark journey" (163), one filled with dangerous landscapes. She never hesitates to record the perilous side of life. "I learned early to keep death in my line of sight," states the narrator in *A Book of Common Prayer*, "keep it under surveillance, keep it on cleared ground and away from any brush where it might coil unnoticed" (121)—a metaphor evocative of a rattlesnake that symbolizes her vision of danger.

The reader senses Didion's vulnerability, even dread, from the opening of her first nonfictional book, *Slouching towards Bethlehem*, published in 1968, four years after she and Dunne were married. Consisting of twenty essays published in various magazines in the mid-1960s, *Slouching towards Bethlehem* alludes to Yeats's 1920 poem "The Second Coming," which Didion quotes in its entirety. Each of the essays demonstrates her lifelong thesis of "atomization," the belief that things are falling apart. "I went to San Francisco," she states in the preface, "because I had not been able to work in some months, had been paralyzed by the conviction that writing was an irrelevant act, that the world as I had understood it no longer existed. If I was to work again at all, it would be necessary for me to come to terms with disorder" (xiii–xiv).

Didion writes about both social and psychic disorder, admitting "there is always a point in the writing of a piece when I sit in a room literally papered with false starts and cannot put one word after another and imagine that I have suffered a small stroke, leaving me apparently undamaged but actually aphasic" (*Slouching towards Bethlehem* xv). Despite the reference to stroke, she rarely worries about heart disease—this was her husband's fear, not her own. Her anxiety is more diffuse, free-floating. Physically ill when writing the title essay, she mentions a pain so intense that it kept her up at night, requiring her to self-medicate by drinking gin and hot water to deaden the pain and then taking Dexedrine to counter the gin. She also refers obliquely to other difficulties during this "troubled time," adding that "working did to the trouble what gin did to the pain" (xvi). She ends the preface by telling us that although she is "bad" at interviewing people and dislikes making telephone calls, she does have unexpected advantages as a reporter. "I am so physically small, so temperamentally unobtrusive, and so neurotically inarticulate that people tend to forget that my presence runs counter to their best interests. And it always does. That is one last thing to remember: *writers are always selling somebody out*" (xvi; emphasis in original).

If writers are always selling somebody out, is writing, then, a hostile act? Didion implies in her Kuehl interview that this may be the case. "It's hostile in that you're trying to make somebody see something the way you see it, trying to impose your idea, your picture. It's hostile to try to wrench around someone else's mind that way. Quite often you want to tell somebody your dream, your nightmare. Well, nobody wants to hear about someone else's dream, good or bad; nobody wants to walk around with it. The writer is always tricking the reader into listening to the dream." In "Why I Write," appearing in *Joan Didion: Essays and Conversations*, she goes even further, asserting that the act of setting words on paper "is the tactic of a secret bully, an invasion, an imposition of the writer's sensibility on the reader's most private space" (5). In Didion's view, the only reader to whom a writer listens is herself: "very possibly I'm committing an aggressive and hostile act toward myself" (Kuehl 144).

There are several problematic implications of this view of writing. To begin with, it clashes with more positive statements Didion makes elsewhere about writing as a healing art, if not to the reader then to the writer, as when she states that she has "always thought of my novels as stories I tell myself. They are cautionary tales. Stories I don't want to happen to me" (Stamberg 23). Writing may be, as she claims, a form of bullying, but it may also be a form of sharing and gifting. If writing may create a false sense of meaning, as she sometimes implies in her essays, it is also a way to prevent the self-disintegration that is one of her greatest fears. She also neglects to mention the ways in which writers empower their readers. Nearly all of the authors she cites in *The Year of Magical Thinking* heighten her understanding of grief and bereavement, knowledge for which she is desperately searching. Writing is also an act of affirmation, as Flannery O'Connor observed: "People without hope do not write novels. Writing a novel is a terrible experience, during which the hair often falls out and the teeth decay. . . . [Writing] is a plunge into reality and it's very shocking to the system. . . . People without hope not only don't write novels, but what is more to the point, they don't read them" (79).

Didion's belief that writers are always selling somebody out raises other troubling questions, including whether writers are selling readers out. There are many ways to betray readers—by not telling the truth, by telling only part of the truth, or by deceiving oneself and therefore deceiving one's readers. Other questions come to mind. In "On Keeping a Notebook," one of the most significant essays in *Slouching towards Bethlehem*, Didion analyzes the motivation behind her writing and the kind of truthtelling to which she is committed. The impulse to write, she suggests, "is a peculiarly compulsive one, inexplicable to those who do not share it, useful only accidentally, only secondarily, in the way that any compulsion tries to justify itself" (132). If writing is mainly a compulsion, does that imply the writer's lack of agency? She does not answer this question. Are writers beset by neurotic conflicts? She seems to imply this. She admits that she has felt compelled to write since she was five years old, and she then informs us that her young daughter will probably never be a writer—not because of a lack of ability but because of a lack of need: "She is a singularly blessed and accepting child, delighted with life exactly as life presents itself to her, unafraid to go to sleep and unafraid to wake up. Keepers of private notebooks are a different breed altogether, lonely and resistant rearrangers of things, anxious malcontents, children afflicted apparently at birth with some presentiment of loss" (132–33).

"Some presentiment of loss": already we can see a foreshadowing of *The Year of Magical Thinking*, along with the terror that is palpable throughout her fictional and nonfictional writings. She elaborates on this feeling in another essay in *Slouching towards Bethlehem* when she identifies with Michael Laski, a Marxist revolutionary who lives outside the political system and who experiences a dread so intense that he turns to "extreme and doomed commitments." She then explains why she feels "comfortable" with such people. "I know something about dread myself, and appreciate the elaborate systems with which some people manage to fill the void, appreciate all the opiates of the people, whether they are as accessible as alcohol and heroin and promiscuity or as hard to come by as faith in God or History" (63). Didion never reveals the origins of her own dread, but she does reveal her need to write, though without implying that literary creativity is an extreme and doomed commitment. "I am still committed to the idea that the ability to think for one's self depends upon one's mastery of the language" (123). Despite paralyzing bouts of writer's block, she remains committed to truthtelling, which is why she keeps a notebook in which she records not factual but subjective reality, how something feels to her. The commitment to subjective reality, she explains, provokes members of her family to reprimand her for not telling the truth, by which they mean "objective truth"—a criticism she readily accepts. "Very likely they are right, for not only have I always had trouble distinguishing between what happened and what merely might have happened, but I remain unconvinced that the distinction, for my purposes, matters" (134).

The essays in *Slouching towards Bethlehem* reveal Didion's admittedly subjective reality, for they seem closer to the entries of a private notebook than to reportage. Among the most personal essays are "On Going Home" and "Goodbye to All That." She opens the former by telling us she is going "home," not to the place in Los Angeles where she, her husband, and their one-year-old daughter live, but to Sacramento in the Central Valley of California where she was raised. Intimating insurmountable cultural differences between her brother and husband, she states that the former refers to the latter as "Joan's husband," and she then concludes, startlingly: "Marriage is the classic betrayal." She immediately qualifies herself, suggesting this is no longer true. Her next statement, however, is only slightly less cynical. "Sometimes I think that those of us who are now in our thirties were born into the last generation to carry the burden of 'home,' to find in family life the source of all tension and drama" (165). She seems distinctly ambivalent toward her own family and childhood. On the one hand, she concedes that she had a "normal" and "happy" family life; on the other hand, she confesses that she was "almost thirty years old before I could talk to my family on the telephone without crying after I had hung up. We did not fight. Nothing was wrong. And yet some nameless anxiety colored the emotional charges between me and the place that I came from" (165). She then hopes that her open and trusting daughter will be spared from the "ambushes of family life" (167). In "Goodbye to All That" she writes about a grim period in her life when she was twenty-eight. "I hurt the people I cared about, and insulted those I did not. I cut myself off from the one person who was closer to me than any other. I cried until I was not even aware when I was crying and when I was not, cried in elevators and in taxis and in Chinese laundries, and when I went to the doctor he said only that I seemed depressed, and should see a 'specialist.' He wrote down a psychiatrist's name and address for me, but I did not go" (237).

Instead, she married—"which as it turned out was a very good thing to do but badly timed" (*Slouching towards Bethlehem* 237). The symptoms of depression continued, though she does not attempt to analyze their causes. Nor does she describe her husband's state of mind during this time. We recall from *Vegas* that Dunne describes the symptoms of his own midlife crisis during this time as an obsession with death, feelings of professional worthlessness, and interpersonal anger; he characterizes his home life as the "familiar season of discontent." Didion's depression manifests itself differently: there is the same feeling of low self-esteem, but she describes feeling isolated, trapped, and "paralyzed by the neurotic lassitude engendered by meeting one's past at every turn, around every corner, inside every cupboard" (166). *Slouching towards Bethlehem* ends inconclusively, with no indication that things have stopped falling apart. Three years have passed since her wedding, and she and her husband now live in Los Angeles. There is a hint of lyricism in the last paragraph, when she describes seeing the moon on the Pacific and smelling the jasmine as they return to California, but she never intimates that her personal or professional tensions have been resolved.

The White Album

The White Album (1979) opens with perhaps Joan Didion's most famous statement—"We tell ourselves stories in order to live" (11), which she later used as the title of her 2006 collection of nonfiction. The affirmative sentence is immediately undercut, however, in the second paragraph, when she reveals that from 1966 to 1971 she began to "doubt the premises of all the stories I had ever told myself, a common condition but one I found troubling." Although she appeared, outwardly, at least, a "competent enough" member of her community, citing several examples of her achievements and honors during these five years, she sensed that something was wrong with her or with her life. "I was meant to know the plot, but all I knew was what I saw: flash pictures in variable sequence, images with no 'meaning' beyond their temporary arrangement, not a movie but a cutting-room experience" (13).

The most revealing flash cut in *The White Album*—indeed, the most candid self-disclosure anywhere in Didion's writings—occurs when she describes, in a nearly four-hundred-word italicized passage, a psychiatrist's report written in the summer of 1968. The report, based on four tests she took when she entered the outpatient psychiatric clinic at Saint John's Hospital in Santa Monica for an attack of vertigo and nausea, characterizes her as a "personality in process of deterioration with abundant signs of failing defenses and increasing inability of the ego to mediate the world of reality and to cope with normal stress" (14).

The report details her emotional alienation; her fantasy life, "virtually completely preempted by primitive, regressive libidinal preoccupations many of which are distorted and bizarre"; and her defense mechanisms, including "intellectualization, obsessive-compulsive devices, projection, reaction-formation, and somatization, all of which now seem inadequate to their task of controlling or containing an underlying psychotic process and are therefore in process of failure" (14). The patient's responses to the four tests—the Rorschach, the Thematic Apperception Test, the sentence completion test, and the Minnesota Multiphasic Personality Inventory—are "highly unconventional and frequently bizarre," filled with "sexual and anatomical preoccupations," and her "basic reality contact is obviously and seriously impaired at times" (14). According to the report, the patient has a "superior intelligence," but she is "now functioning intellectually in impaired fashion at barely average level" (14). Emphasizing her "fundamentally pessimistic, fatalistic, and depressive view of the world around her," the report concludes with a statement that has both existential and psychiatric implications: "It is as though she feels deeply that all human effort is foredoomed to failure, a conviction which seems to push her further into a dependent, passive withdrawal. In her view she lives in a world of people moved by strange, conflicted, poorly comprehended, and, above all, devious motivations which commit them inevitably to conflict and failure" (14–15).

How do we interpret Didion's psychiatric profile? Do we read it straightforwardly, as an indication that her life was so out of control during this period that it was a miracle she could still function—as if she were writing her own version of *Vegas*? Or do we read it ironically, as an example of how out of touch psychiatry was in the 1960s? Or might there be a degree of truth in both readings? If this passage appeared in *Lolita*, there would be no question that Nabokov was mocking Freud, the "Viennese witch doctor." The difference between therapist and the rapist, Humbert avers in *Lolita*, with his creator's approval, is a matter of spacing. If this passage appeared in *One Flew over the Cuckoo's Nest*, we would interpret it as a statement about a "mad society" against which the inmates like Randall McMurphy and Chief Bromden would be justified in rebelling, a reading that R. D. Laing would endorse in his influential antipsychiatric text *The Divided Self*. Is Didion ridiculing the mental health profession, which in the 1960s enjoyed the height of its power and prestige? If this passage appeared in Doris Lessing's novel *The Golden Notebook*, we could see how writing about a psychological breakdown is one of the best ways to heal the splits and false dichotomies within the self. Didion's statement in *The White Album* that Lessing looms through the novel "as a woman driven by doubts not only about what to tell but about the validity of telling it at all" (125) describes herself as well.

Nowhere in Didion's writings do we see her in the process of self-deterioration, not even in *The Year of Magical Thinking*, where she *tells* us that she was "incapable of thinking rationally" (35) but *shows* us remarkable self-control. A social worker describes her, minutes after Dunne's death, as a "pretty cool customer" (15), and though she later repeats this comment three times, each time with the intention of ironically undercutting it, she remains composed. Her novels do not reveal a fantasy life filled with distorted and bizarre libidinal preoccupations—though this characterization is true of her *husband's* novels, which record his sexual and anatomical preoccupations. And yet there is one striking way in which the psychiatric report is true: throughout Didion's writings her vision has remained "fundamentally pessimistic, fatalistic, and depressive." Many of her novels and essays are undeniably dark, stark, and bleak. For this reason, it is startling to hear her observe toward the end of *The Year of Magical Thinking* that her impression of herself "had been of someone who could look for, and find, the upside in any situation. I had believed in the logic of popular songs. I had looked for the silver lining" (171).

However she viewed it at the time, the psychiatric report is now one of the narratives that no longer make sense to Didion, if it ever did. It is not a story she tells herself in order to live. The psychiatric report is a counterstory she must resist if she is to continue to live and write. Indeed, if she felt, as the report claims, that "all effort is foredoomed to failure," then she would not have written *The White Album*. However depressed she may have been during this time—she tells us that during these years she published two books, wrote magazine articles twice a month, fulfilled all her responsibilities as wife and mother, and was even named in 1968 a *Los Angeles Times* "Woman of the Year"—she was not only clearly functioning but also astonishingly creative.

Didion reveals in *The White Album* other debilitating illnesses from which she suffered during this time, including recurrent migraine headaches so severe that they would make her "insensible to the world around me" (168). These migraines began when she was eight years old and intensified when she was in her thirties. Migraines, she writes, are "central to the given of my life" (168). "That no one dies of migraines seems, to someone deep into an attack, an ambiguous blessing" (171). Without medication, she would be able to function perhaps one day in four; even with medication, the only remedy is to take to bed immediately and wait until it passes. Her husband also suffers from migraines, she informs us, "which is unfortunate for him but fortunate for me: perhaps nothing so tends to prolong an attack as the accusing eye of someone who has never had a headache" (171). The other illness she mentions during the late 1960s was a series of visual disturbances that a neurologist diagnosed as multiple sclerosis, a chronic disease of the central nervous system. To my knowledge, Didion never refers to this disease in her later writings, suggesting either that she was misdiagnosed or that the illness has not progressed.

Run River and *Play It as It Lays*

The two books Didion published between 1966 and 1971, the years when she doubted the premises of the stories she told herself, were *Slouching towards Bethlehem* and her second novel, *Play It as It Lays*, published in 1970. She doesn't discuss her first novel, *Run River*, published in 1963, but we can see in this story a movement toward self-disintegration. The female characters in both novels reveal some of the symptoms described in the psychiatric report—estrangement from the world and oneself, a tenuous hold on reality, a depressive worldview, and the conviction that all human effort is foredoomed to failure.

Not that the two main female characters in *Run River*, Lily Knight McClellan and her sister-in-law, Martha McClellan, are authorial in the way that Des Spellacy and Jack Crawford are to Dunne. The two women are not capable of writing a story about their lives, as Des and Jack could write about their own lives if they wished. Nor do Lily and Martha see life through Didion's nuanced vision of sympathy and criticism, as Des and Jack embody Dunne's vision. Rather, the novelist projects upon Lily and Martha personality traits with which she is intimately familiar. Set in the Central Valley of California, where Didion grew up, *Run River* focuses on two families descended from nineteenth-century pioneers. Lily, the compliant daughter of a prominent state senator, marries Everett McClellan, a Stanford graduate who decides to return to his large family estate near Sacramento to make his fortune growing hops. His sister, Martha, is as rebellious as Lily is conformist. Martha knows what she doesn't want, a life like that of her family, but she hasn't found anyone or anything to which she can commit herself. Early in the story Martha is reading Burton's *The Anatomy of Melancholy*, listed as number twenty-two on Everett's college reading list. "Melancholia's one study you don't need any lessons in," her father sarcastically shouts to her (59)—a statement that can also be applied to Didion.

Lily, too, is a depressive, even before she makes a disastrous marriage to Everett. After her father and his girlfriend are killed in an auto accident, Lily sinks into a depression that not even medication can help. Everything in *Run River* falls apart, including Lily and Everett's marriage and Martha's hope of finding meaning in her life. Each character is a prisoner of self-absorption, condemned to brood over past grievances that can be neither forgotten nor forgiven. Martha drowns at the end of the novel in a boating accident on the flooded river, and Everett, deranged by grief, kills Ryder Channing, who has had affairs with both Martha and Lily. He then turns the gun on himself.

Didion's next novel, *Play It as It Lays*, offers a memorable portrait of a woman numbed by grief and loss. Maria Wyeth is thirty-one years old, an actress married to film director Carter Lang, and the mother of a four-year-old daughter, Kate, who is hospitalized for a brain disease that is never fully disclosed. "I talk about Kate to no one here," Maria confides as the story opens. "In the place where Kate is they put electrodes on her head and needles in her spine and try to figure out what went wrong. . . . Kate has soft down on her spine and an aberrant chemical in her brain. Kate is Kate. Carter could not remember the soft down on her spine or he would not let them put needles there" (2–3). Throughout the story she mourns the loss of her child, whose illness she regards as permanent and incurable. Maria's grief transforms her into a helpless child: "she went upstairs and lay face down on Kate's empty bed, cradled Kate's blanket, clutched Kate's baby pillow to her stomach and fought off a wave of the dread" (21).

Everything in Maria's life is falling apart, including her marriage and acting career. She embodies the dread and atomization Didion discusses in *Slouching towards Bethlehem*. Maria is a catastrophizer, always expecting the worst. "She realized that she expected to die. All along she had expected to die, as surely as she expected that planes would crash if she boarded them in bad spirit, as unquestionably as she believed that loveless marriage ended in cancer of the cervix and equivocal adultery in fatal accidents to children. Maria did not particularly believe in rewards, only in punishments, swift and personal" (*Play It as It Lays* 72). To add to her troubles, she is pregnant without knowing the father of her child, and she consents to an abortion only because her husband threatens to take Kate away from her. Maria embodies a radical disconnection that cuts her off from everyone and everything. She is horrified by her mother's death in the desert, her daughter's endless screams, and her aborted baby. Apocalyptic violence, however, strangely comforts her. The "notion of general devastation," whether caused by an earth slide, flood, or prediction of a massive earthquake, "had for Maria a certain sedative effect," suggesting an "instant in which all anxieties would be abruptly gratified" (104).

Among Maria's most intriguing qualities that unite her with the novelist is her mystical apprehension of the universe. One of these moments occurs toward the end of the story when she finds herself "thinking constantly about where her body stopped and the air began, about the exact point in space and time that was the difference between *Maria* and *other*" (171–72). She seems to have an almost supernatural extrasensory perception. "She began to feel the pressure of Hoover Dam, there on the desert, began to feel the pressure and pull of the water. When the pressure got great enough she drove out there. All that day she felt the power surging through her own body. All day she was faint with vertigo" (172). The reference to vertigo reminds us of the flash cut in *The White Album* when Didion tells us about the attack of vertigo and nausea that compelled her to enter the outpatient psychiatric clinic of Saint John's Hospital. We may also recall Dunne's description in *Vegas* about the headache his wife experiences when she reads a French cookbook: "The particular rhythm of the sentences. They upset my alpha waves" (11).

Not that Maria may be equated with her creator. Rather, Didion knows her character well, and she projects some of her own perceptions and sensitivities onto her. Ellen G. Friedman's observation that "Didion's work mirrors a melancholy and deprived world, a world that is without joy, suspicious of good works and optimism" (90) applies to Maria and many other characters in Didion's stories, including those in *The Year of Magical Thinking*. Maria has, in the words of her husband's friend, a "very self-destructive personality structure" (*Play It as It Lays* 157), but there is no evidence from Didion's psychiatric report nor from her own writings that she herself was suicidal. As I was nearing the end of the novel, I recall predicting that Maria would commit suicide. She unexpectedly survives at the end, though she enables another character, film producer BZ, to commit suicide by taking a fatal overdose of Seconal. Her reasons for declining to take her own life are never entirely clear, yet she has surprising strength and resiliency, as Didion suggests in the *Paris Review* interview. "There was a certain tendency to read *Play It as It Lays* as an autobiographical novel, I suppose because I lived out here and looked skinny in photographs and nobody knew anything else about me. Actually, the only thing Maria and I have in common is an occasional inflection, which I picked up from her, not vice versa—when I was writing the book. I like Maria a lot. Maria was very strong, very tough." Didion observes that only after finishing *Play It as It Lays* did she realize she had written the same ending as in *Run River*: "The women let the men commit suicide" (Kuehl 153).

Rereading *Play It as It Lays* after reading *The Year of Magical Thinking*, one is struck by a terrible irony. Maria's constant worry over her child is a constant fear in Didion's writings, long before her own daughter's death. "The death of children worries me all the time," Didion admits in the *Paris Review* interview. "It's on my mind. Even *I* know that, and I usually don't know what's on my mind. On the whole, I don't want to think too much about why I write what I write. If I know what I'm doing I don't do it, I can't do it" (Kuehl 160). To date, Didion has not created a fictional child whom readers can *see*: as the novelist acknowledges in the *Paris Review* interview, she was unable to imagine Kate as a fictional character; hence, for most of the novel, Kate is confined to a hospital. But that doesn't prevent Didion's fictional mothers from worrying about losing their children.

It is not simply the death of a child, however, that worries Didion. Nearly all novels reflect the fear of loss, but her stories reveal a heightened awareness of this theme, including *Where I Was From*, published in 2003, two years before *The Year of Magical Thinking.* Part memoir, part cultural history of California, the book offers a moving portrait of Didion's relationship with her family. She tells us early in the story that her mother usually ended telephone conversations in the middle of a sentence, partly to economize on the cost of long distance conversations, but their last phone conversation, the afternoon before her death, two weeks short of her ninety-first birthday, was different. "It did not occur to me until morning, when my brother called, that in this one last instance she had been just too frail to keep the connection." She then adds, in two staccato sentence fragments, "Maybe not just too frail. Maybe too aware of what could be the import of this particular goodbye" (204). Didion's observation about her mother's death now seems, in retrospect, strikingly prophetic of her response to her seventy-one year-old husband's death in midsentence, "There is no real way to deal with everything we lose" (225).

The Year of Magical Thinking

For the writer, however, the way to deal with loss is through writing, and that is precisely what Didion does in *The Year of Magical Thinking.* One could not have predicted she would write a book about her husband's death, but it is not surprising in retrospect that she did. In *Democracy* she quotes Kierkegaard's observation: "Life can only be understood backwards, but it must be lived forwards" (27). Another statement from the same novel, this time expressed by Didion herself, is no less striking. "When novelists speak of the unpredictability of human behavior they usually mean not unpredictability at all but a higher predictability, a more complex pattern discernible only after the fact. Examine the picture. Find the beast in the jungle, the figure in the carpet" (215).

A close reading of Didion's and Dunne's writings allows us to see the beast in the jungle, the figure in the carpet. Each had a different beast: free-floating anxiety combined with dread and a sense of foreboding for Didion, fear of a cardiac catastrophe for Dunne. He was well aware of the beast in the jungle for decades prior to his fatal heart attack, and he kept returning to this event in his books, as if writing about his fear would exorcise it. He would no doubt agree with Hemingway's response to the question whether he had an analyst: "Sure I have. Portable Corona number three. That's been my analyst" (Hotchner 152). Writing is no less therapeutic for Didion, as Michiko Kakutani pointed out in 1984. "One suspects that writing holds for her a kind of talismanic power—the process of putting her life on paper somehow helps to exorcise private demons. Writing, after all, is a means of creating a momentary stay against confusion, of making order out of disorder, understanding out of fear" (32).

Death is always a shock for relatives and friends. Dunne's medical interventions enabled him to live twenty years longer than his father, and notwithstanding her self-blame, there was nothing Didion could have done to prolong his life. For those who believe, as I do, that life is a tragedy filled with joy, *The Year of Magical Thinking* focuses largely on the former and ignores the latter. This was her choice as a writer, as well as her way of grieving, to emphasize the fundamentally pessimistic, fatalistic, and depressive view of the world around her. In doing so, she was consistent with her lifelong vision. And so she was, paradoxically, affirming agency while simultaneously following her obsessions and compulsions.

Didion's quest for control is reflected in her prose style. "The way I write is who I am, or have become," she states in *The Year of Magical Thinking* (7), and she conveys her obsessive-compulsive vision of life, always seeking but never achieving complete control, through deliberate repetition. The opening four lines of the book read more like poetry than prose, partly because they are one-line paragraphs, like so many others in the book:

> *Life changes fast.*
> *Life changes in the instant.*
> *You sit down to dinner and life as you know it ends.*
> *The question of self-pity.* (3)

In "Why I Write" Didion tells us that she uses white space as a structuring principle in *Play It as It Lays*—she tried to write a book "in which anything that happened would happen off the page, a 'white' book to which the reader would have to bring his or her own bad dreams" (7). White space is also a structuring principle in *The Year of Magical Think-*

ing. White space surrounding the short one-sentence paragraphs creates a terse, elliptical style that describes but doesn't analyze, a minimalist approach she uses effectively in many of her books. The prose style reveals a mind fixated on grief.

Despite a long history of mistrusting all forms of psychiatry and psychoanalysis, Didion quotes sympathetically several passages from "Mourning and Melancholia." She agrees with Freud that mourning is not inherently pathological and quotes the following two sentences from his essay, omitting the middle sentence: "Each single one of the memories and expectations in which the libido is bound to the object is brought up and hypercathected, and detachment of the libido is accomplished in respect of it. Why this compromise by which the command of reality is carried out piecemeal should be so extraordinarily painful is not at all easy to explain in terms of economics. It is remarkable that this painful unpleasure is taken as a matter of course by us" (*S.E.* 14:245).

Didion endorses Freud's assertion that the bereft must give up all their attachments to the deceased. She knows that memory is wrenching and likens Freud's emphasis on the "work" of grief to what she calls the "vortex," the mysterious way in which all of her memories seem to lead to her husband's death and her daughter's illness. "The way you got sideswiped was by going back" (*The Year of Magical Thinking* 53), she cautions herself, but she is unable to avoid brooding over and writing about traumatic loss. Unable to think about the past without being overwhelmed by grief, she does not have the benefit of what her husband calls in *Playland* a "lingering death," which gives "both the victim and the survivors time to prepare" (26). Still reeling from the suddenness of her husband's death, she identifies with Melanie Klein's paradoxical observation that "The mourner is in fact ill, but because this state of mind is common and seems so natural to us, we do not call mourning an illness. . . . To put my conclusion more precisely: I should say that in mourning the subject goes through a modified and transitory manic-depressive state and overcomes it" (*The Year of Magical Thinking* 34). She identifies with Freud's and Klein's statements because she now experiences the power of grief to derange the mind; she finds herself "thinking as small children think, as if my thoughts or wishes had the power to reverse the narrative, change the outcome" (35).

Didion's greatest indebtedness to Freud is his discussion of "magical thinking," which lies at the heart of *The Year of Magical Thinking.* The word "magic" appears dozens of times throughout Freud's writings, but his most important discussion of magical thinking occurs in his 1913 book *Totem and Taboo,* where he defines the "omnipotence of thought." "Primitive men and neurotics," Freud suggests, "attach a high valuation—in our eyes an *over*-valuation—to psychical acts. This attitude may plausibly be brought into relation with narcissism and regarded as an essential component of it. It may be said that in primitive men the process of thinking is still to a great extent sexualized. This is the origin of their belief in the omnipotence of thoughts, their unshakable confidence in the possibility of controlling the world and their inaccessibility to the experiences, so easily obtainable, which could teach them man's true position in the universe" (*S.E.* 13:89). Nowhere is magical thinking more evident than in the belief that we can will ourselves into saving another person from death. Magical thinking may take many forms, including the denial that death has occurred and the belief in the possibility of "undoing" or reversing death.

Didion chronicles her own year of magical thinking, and this is one of the greatest achievements of her book. "It was in fact the ordinary nature of everything preceding the event that prevented me from truly believing it had happened, absorbing it, incorporating it, getting past it" (*The Year of Magical Thinking* 4). Unlike John Bayley and Donald Hall, she does not describe how marriage has changed her life. Only rarely do we see marital joy, as when she ends the book with a memory of them swimming together in a cave in the Far East a quarter of a century earlier, Dunne telling her how to ride the waves. Nor does she describe in detail, as Bayley and Hall do, strategies for survival, perhaps because the suddenness of her husband's death has left her unprepared for the future. What we do see, however, is her continual effort to remain in control of her life during a time when she felt out of control. And it is writing that enables her to regain control, as she explains in an uncharacteristically long sentence at the beginning of her story. "This is my attempt to make sense of the period that followed, weeks and then months that cut loose any fixed idea I had ever had about death, about illness, about probability and luck, about good fortune and bad, about marriage and children and memory, about grief, about the ways in which people do and do not deal with the fact that life ends, about the shallowness of sanity, about life itself" (7). Or as she says later, more tersely: "*Read, learn, work it up, go to the literature. Information is control*" (94; emphasis in original).

Had Didion read *Beyond the Pleasure Principle*, she would have immediately agreed with one of Freud's most important theories, not his notion of an innate human "death wish," which has never received clinical or empirical support, but his repetition-compulsion principle: the need to repeat traumatic events to master them. This compulsion to repeat, to convert an intolerable passive situation into active mastery, is more instinctual than the pleasure principle that it overrides. She does not discuss the repetition-compulsion principle, but she recognizes its presence in *Dutch Shea, Jr.*, when Dunne's eponymous character relives his daughter's horrific death. "I now see what I failed to see in 1982, the year *Dutch Shea, Jr.* was published: this was a novel about grief. The literature would have said that Dutch Shea was undergoing pathological bereavement. The diagnostic signs would have been these: He is obsessed with the moment Cat died. He plays and replays the scene, as if rerunning it could reveal a different ending" (*The Year of Magical Thinking* 51). No less than Dutch Shea, or Donald Hall, Didion replays her loved one's death again and again, as if by doing so she can reverse it, undo it. When her magical thinking fails to bring him back to life, she does the next best thing: she writes a book about her confusion following unexpected loss, transforming his corporeal absence into linguistic presence.

Believing, with Freud, that knowledge is power, Didion researches the subject of mourning and bereavement as if it were a doctoral dissertation, complete with full bibliographical citations, and she reads many of the same books that I did after my wife's death. She begins with Philippe Ariès's *The Hour of Our Death*, which points out that the main characteristic of death in the *Chanson de Roland* is that death usually gives advance warning. "Gawain is asked: 'Ah, good my lord, think you then so soon to die?' Gawain answers: 'I tell you that I shall not live two days'" (*The Year of Magical Thinking* 26). This statement appears like a leitmotif throughout her book. She next quotes Eric Lindemann's 1944 study describing the physical symptoms of illness experienced by grievers, including tightness in the throat and choking, both of which afflict Didion herself. Then she cites Geoffrey Gorer's 1965 book *Death, Grief, and Mourning in Contemporary Britain*, which discusses the changing cultural rituals of bereavement. She quotes Gorer's observation about the dangerous trend in both England and the United State to "treat mourning as morbid self-indulgence" (*The Year of Magical Thinking* 60). She might have quoted a more significant statement by Gorer: "At present death and mourning are treated with much the same prudery as sexual impulses were a century ago" (Gorer 111). She also quotes Sherwin Nuland's graphic *How We Die* to describe, in Nuland's words, how a cardiac patient's eyes "become unresponsive to light and then widen until they are large fixed circles of impenetrable blackness" (*The Year of Magical Thinking* 90).

Not all of Didion's references to the published research on grief and bereavement are sympathetic, however. She is most critical of Vamik D. Volkan, a professor of psychiatry at the University of Virginia who has devised a treatment for "pathological mourners" called "re-grief therapy" in which a patient is encouraged to "keep the lost one alive." She reacts defensively to Volkan's therapeutic strategy, as if he were blaming her for Dunne's death and Quintana's illness, and she demands to know whether he was there when she did everything she could to help her family. She becomes furious with Volkan, then catches herself, stops, and acknowledges her "irrational anger toward him" (*The Year of Magical Thinking* 56–57). Her anger toward Volkan and his re-grief therapy recalls her unsympathetic portrayal of psychiatry in *The White Album*, when she quotes her own psychiatric report. No psychotherapist in any of Didion's fictional stories offers real help or insight.

Some of Volkan's statements, however, make sense. He finds that ambivalence toward the dead is a central element among pathological mourners, something that is true for Didion's and Dunne's fictional characters. He also finds that the pathological mourner "invests some objects with magical and symbolical powers that permit a link with the dead" (Volkan, "'Re-Grief' Therapy" 336), which is also true for Didion's and Dunne's fictional characters. Several of Volkan's clinical observations are borne out in *The Year of Magical Thinking*. Volkan stresses the importance of funeral rites, including seeing a coffin lowered into the ground, as a way to accept the finality of death. Didion has Dunne's body cremated, and his ashes are then ceremonially placed in the Cathedral Church of Saint John the Divine in New York City during a memorial service attended by a Catholic priest and an Episcopal priest. Volkan also recognizes the power of magical thinking, which is Didion's central thesis in her memoir. "Since the established pathological mourner is in a state of chronic hope (as well as dread) of reunion with the dead, we help him, during the first phase of this therapy, to make rational distinctions between what actually belongs to himself and what actually belongs to the one he has lost" ("'Re-Grief' Therapy" 337). In a later article, Volkan returns to the subject of complicated grief, exploring how it may be the inspiration for creativity. "Complicated mourning still remains in such individuals, but now is expressed in art. It is not proper to refer to someone who created such a thing as the Taj Mahal as 'pathological'" ("Individuals and Societies" 51). To his credit, Volkan never attempts to pathologize art.

Why Didion's anger toward Volkan? She accepts the distinction he and other clinicians make between "uncomplicated" and "complicated" (or "pathological") grief, and she has no difficulty characterizing Dutch Shea Jr.'s response to his daughter's violent death as "pathological bereavement." But it is easier to attribute complicated grief to a fictional character than to oneself. Significantly, when Didion discusses complicated grief she dwells on one of its major causes, the survivor's unusual dependence on the deceased spouse, but she ignores another major cause, emotional ambivalence. And yet her tendency toward self-blame is one of the major symptoms of emotional ambivalence. Examples of self-blame abound in *The Year of Magical Thinking.* She consents to an autopsy out of the mistaken belief that his death might have been preventable, and then she worries that he will not be able to return to life if his organs have been removed. She relives every mistake and, more ominously, converts every action and nonaction into a mistake. She worries about how he will judge her if he reappears. She tells us repeatedly that she failed to appreciate the significance of her husband's premonitions of death, as if a different response on her part would have led to a different outcome. Didion does not refer to John Bowlby's research on attachment behavior, but two of the four examples he cites of "pathological variants of adult mourning" characterize *The Year of Magical Thinking*: "unconscious reproach against the lost person, combined with conscious and often unremitting self-reproach," and "persistent disbelief that the loss is permanent" (*Loss* 15–16).

We see remarkably little if any ambivalence in Lewis's, Bayley's, and Hall's memoirs of their spouses; Didion's ambivalence toward her spouse is apparent. This ambivalence affects her comments about him as a writer. She quotes his statement shortly before his death that "everything he had done . . . was worthless" (81), never reminding us that he was one of the most accomplished writers of his generation. At times her self-blame and guilt seem all-consuming. She may also have felt guilty that the "novelist" in her took precedence over the wife. If so, she should recall her tough-minded advice to Dunne in *Vegas* that he should go on a date with a nineteen-year-old because it's "research." In other words, the writer must do whatever it takes to get the story. There may be another meaning behind Didion's tendency toward self-blame in *The Year of Magical Thinking.* Freud interpreted "moral masochism" as the superego's need to punish the ego for Oedipal fantasies, real or imaginary, but contemporary relational psychoanalysts view masochism differently, as a pre-Oedipal response to separation from the mother. Turning pleasure into pain and pain into pleasure, masochists remain dependent on the other while simultaneously controlling the other. An author's self-inflicted pain usually has the effect of awakening the reader's sympathy, especially when the self-blame has little or no basis in reality. Masochism is, paradoxically, both a denial and confirmation of the power of omnipotent fantasy—another manifestation of magical thinking. Most readers will feel an enormous outpouring of support for Didion, who has suffered two grievous losses, but some readers may feel she manipulates them into sympathy. Recall her statement in the *Paris Review* interview that the act of setting words on paper "is the tactic of a secret bully, an invasion, an imposition of the writer's sensibility on the reader's most private space." Her view of writing as an "aggressive and hostile act toward myself" suggests a sadomasochistic view of literary creativity, one that I find inherently troubling.

Didion derives comfort and knowledge not from the psychotherapists, whose jargon-filled language offends her, but from literary writers. No surprise here. She mentions C. S. Lewis's *A Grief Observed*, written immediately after his wife's death from cancer. Unlike Lewis, her spouse's death did not precipitate a religious crisis—she had lost her religious faith decades earlier. She also refers to Thomas Mann's *The Magic Mountain* to see how Hermann Castorp reacted to his wife's death. Not well, as Mann writes: "His spirit was troubled; he shrank within himself; his benumbed brain made him blunder in his business, so that the firm of Castorp and Son suffered sensible financial losses; and the next spring, while inspecting warehouses on the windy landing-stage, he got inflammation of the lungs. The fever was too much for his shaken heart, and in five days, notwithstanding all Dr. Heidekind's care, he died" (*The Year of Magical Thinking* 44). Didion discovers what thanatologists have observed for years: widows and widowers suffer a much greater incidence of serious illness and premature death than those whose spouses are still alive. She also quotes Auden's poem "Funeral Blues," which depicts the grim reaper's power to disrupt every aspect of life, and *Leftover Life to Kill*, Caitlin Thomas's memoir about life after her poet-husband's death. "I remember being dismissive of, even censorious about, her 'self-pity,' her 'whining,' her 'dwelling on it.' *Leftover Life to Kill* was published in 1957. I was twenty-two years old. Time is the school in which we learn" (*The Year of Magical Thinking* 198).

Surprisingly, Didion is moved by the pragmatic wisdom of Emily Post, whose 1922 book of etiquette "spoke to" her when she read it on the Internet. She quotes several sentences from the section on "Funerals," including how to sit inconspicuously in the rear of a church during a funeral service and how to comfort the bereaved. "Those who are in great distress want no food, but if it is handed to them, they will mechanically take it, and something warm to start digestion and stimulate impaired circulation is what they most need"—to which Didion responds, "There was something arresting about the matter-of-fact wisdom here, the instinctive understanding of the physiological disruptions" (*The Year of Magical Thinking* 59). I also found such practical information useful. In *Dying to Teach* I quoted with amusement a statement by Katherine Ashenburg in her book *The Mourner's Dance*: "Caterers will tell you that people eat much more at a funeral than at a wedding" (Ashenburg 25).

The most revealing of Didion's literary references is her discussion of Euripides's *Alcestis*, a play which she had first read when she was sixteen or seventeen and then decided to reread following her husband's death. After giving a brief summary of the play—a young king, Admetus, has been sentenced to death but then persuades his wife, Alcestis, to take his place—Didion elaborates on the guilt, shame, and self-pity he later experiences. The play ends happily—Alcestis is restored to life, though through a clumsy plot device, she is not able to speak. Didion misremembered the ending, judging Alcestis's silence as deliberate, suggestive of the anger or indignation over being talked into sacrificing her life for another person. Didion's misremembered ending, she believes, is in some ways a "better (more 'worked out') story, one that at least acknowledges that death 'changes' the one who has died, but it opens up further questions about the divide. If the dead were truly to come back, what would they come back knowing? Could we face them? We who allowed them to die? The clear light of day tells me that I did not allow John to die, that I did not have that power, but do I believe that? Does he?" (*The Year of Magical Thinking* 152).

Didion never tells us whether she wondered how her husband would feel reading *The Year of Magical Thinking*, nor does she tell us how she feels now that she has completed the book. Other questions linger. Does she still believe that writers are always selling somebody out—and, if so, whom has she betrayed? To what extent did writing the book help her recovery? As she crosses Lexington Avenue in Manhattan exactly one day and a year after Dunne's death, she reaches two noteworthy conclusions, both of which signal the end of her year of magical thinking. "I know why we try to keep the dead alive: we try to keep them alive in order to keep them with us. I also know that if we are to live ourselves there comes a point at which we must relinquish the dead, let them go, keep them dead" (225–26). She accepts Freud's belief that we must let go of the dead, never considering the view held by contemporary continuing bonds theorists that it may be therapeutically helpful to maintain a relationship with the dead. We see in *The Year of Magical Thinking*, as we do in John Bayley's and Donald Hall's memoirs, some evidence for the dual process model of coping with bereavement. That is, we see both loss-oriented coping, which includes rumination about the deceased and the circumstances surrounding the death, and restoration-oriented coping, which includes taking care of oneself and developing a new identity as a widow or widower. "At times the bereaved will be confronted by their loss, at other times they will avoid memories, be distracted, or seek relief by concentration on other things" (Stroebe and Schut 215–16). Didion's decision to write *The Year of Magical Thinking*—researching the vast literature of bereavement, recording the details of her husband's death, reflecting on their lives together, discussing his books, imagining her life without him, and creating a narrative with a forward movement—reveals both loss-oriented and restoration-oriented coping. Ironically, despite her decision to "relinquish the dead," she remains closely attached to the memory of her husband through the countless interviews she has given on *The Year of Magical Thinking* and through her active participation in the Broadway play based on her memoir. Writing the memoir and the screenplay reveals her effort to keep alive his memory as well as her attempt to move forward in the process of bereavement.

Didion tells us near the end of *The Year of Magical Thinking* that she does not want to finish the book, perhaps because she does not know what to do afterward. What will her life be like after her husband's death? She hints obliquely that Dunne himself raised this question repeatedly: What will she do with her life "*when something happens to me,*" he euphemistically asks her. "Nothing will happen to you, I would say" (196; emphasis in original). She refuses to answer his question, and he then offers his own unsolicited advice. "*If it does*, he would continue. If it did, for example, I was not to move to a smaller apartment. If it did I would be surrounded by people. If it did I would need to make plans to feed these people. If it did I would marry again within the year." Understandably dismayed, she responds, "*You don't understand*" (*The Year of Magical Thinking* 196–97; emphasis in original). The first three injunctions are vastly different from the fourth one. Did he actually wish her to remarry within one year? It's hard to imagine anyone seriously offering this advice to a spouse, and it's even harder to imagine a widow or widower acting on this advice without feeling survivor or recovery guilt.

Didion never entirely overcomes her anger, guilt, and self-pity in *The Year of Magical Thinking.* Nor is this surprising, since bereavement of a lost spouse is often a lifelong process. How could it not be? She is too honest a writer to gloss over these vexing emotions. Nor does she attempt to resolve her grief or contemplate a future without her husband, as Thomas Larson notes: "Didion intrudes into the story with so much self-doubt and so many questions that, despite the progression of the unfolding year, there's no closure" (46). At the beginning of the book she confesses that she is "not the ideal teller" of the story, but there is no ideal teller for any story, particularly one about sudden spousal loss. Her account of bereavement is the best she could write under the circumstances. Indeed, no spousal loss memoir is more successful in capturing the complexities of magical thinking, the sense of shock, bewilderment, disbelief, and denial arising from sudden loss. For a writer who claims she was unable to read an obituary months after her husband's death, it is remarkable that she completes the book in a year. *The Year of Magical Thinking* captures the immediacy of sudden loss, when one is overcome by emotions; because it was written so quickly, it does not convey the reflections on loss that come only with time.

Unlike Lewis and Bayley, Didion does not describe the movement from companionship in grief to companionship in joy, but she does show how the process of writing can help the bereaved. However grief-stricken Didion was, she needed to write about her experience, and in doing so, she demonstrates, almost against her own self-perception, that she has regained a degree of control over her life. In the process, she helps to educate the reading public about the process of spousal bereavement. As Peter D. Kramer suggests in an October 17, 2005, review in *Slate*, Didion's memoir "may do for grief what William Styron's *Darkness Visible* did for depression." Didion has always been a highly intellectual writer, tightly in control of her emotions, a pretty cool customer, as the social worker observed, one who sees irony everywhere. Her memoir is emotionally charged in ways that her more cerebral novels are not. If, as she asserts, she was "born fearful," believing that "some events in life would remain beyond my ability to control or manage them" (*The Year of Magical Thinking* 98), when writing the memoir she was able to call upon resources that she may not have thought she had. These writerly resources have never failed her, including the belief that knowledge is power. *The Year of Magical Thinking* is fascinating for what it reveals and conceals about a celebrated literary marriage in which both wife and husband take turns in writing about each other's lives and, in the case of John Gregory Dunne, death. Unable to prevent her husband from dying, Didion writes a memoir that affirms the haunting title of his last novel, *Nothing Lost*, and in doing so, she becomes one of those writers on whom nothing is lost.

FIVE

CALVIN TRILLIN AND ALICE STEWART TRILLIN

"I Wrote Everything for Alice"

Calvin Trillin, the popular *New Yorker* humorist, food critic, journalist, and novelist, described by the *Boston Globe* as "America's quietest great writer," has written more than twenty books on wide-ranging topics, but the subject to which he returns repeatedly is his beloved wife, Alice Stewart Trillin. Her name appears in the titles of two of his books, *Alice, Let's Eat*, published in 1978, and *Travels with Alice*, appearing in 1989. She—and sometimes their two daughters—is the dedicatee of several other books, including his 2001 novel *Tepper Isn't Going Out*: "I wrote this for Alice. Actually, I wrote everything for Alice." The dedication is poignant, for in the same year, on September 11—the day of the infamous terrorist attacks against the United States—she died, at the age of sixty-three. Trillin's memoir of spousal loss, *About Alice*, a slender volume of seventy-eight pages that first appeared in the March 27, 2006, issue of the *New Yorker*, was published later that year. As he notes, the headline on her *New York Times* obituary described her as "Educator, Author and Muse" (16). It is clear from his writings that she was indeed the major inspiration in his life and art.

Many grateful readers sent condolence cards to Trillin asserting that they knew his wife from his writings. They may have known the Alice starring in his often sitcom-like writings about her, but they didn't know the real woman, who was far more complex than the caricature appearing in his books. A fuller portrait emerges in her own writings. She wrote about her experiences with illness in two revealing essays and a children's book. "Of Dragons and Garden Peas" appeared in a 1981 issue of the *New England Journal of Medicine* and focused on her experience as a lung cancer patient. She later published a children's book, *Dear Bruno*, in which, speaking in a simple, heartfelt voice, she expresses the fear engendered by life-threatening illness and the hope arising from medical progress from which so many patients, including herself, have benefitted. Her essay "Betting Your Life," published in the January 29, 2001, issue of the *New Yorker*, explores the terrifying medical crisis that occurred in 1990, when a bone scan indicated five portentous "lights" that seemed to be tumors. Amid the wildly conflicting advice of her physicians, some of whom urged immediate radical surgery while others recommended a cautious wait-and-see policy, her decision involved nothing less than betting her life. In all three texts she writes from the point of view of patient and survivor. She did indeed survive lung cancer, although she was given only a 10 percent chance of recovery at the time of her diagnosis. Ironically, the radiation therapy that saved her life was also responsible for weakening her heart, and she died of congestive heart failure while awaiting heart transplant surgery.

I had only a passing familiarity with Calvin Trillin—and no knowledge of Alice Stewart Trillin—until I read *About Alice*. I found the memoir moving but unsatisfying, since it tells us so little about the author's feelings about his wife's death. Unlike C. S. Lewis, John Bayley, Donald Hall, and Joan Didion, Trillin doesn't describe the impact of his spouse's illness on his life or any of the dark emotions surrounding loss. He neither observes his sorrow nor imagines companionship in grief. Unlike Joan Didion, we learn nothing about his year of magical thinking, if he had one. Why, I wondered, did he omit any mention of shock or anger or grief? How has he coped with her death? In what ways has she continued to be his muse? These questions intrigued me, and I decided to read all of his books to learn more about Trillin's life. I found the light-hearted books fun to read, but I was more interested in his "serious" books, including the two memoirs he wrote in the 1990s: *Remembering Denny* (1993), a story about a brilliant Yale classmate who unexpectedly committed suicide, and *Messages from My Father* (1996), a loving portrait of Trillin's father. These two memoirs cast much light on *About Alice*, revealing not only the importance of family to him but also the link between his past and present. After reading all of Trillin's books, I then read his wife's publications. It's fascinating to read their writings together, for they demonstrate remarkably different points of views and voices. They are both polished and graceful writers, but they are strikingly different from each other. Each reveals and conceals different aspects of the story of her illness, recovery, and relapse. What they conceal is as intriguing as what they reveal. They were fiercely protective of each other and their two daughters, which is not surprising, but they were both cautious self-disclosers, which is surprising given the subjects on which they wrote. Their writings have wide appeal, especially to those who have lost a spouse.

Trillin's first reference to his wife appears in his fourth book, *American Fried*, published in 1974. He dedicates the book to "Alice and Sarah and Abigail (who, when she was four, reacted to polishing off a particularly satisfying dish of chocolate ice cream by saying, 'My tongue is smiling'"). The book is subtitled "Adventures of a Happy Eater," but it could have also been subtitled "Adventures of a Happy Writer." The tone is playful, bantering, light-hearted; he is in love with his family, ecstatic about the joy of eating, and optimistic about life. He begins his lifelong process of mythologizing Alice as a no-nonsense woman from the East who nevertheless agrees with him that the best hamburgers in the world are served in his hometown of Kansas City—though she warns him "not to indulge in any of that hometown nostalgia while I'm eating. You know it gives me indigestion" (30). She is a stern moralist, the voice of conscience, the embodiment of restraint. In simplistic Freudian terms, he represents the claims of the id, she the demands of the superego. When he asks her "whether or not she should take advantage of having a number of immigrant Chinese students in an English class she was teaching at City College by trying to worm some restaurant information out of them," her response is curt and unambiguous: "I'm ashamed of you" (164–65).

Like her husband, Alice is a staunch social and political liberal, telling him that she had recently read in the *New York Times* that Tricia Nixon Cox's favorite recipe is chicken divan—and that the president "doesn't eat ketchup on his cottage cheese any more" (167)—which allows Trillin a few pages later to tell us about a "tense moment" arising the first time their older daughter asked for ketchup. "'How did you know about ketchup?' Alice asked, after informing her that we didn't have any. 'Those wild kids down the street probably told her,' I said. 'Maybe we oughtn't to let her play with them any more'" (170). Only a purist, we infer, a person of uncompromising taste, will ban ketchup from the kitchen in order to protect her children from adulteration. Disclosing that he is a food critic who cannot cook, Trillin is quick to give his wife credit for being a superb cook. "I'm a specialist; I just eat. Because of Alice, though, I don't even have to leave home to eat dishes—from a subtle poached salmon to a sausage concoction called Lunenberg Leftovers—that could make the average plastics salesman forget the cost of a between-the-teeth gold inlay" (169).

Alice, Let's Eat

Trillin continues his love affair with food, life, and his wife in *Alice, Let's Eat*. Once again the tone is mirthful, implying that everything is sunny in his world. The opening sentence seems to parody the subgenre of confessional narratives. "Now that it's fashionable to reveal intimate details of married life, I can state publicly that my wife, Alice, has a weird predilection for limiting our family to three meals a day. I also might as well admit that the most serious threat to our marriage came in 1975, when Alice mentioned my weight just as I was about to sit down to dinner at a New Orleans restaurant named Chez Helène" (3). She continues to be the voice of wisdom and restraint, though he concedes that she "tempers her rigidity" with a "broad view of what constitutes an hors d'oeuvre." He lists her many excellent qualities—tenacity, imagination, and generosity—while acknowledging her shortcomings: "I should also say that I consider her failure with the children half my own: no one person could be responsible for engendering in two innocent little girls a preference for frozen fish sticks over fish" (6–7). Unlike her husband, Alice is a saver rather than a spender, an exponent not of wish fulfillment but of the reality principle. She is also a tireless exposer of vanity, pretentiousness, and waste.

Reading *Alice, Let's Eat*, one would never guess that it was published the year of Alice's lung cancer diagnosis, a disclosure Trillin makes first in his 1998 book, *Family Man*, written two decades after her diagnosis, and then repeats in *About Alice*:

> The summer after her operation, I was finishing the second of what turned out to be three books about eating—a series we eventually came to refer to around the house as the tummy trilogy. The work I did on the final drafts of the book was dominated by additional

> references to Alice. . . . At the time I thought that increasing Alice's role was a way to help knit together a book. . . . Aside from trying to focus the book, though, I suppose I was conscious that spreading Alice from beginning to end in her usual George Burns role was a way of declaring, mainly to myself, that we were not accepting the prognosis that would have made her a tragic character. Also, tragic characters did not happen to be my specialty. If Alice had been married to a different sort of writer, she might have been presented in the sort of role Ali McGraw played in *Love Story*, instead of in a role she has sometimes described as 'a dietician in sensible shoes.' It does seem unfair, I told Alice years later, but we all have to construct our little stories with the tools available to us. (*Family Man* 27–28)

By revealing in *Family Man* that he—and presumably she—did not accept the prognosis of death, Trillin acknowledges a counterphobic impulse behind *Alice, Let's Eat*. Writing was a way to defy the possibility of death and master their fear of loss. And yet he did not include this revelation in *Alice, Let's Eat*, almost certainly because she was still too close to the surgery to know whether it would be successful. A quarter of a century later, however, she had withstood the test of time, and he could write about her illness and recovery.

Trillin's reference to George Burns and, by implication, his zany wife, Gracie Allen, is instructive, for not only was Alice her husband's "straight man"—the team's "George Burns"—but both men wrote and spoke a great deal about death. Trillin doesn't mention George Burns's 1991 memoir, *Gracie: A Love Story*, which conveys the theme of love and loss through death-defying humor. I read the book only after Trillin's reference to George Burns, and I was delighted by the scores of witticisms. "A lot of people ask me why I tell jokes about dying," explains Burns. "Death is part of life, and it doesn't do any good to worry about it. In fact, I once knew a man who was so worried about dying that he had a heart attack caused by worrying about having a heart attack" (117). This joke may be apocryphal, but there is a long tradition of gallows humor from which Burns borrows. His ability to modulate from the serious to the silly is evident when he tells us that "Gracie died in 1964, and I still go to Forest Lawn Cemetery once a month to see her. I stand in front of her marble monument and tell her everything that's going on in my life. I told her I was writing this book about her, for instance; evidently she didn't mind, she didn't say anything" (117–18). I never understood why, after her death, Burns closed every show with the words, "Good-night, Gracie," always with a smile on his face. After Barbara's death, however, this need for connection seems obvious to me.

The Calvin Trillin and Alice Stewart Trillin team is not precisely Burns and Allen in reverse, but there are noteworthy parallels. Gracie played the role of a ditsy blonde who deliberately confused literal and metaphorical meanings of words, and who simultaneously endorsed and poked fun at negative stereotypes of women, as we can see from this exchange in Burns's memoir. "Gracie, why should I give your mother a bushel of nuts? What'd she ever give me?" "Why George, she gave you me. And I'm as good as nuts." Her public persona was the opposite of her real personality—in life she was an intelligent, highly disciplined master artist with a perfect sense of timing and delivery. These artistic qualities enabled her to be part of the longest-running comedy team in the United States. Burns was smart enough to allow her to get the final laugh, though sometimes he could laugh at himself, as when he offers the following information about their marriage. "Sex is certainly a very important part of any marriage. Gracie and I had a wonderful life together, and a wonderful marriage, and sex was part of it, but not the major part. Probably the most important thing about sex is that it helps sell a lot of books. Fortunately Gracie married me for laughs, not for sex. Of course she got both of them—when we had sex, she laughed" (69).

Trillin *never* writes about his sexual relationship with his wife—it is one of the many subjects out of bounds for him—but he does construct his wife as a "straight man" who comments on her husband's self-indulgences. In a review of *Alice, Let's Eat* published in the *Nation*, Alice refers to herself as "someone who has been assigned the role of heavy in her husband's book," a role she relishes. Exemplary in her wisdom, compassion, and tolerance, she is an icon of human perfection: a model wife, mother, and citizen. She is his foil in countless ways: he is self-indulgent, she self-restrained; he is peevish, she amiable; he is sometimes out-of-control, she composed. And yet she never comes across as puritanical, self-righteous, or ascetic. He tells us in *About Alice* that "she saw no reason to live like a graduate student if you didn't have to" (55).

Trillin refers to Alice in several books after her lung cancer surgery. One suspects that by writing about her, he hoped he could keep her alive, cancer-free. In his books published in the 1970s and 1980s, he continues his light-hearted tone, never intimating to readers her brush with death. He describes her in his 1982 book *Uncivil Liberties* as the family intellectual, knowing, unlike him, the meaning of words like "holistic" and "heuristics." Nor is he motivated, as she feels he should be, to look up the meanings of these words in a dictionary. "I realize that passing up words like 'holistic' may strike some people as laziness or even philistinism, but I have always liked to think of it as a sort of negative act of character. The speed of trends being what it is these days, after all, about the only way a citizen can exhibit an independent spirit is to remain totally inert" (15). Is it merely a coincidence that he chooses a word that is often associated with holistic medicine, a philosophy of health based upon the whole person? He then pokes fun at Alice for not being able to spell the words *occurred* or *commitment*: "I don't mean she didn't have any; she couldn't spell it. I have never been able to spell "commitment" myself" (32). But in just about every other way she is perfect. "Alice can explain foreign movies and decipher road maps. I suspect that in a pinch she might be able to rewire a lamp" (33). She also has an astute understanding of politics, realizing that sooner or later, "every administration makes you nostalgic for the preceding one" (203–4)—an observation for which her husband takes credit in *A Heckuva Job* (4). She prefers the image of Rosalynn Carter—"pretty tough American woman in her own way"—to the smiling Nancy Reagan, who, Trillin can't avoid mentioning, "was the only one who knew the secret of how simple-minded her husband is" (206). And yet Alice has, despite her middle-class background, a natural aristocratic sensibility, which is one of the reasons Trillin refers to her in his 1983 book *Third Helpings* as *la principessa* when traveling in Italy: "I find it improves the service" (135).

Alice appears in Trillin's next book, *With All Disrespect: More Civil Unliberties*," published in 1985. In the opening chapter he asks his wife, "What if I got kidnapped and they called demanding ransom money?"—to which she pragmatically responds, "You're not going to get kidnapped. . . . Why can't you just worry about high interest rates or acid rain or The Bomb, like normal people?" (7). Later in the book, when he discusses *Forbes* magazine's list of the four hundred richest people in the United States, he confesses that his "heart went out to the person who was four hundred and first. "You must get over this," Alice replies; "It's misplaced sympathy" (70). Two pages later she declares sarcastically, "I suppose you're going to say, 'The rich are different from you and me,'" which he helpfully—and incorrectly—glosses: "She was referring, of course, to that famous exchange between two great American literary figures—when Zane Grey said to Will Rogers, 'The rich are different from you and me,' and Rogers replied, 'Yes, they don't wear cowboy boots'" (72). Only a pedant would point out that the famous literary exchange involved Hemingway cruelly making fun of Scott Fitzgerald's admiration for the wealthy. In the chapter called "Alice as Tamperer," Trillin returns to his wife's nagging concern over his weight, accusing her of making an upward adjustment of the scale that he uses to weigh himself "every year or so." Writing about these small health worries, he avoids disclosing the larger ones about which he has not yet written.

Although Trillin claims in *Family Man* that "tragic characters did not happen to be my specialty," he acknowledges in his 1984 book *Killings* the "appeal sudden death has for reporters"—at least for *this* reporter. "It gives us an excuse to be there, poking around in somebody's life" (xv)—in short, what John Gregory Dunne calls "scavenging." He admits he has "always been attracted by stories of sudden death" (ix), but the only reason he gives for this attraction is that the deaths "sounded interesting" (xi). Unlike Dunne, Trillin's fascination for murder has nothing to do with an interest in violence; rather, the stories in *Killings* "are meant to be more about how Americans live than about how some of them die" (xix). The character sketches in *Killings* could be called "human-interest stories," he adds, but he dislikes the journalistic term because it conjures up an image of a "motherly cocker spaniel adopting orphaned ducklings" (xix). He makes no mention of other types of deaths, such as from illness, for example, which also reveal how people live—a subject that he avoids even when eulogizing his wife in *About Alice.*

Trillin writes about Alice in his next two books, *If You Can't Say Something Nice*, published in 1987, and *Travels with Alice*, which appeared two years later. The title of the 1987 book refers to Alice's belief that one should observe the golden rule—not to talk (or write) negatively about other people—a rule which, if observed, would result in the end of literature. She occupies a larger role in the 1989 book in which, about to turn fifty—"what I suppose you could call a half century, although that was not a term we used regularly around the house" (185)—she remains youthful, seemingly impervious to the aging process.

Remembering Denny

Trillin doesn't write about Alice in his 1993 book *Remembering Denny*, but we learn a great deal about his own life and, indirectly, about his marriage. *Remembering Denny* is his most substantial book to that date, striking emotional chords absent from his earlier books. Part memoir, part eulogy, and part detective story, *Remembering Denny* seeks to understand the suicide of Roger D. Hansen, Trillin's Yale classmate whose future seemed so bright that friends predicted he might become president of the United States. Trillin admits that "poking around in other people's lives is nothing new for me, of course—I've done that for a living for a number of years—but ordinarily the people in question are strangers. This was something different, something quite a bit closer to those heart-to-hearts that my father—and I after him—had always tried to avoid" (67). Trillin later acknowledges that one of his major assumptions in the 1950s was that young men were sent away to college to distance themselves from their parents. That was why he was sent to Yale: so that he could achieve the American dream, something denied to his immigrant Jewish father, who struggled with his small business in Kansas City. Despite his aversion to "heart-to-hearts," both as a son and as a father, Trillin succeeds in *Remembering Denny* in probing the many reasons for his friend's suicide, in the process revealing the psychic forces that strengthen or weaken the will to live.

Only after he graduated from college did Trillin realize the central importance of family. "In fact, when I reached a certain age, around my late thirties or early forties, it even occurred to me that one elemental fact of life separating the people I knew into groups had to do with their relationship with their family of origin: those who, in one way or another, took care of their parents and those whose parents still more or less took care of them" (*Remembering Denny* 76). Denny was in neither category, and his suicide compels Trillin to meditate on the importance of parent-child relationships. Not that he had ever taken his own parents for granted. There is no evidence in any of Trillin's writings that he was ever in serious conflict with his parents. Nor did he fail to appreciate their love and support. But there were times, he admits, when he feared his identity was disappearing, especially immediately after college graduation. "I didn't know what I wanted to do, and the one thing I was clear about not wanting to do was to start being a grownup" (120). This was the time when he began to lose his direction in life, as Denny apparently did. Denny's crisis of faith arose after writing an influential book. In a passage that has the ring of authenticity, Trillin tells us that a lack of self-confidence in a writer may be fatal: "I suppose that there are endeavors in which self-confidence is even more important than it is in writing—tightrope walking comes immediately to mind—but it's difficult for me to think of anybody producing much writing if his confidence is completely shot" (162–63).

Trillin reaches no earth-shattering epiphanies about Denny's rise and fall, though he does endorse Cyril Connolly's statement that "whom the gods wish to destroy they first call promising" (*Remembering Denny* 208). Denny was one of these promising young men. The heroic values for Trillin are those derived not from the bitch-goddess success but from his father. "He raised me not to become him, of course, but it had often occurred to me that a reporter could do worse than aspire to a standard of behavior reflected in my father's approach to being a grocer—give good weight, refuse to buckle under to pressure from the chain stores, treat with contempt the wartime temptation to get rich by cutting a few corners" (166–67). Trillin's conclusion is that although his parents could not bequeath to him a "Grand Plan" for success, they endowed him with something far more important: "the security that comes from knowing for sure that they believe you to be a special case" (210).

Messages from My Father

Unlike Denny, Trillin had a happy childhood. Tolstoy's opening sentence in *Anna Karenina*—"Happy families are all alike; every unhappy family is unhappy in its own way"—is only partly correct, for happy families are always different too. If Trillin could not write seriously about his own wife and children in the 1980s and early 1990s without invading their privacy, he could write about his happy parents, especially his father, who gave him life. This is what he does in *Messages from My Father*, published in 1996, his next major book after *Remembering Denny*. The two biographical studies are thematically linked. *Messages from My Father* continues Trillin's probing investigation into the importance of family. The book is mainly about his relationship with his father and only secondarily about the author's relationship with his wife, but the two are closely connected in expected and unexpected ways. A man may marry a woman who reminds him of his mother, just as a woman may marry a man who reminds her of his father. Trillin, however, seems to have married a woman who reminds him of his father, a man who continues years after his death to exert a powerful influence on his son.

Abe Trillin moved with his family to Missouri in 1909 at the age of two. "His family—then known as Trilinsky—was from a place that was always described as 'near Kiev'" (*Messages from My Father* 7–8). Life in the hardscrabble American Midwest was only slightly better than in the old country. Abe Trillin was a second-generation grocer, and his life as a small businessman was filled with endless headaches and heartaches exacerbated by the Great Depression, which had a formative influence on his attitude toward money. He struggled financially so that his son would be able to go into another line of work. The father was proud of his Jewish heritage, which was linked inextricably to his identity, but he suspected that an ethnic name might make it more difficult for his son to pursue the American dream. He not only changed the family name but also gave his son a name that he thought, incorrectly, in his son's opinion, would be more appropriate for a Yale student. "My parents were willing to name me Calvin, but not to call me Calvin; I was known as Buddy from the start. [My sister] Sukey had also been given what my parents must have thought of as a fancy name, Elaine Sue, and it, too, was as rarely used as our dining room" *(Messages from My Father* 71). Abe Trillin began saving for his son's college education when he was a young boy. "My father's Grand Plan, I think, began with my going to Yale—not on a shoestring, but in the way the sons of the industrialists went to Yale. I would then be not simply a real American, unencumbered by poverty and Old World views, but a privileged American—an American whose degree could give him a place on some special, reservations-only escalator to success" (73).

Every portrait, Oscar Wilde quipped, is a self-portrait. If Trillin's picture of a father's unwavering belief in the American dream and the green light of success conjures up the image of a Jewish James Gatz, who reinvents himself into Jay Gatsby to win the golden girl, this story ends differently from *The Great Gatsby*. Calvin Trillin wins both the love of a beautiful woman and achieves success, not as a wealthy, unscrupulous gambler, but as an esteemed writer, a man who, unlike Fitzgerald's doomed hero, never denies his unromantic past. One reason for his success is surely his father, who bequeathed to his son family values, morality, and a wry, self-mocking humor. Trillin brings his father to life in the memoir, allowing us to see the qualities that his son admired and emulated. We see the father's unassuming dignity and strength, his lifelong devotion to work and family, his simplicity (which is never simplemindedness) and innocence. There is nothing pathetic or feeble about Abe Trillin, as there is about James Gatz's father, nothing that might awaken embarrassment or shame or resentment in a son eager for assimilation and success.

Abounding in ethnic humor, in Jewish wry, *Messages from My Father* reveals the large and small ways in which Calvin Trillin finds himself practicing his father's beliefs, including the "no kvetching" policy. "If I noticed ominous symptoms while working in the yard, I wouldn't consider it kvetching to call the doctor. On the other hand, my attitude toward kvetching is so much of a standing joke in my own family that if my daughters are complaining about something[,] they provide my response before I can open my mouth: 'I know, Daddy—'Pull up your socks'" (113). Alice also practices the no-kvetching policy. Trillin tells us in *About Alice* that rather than complain about a problem, his wife would quietly work to solve it, a characteristic he traces back to her efforts as a young woman to respond constructively to her parents' many financial problems.

Abe Trillin died in 1967 at the age of sixty, when his son and daughter-in-law were vacationing in a small resort on the coast of Kenya. "The funeral is sort of a blur now," he writes. "I do remember that in the eulogy the rabbi—the successor to Rabbi Hadas—said that when he visited my father in the hospital once and they'd had a talk about the new novel by Chaim Potok, he understood that my father wasn't truly under the impression that the author's name was Chaim Potok" (*Messages from My*

Father 108). Another writer might be embarrassed by his father's lack of literary sophistication, but Trillin is not. At his mother's request, he went to the synagogue every evening to recite kaddish, the ancient Jewish funeral prayer. "Mildly resentful at having to perform what seemed to me a public relations function, I viewed my fellow mourners—mostly men nearer my father's age—as people honoring their obligations in the most cursory way" (109). He never discloses his grief over his father's death nor his family's reaction to the loss, but there is never any doubt about the extent to which Trillin honors his father's memory in this loving memoir.

Family Man

Trillin's next book, aptly named *Family Man*, offers his fullest discussion of the subjects about which he will—and will not—write. He reveals for the first time his extreme cautiousness with respect to self-disclosure and personal writing, his refusal to sacrifice his family's privacy for the sake of art. He writes from the point of view of author, literary critic, and even, to a limited extent, psychobiographer, drawing a relationship between the writer's art and life. "There is often a connection between the way someone writes about his own family and the way he's written about the family he came from. It's common these days for memoirs of childhood to concentrate on some dark secret within the author's ostensibly happy family. I've admired some of those memoirs, but I've always known that I wouldn't be writing one of them. The material just wasn't there" (21). He recognizes that writers of these sensationalistic memoirs might be suspicious of his claim that he had a happy childhood, rejecting his published statements that he never heard his parents yell at each other. He playfully invents traumatic childhood memories only to dismiss them as fictional.

Trillin labels himself a "moderate" on the "reveal-o-meter" of self-disclosure. At one extreme are those writers "who can work in, say, a husband's sexual dysfunction or at least a daughter's humiliation at the hands of a prom date into an article whose ostensible subject is the changing American views of cranberry sauce and turkey stuffing as holiday side dishes." At the other extreme are those writers "who believe that any mention of your family in print is exploitation on the order of a lounge comic doing cheap jokes about his wife" (*Family Man* 25). Trillin points out that cultural and generational factors explain the differences in self-disclosure. "Around our house, we sometimes refer to people who are uncomfortable with writing about their private lives as 'fifties guys.' People at the other end of the spectrum are likely to have grown up at a later time or to have been raised in those small patches of the East Coast and the West Coast where anyone who does not come right out and say that he deeply resents his father for sleeping with his mother is assumed to be dissembling" (25).

Trillin doesn't identify specific writers at either end of the spectrum, nor does he indicate whether he has been criticized for being a "moderate" self-discloser. But he does elaborate on how he and his family regard his own writing. He distinguishes between his use of third person narration to write about strangers who have met violent deaths, on the one hand, and his use of first person singular to write about his father, wife, and children, on the other hand. "Alice and the girls began appearing only in lighter pieces—pieces about travel or eating or the little domestic dramas that in the American tradition (and certainly in the tradition of our family) tend to be about the manipulation of the father" (*Family Man* 25–26). The Alice persona in his books parallels the real Alice, especially with respect to her legendary restraint—"except, perhaps, when it came to ice cream." He then discloses her lung cancer diagnosis in 1976, when their girls were seven and four. Twelve years later, when she appeared to be in excellent health, he wrote a poem to her on her fiftieth birthday. Some of the stanzas of this poem he often recited in public; other stanzas he would not recite in public "because they involve matters that are for me, a fifties guy at heart, private" (*Family Man* 28). He was also protective of his children's privacy, especially when they were teenagers—always a time of heightened self-consciousness and embarrassment.

Most of Trillin's disclosures about his wife in *Family Man* are "moderate," but he makes two revealing observations. The first is that Alice has an "almost instinctual attraction for avoided subjects" (55). The example he cites reflects her interest in health issues—such as the "morbid connection between sugar and rotten teeth" that she kept bringing up during dinner with an out-of-town guest reputed to be a "sugar baron"

(55). The second is her emotional response to events such as weddings. "She cries even if the match being sanctified has long been spoken of as one that is unlikely to have much of a future. If the groom is well known as a cad, she cries anyway" (134). She even cries at school plays, he adds: "She has a weakness for any event that can be seen as one of life's landmarks" (134). He could not have known when writing *Family Man* in 1998 that Alice's fondness for life's landmarks, especially weddings, would form one of the most moving moments in *About Alice*, when he describes her joy, just days after unsuccessful heart bypass surgery, in attending her daughter Abigail's wedding.

Entertaining and enlightening, *Family Man* takes on special significance because it is the last book Trillin published before his wife's death. His comic novel *Tepper Isn't Going Out* was published in 2001, the year of her death, and contains the dedication I quoted earlier: "I wrote this for Alice. Actually, I wrote everything for Alice." His next book, *Feeding a Yen*, appeared in 2003 and contains on the title page an arresting statement that functions as both death announcement and dedication: "For more than thirty-five years, my companion at the table was my wife, Alice. Although I did once describe Alice as having 'a weird predilection for limiting our family to three meals a day,' her knowledge and enjoyment of food had a lot to do with the pleasure I took in writing about eating. Partway through this book's adventures, which took place over several years, her name no longer appears. She died in September 2001. I know she would have expected this dedication to be shared with our first grandchild, Isabelle Alice Trillin-Lee, who, as it happens, has already shown signs of being a good eater."

About Alice

Writing teachers routinely tell their students that the two most important sentences in a story are the opening and closing ones. *About Alice* opens abruptly, even startlingly, without explanatory material: "There was one condolence letter that made me laugh. Naturally, a lot of them made me cry" (5). Laughter and tears, joy and sorrow: such is the experience of life. The closing sentences strike the same tone of sorrowful joy as Trillin reminds us that his wife lived, "against horrifying odds," for twenty-five years after her cancer diagnosis. "I know what Alice, the incorrigible and ridiculous optimist, would have said about a deal that allowed her to see her girls grow up: 'Twenty-five years! I'm so lucky!' I try to think of it in those terms, too. Some days I can and some days I can't" (78). *About Alice* contains far more joy than sorrow, however, and apart from the opening and closing sentences, there are few moments of sadness. Unlike John Bayley's memoirs of Iris Murdoch and Donald Hall's memoir of Jane Kenyon, Trillin's includes few details of the ways in which illness affected his wife's life, physically or psychologically. Nor does he describe the shock and horror of unexpected death, as Joan Didion does in *The Year of Magical Thinking*. For the most part, Trillin's memoir dwells on the lighter sides of Alice's character and their marriage, though we see her seriousness as well. The memoir only hints at the darker emotions of bereavement.

Much of what we learn about Alice we have read in the earlier books, but there is enough new material to satisfy Trillin devotees. In his earlier books he implies she was his muse, but he now gives a concrete example of her literary expertise. This expertise is not surprising, since she spent a year in the graduate program in English at Yale, was an accomplished writer herself, and taught composition at two universities. She was not reluctant to make constructive criticisms. Reading a rough draft of *Remembering Denny*, she wrote a detailed memo in which she suggested, in his words, that "the book would be much improved if I'd write it less as an observer and more as someone who had a lot in common with the subject. I pretty much started the book over again" (*About Alice* 32). In the composition textbook she wrote, *Teaching Basic Skills in College*, she talks about the challenges and excitement of teaching, and one infers that she was an excellent teacher—and critic. She knew how to take and receive criticism. There is no hint of any professional competition between the two writers—he admired her literary judgment and generally acceded to it. "You could say, I suppose, that she was in the English-language business, and I was her sideline—the pro-bono case being handled by a high-powered corporate lawyer. That sort of help wasn't easy to turn down" (34).

We learn about other aspects of Alice's life as well. Trillin acknowledges that the "role she played in my stories was based on the role she played in our family—our daughters and I sometimes called her T.M., which stood for The Mother"—but she didn't play it in the broad strokes of a sitcom mom (*About Alice* 4–5). He also writes about her "child's sense of wonderment" (5) and her active engagement with people's lives, particularly those who were cancer patients, whom she always tried to befriend. She could be "bossy" (8) and "direct" (43). She "hated" cigarettes, and she knew that lung cancer kills more women than breast cancer and ovarian cancer combined. She herself was a nonsmoker, but her parents were addicted to smoking, and her lung cancer may have been caused by secondary smoke. For this reason, she enforced a no-smoking policy for her children. "The girls were only four and seven when Alice was operated on, but when they got old enough to understand she sat them down and told them that, given her illness, we had to face up to the possibility that a genetic predisposition to lung cancer existed in our family. Everything else that could be a part of a teenager's life was discussable, she said, but cigarette smoking was out. She was at that moment at her bossiest, and both girls took her at her word" (48–49).

Anyone who is a parent knows how difficult it can be to convince children to avoid actions that may be harmful to their health, especially those that are culturally acceptable and legal, such as smoking and excessive drinking. Trillin doesn't tell us whether their children objected to their mother's smoking ban and, if so, what the outcome was. Alice had a close relationship with her daughters, but it was not conflict-free. As in *Family Man*, Trillin reveals himself as a moderate self-discloser. "Sarah, in describing the complicated relationship that she, in particular, had with her mother, said at Alice's memorial service that at the center of it was the fact that 'we both wanted desperately love, approval, and admiration from each other.' That meant that it was easy for them to wound each other even with an offhand comment. At times, Sarah said in that speech, Alice had told her that their conversations had made her feel like 'a nerd around the too-cool cheerleader.' At times, Sarah would feel that Alice expected her and Abigail to sail through perfect lives" (*About Alice* 63–64). Trillin then quotes a letter Alice wrote to her children in which she talks about getting through the rough patches of life: "'As you get older,' she wrote, 'you will begin to understand that we love you not because you are perfect, but because you are decent and loving and honest and will always deal with what life brings you with courage'" (64).

It is not easy for anyone of any age, especially children, to admit in a eulogy ambivalence toward deceased parents, nor is it easy to include this information in a published memoir. Almost certainly, Trillin asked for and received permission from his daughter—probably *both* daughters—to use this personal material for his book. Interestingly, there is no mention in the memoir about Abigail's eulogy of her mother, if she wrote one, or of his own. I don't know how common it is for writers to eulogize their deceased spouses—I suspect most do not. Trillin does include part of Sarah's eulogy as well as an undated letter Alice had sent to her daughters, which he first contextualizes. "Alice always said that parents had a huge influence on children when it came to what she called 'the big things.' Essentially, she meant values. In a letter to the girls, she once included among the messages we'd been trying to send them 'to worry about being kind and generous to other people, to be honest with yourself and with others, to find meaning in the work you do, not to over-value financial success.' Although we never discussed it in these terms, I think she believed in the transformative power of pure, undiluted love" (64–65).

About Alice affirms on every page the transformative power of love, and this is one reason for the book's extraordinary appeal. Trillin reports being surprised by the number of readers who felt they knew his feelings for Alice. "I got a lot of letters like the one from a young woman in New York who wrote that she sometimes looked at her boyfriend and thought, 'But will he love me like Calvin loves Alice?'" (6). It is not only Calvin's love for Alice that is apparent but also Alice's reciprocal love for her husband, their daughters, their friends, their well-wishers, and for life itself that shines through. Her excitement over her daughter's wedding in the spring of 2001, which she attended just hours after being released from a hospital after complications arising from emergency open-heart surgery, reveals her joy for life.

Life is in the foreground in *About Alice*, with death remaining in the distant background. Trillin quotes a letter Alice wrote to a friend in which she cites a statement by Ernest Becker, whose book *The Denial of Death* won the Pulitzer Prize in 1974: "To live fully is to live with an awareness of the rumble of terror that underlies everything" (*About Alice* 9). That rumble lies in the distance here. There are only three moments when Trillin's composure is shaken, apart from the book's opening and closing sentences. The first occurs when he recalls a surgeon telling Alice in June 1976 that she had a "ten-percent chance." Trillin is unable to fathom the meaning of the words. "I didn't quite understand what he was talking about. I thought I'd missed something. I asked, 'Ten-percent chance of what?' And he said, 'Ten-percent chance that she'll survive.'" Nor did his shock easily disappear. "For some years, that conversation with the surgeon was unsafe territory for me if I intended to keep my composure. I couldn't talk about it, and I tried not to think about it" (68). The second incident occurred a few years after that surgery when he found himself walking through an airport and, "apropos of nothing, the possibility that things could have gone the other way in 1976 burst into my mind. I could see myself trying to tell my girls that their mother was dead. I think I literally staggered. I sat down in the nearest chair. I wasn't in tears. I was in a condition my father would have called pole-axed" (71). After a few minutes he regained his composure, reminding himself that Alice was now healthy.

The third incident arose following the open-heart surgery, when Alice made him promise not to delay their daughter's wedding. In the spring of 2001, ten months after Sarah's wedding and a month before Abigail's wedding in New York City, a routine X-ray indicated that Alice needed immediate heart bypass surgery. The operation was unexpectedly difficult because the radiation treatment for lung cancer a quarter of a century earlier had damaged the heart. She remained in the hospital for several days, but after she was released she had to return because of medical complications. She insisted that, no matter what happened to her, the wedding must go on as scheduled. "'You have to promise now,' she said. "I managed to nod" (75–76). Alice was able to attend her daughter's wedding, marching joyfully down the aisle, and the next day she wrote friends a detailed account of the happy event, closing with the words, "Life doesn't get much better than this" (76). Four months later she was dead.

Trillin doesn't describe what the last few months of Alice's life were like for her or her family, nor does he write about the moment of her death. He also avoided writing about his life as a widower. We learn nothing about the aftermath of grief, his way of coping with her absence, his changed relationship to his children. Perhaps he avoided these questions because he felt they were not part of Alice's story. Or perhaps these questions are still too emotionally charged for him to write about—unsafe territory. Neither he nor Alice was religious, and there is no hint of religious comfort or consolation for either of them. *About Alice* is a story of love, death, and gratitude for the extra twenty-five years husband and wife had with each other. The last sentence reminds us, however, that it is not easy to remain grateful in the presence of devastating loss.

Trillin quotes Alice as describing herself as an "incorrigible, even ridiculous optimist" (*About Alice* 69), and that's how he portrays her in his memoir, but in her own writings she comes across as much more cautious and subdued. She is indeed hopeful about life, finding pleasure in countless activities, but she has a heightened awareness of the precariousness of health. This aspect of her life does not come out in her husband's writings, but it is evident everywhere in her own. She writes with a strong personal voice that is unmistakably different from her husband's. Whether her audience is rhetoric and composition scholars, physicians, children, or sophisticated readers of the *New Yorker*, she speaks with a quiet, self-assured authority, idealistic about the possibility of education but realistic in her awareness of the gap between theory and practice. Her experience with lung cancer taught her that every day is a gift, one for which she was grateful. As an educator, she believed in the power of reading, writing, and speaking. Unlike her husband, she was not reluctant to enter the unsafe territory of illness and suffering.

"Of Dragons and Garden Peas"

Based on a talk she gave to students at the Cornell and Albert Einstein medical schools, "Of Dragons and Garden Peas" focuses on the "special place" she came to call "The Land of the Sick People." She entered this realm in 1976 when, at the age of thirty-eight, she discovered she had lung cancer. This special place was disconcerting not because it was terrifying but because it was so ordinary and banal. "I didn't feel different, didn't feel that my life had radically changed at the moment the word *cancer* became attached to it. The same rules still held" (699). What changed, however, were people's perceptions of her. Their behavior toward her also changed, not in dramatic but in subtle ways. "I had become special, no longer like them" (699). Aware that others now saw her differently, she did not know what her public persona should be.

Should she be, like so many others, an angry patient? A good patient? A brave patient? None of these roles felt comfortable to her. She admits, with endearing honesty, that she was afraid to be the brave patient because she didn't know whether she could sustain this role in the event her cancer returned.

Hope is especially important, she states, because the universal fear of death "makes it essential to maintain a distance between ourselves and anyone who is threatened by death. Denying our connection to the precariousness of others' lives is a way of pretending that we are immortal" ("Of Dragons" 699). We need this deception, she continues, but it only makes it harder for those who are seriously ill or dying. Cancer embodies the existential paradox that we all know but seldom admit: "we feel that we are immortal, yet we know that we will die" (699).

Two years after her cancer surgery, she watched her best friend "live out my worst nightmares" ("Of Dragons" 699). She doesn't name her friend, who succumbed after eight cancer surgeries, but her husband does in *About Alice*: Mina Shaughnessy, Alice's colleague, first at Hofstra College in Long Island and then at City College of CUNY. Alice had dedicated her textbook, *Teaching Basic Skills in College*, to the memory of Mina Shaughnessy. Her cancer was diagnosed in 1977, a year after Alice's cancer diagnosis, but she had had a hysterectomy several years earlier, and she understood Alice's terror. Shaughnessy's biographer Jane Maher quotes a statement made by Alice indicating how Mina comforted her in the hospital:

> Mina knew how afraid I was. . . . She not only brought orange juice, she brought herself and her revelations about how she had felt fourteen years earlier when she had had a hysterectomy performed. She had been exactly my age—thirty-eight—and she had been terrified (and also unable to have children afterwards).
>
> She shared all of this with me, and also the assurance that the terror gradually goes away. Mina never tried to underestimate or ignore my illness or engage in platitudes as so many people do with cancer. And as I began to recover, and we became more hopeful that the cancer hadn't metastasized, she celebrated with me. (Maher 174)

Fourteen years older than Alice—"in a way a mentor and in another a big sister" (*About Alice* 36), Mina Shaughnessy died in 1979 of kidney cancer. Why doesn't Alice name her colleague in the *New England Journal Medicine* article, published two years after her death? Perhaps because she felt uncomfortable revealing in public that she was angry at her friend for dying. "I felt that she had let me down, that perhaps she hadn't fought hard enough. It was important for me to find reasons for her death, to find things that she might have done to cause it, as a way of separating myself from her and as a way of thinking that I would somehow have behaved differently, that I would somehow have been able to stay alive" ("Of Dragons" 700).

How do we respond to a best friend's death from cancer, especially if we also had—and perhaps still have—cancer? This is the next question Alice raises. For one who values human agency, as she does, how does one then acknowledge the limitation of the will to live? "My friend who died wanted to live more than anyone I have ever known. The talisman of will didn't work for her" ("Of Dragons" 700). Nor did that talisman work completely for Alice, though she didn't know it at the time. What does work for her, to a limited extent, are stories of survival, which can instill hope in the seriously ill and forge a connection between the living and the dying. This is presumably why she wrote "Of Dragons and Garden Peas": to tell doctors and patients alike that "The Land of the Sick People" is as ubiquitous as life itself. "We all know, at least, that the dragons are never quite dead and might at any time be aroused, ready for another fight. But our brave act is important. It is one of the ways we stay alive, and it is the way that we convince those who live in "The Land of the Well People" that we aren't all that different from them" (700). It is for this reason that the book cover of *Dear Bruno*, artfully illustrated by Edward Koren, contains the image of a dragon, apparently vanquished by a smiling knight who has just injected it with a magical potion—chemotherapy. The dragon is down but not quite dead, for one of its eyes is portentously half open, a recognition that it may suddenly spring to life in the future and devour the knight.

Alice Stewart Trillin writes best about the not-quite-slain dragon, and this is one of the major differences between her writings and her husband's. Her close encounter with death has brought her to the dragon—she knows how frightening it looks, how its half-opened eye can haunt one's waking and sleeping moments. Most people in her situation would understandably try to distance themselves from the dragon, doing everything they can to deny or repress its existence, but she writes about it and, in doing so, achieves a degree of control over it. She doesn't explicitly mention a counterphobic motive behind her writing, but she does quote a statement made by William Saroyan: "Why am I writing this book? To save my life, to keep from dying, of course. That is why we get up in the morning" ("Of Dragons" 701). Writing about death encourages introspection while paradoxically shielding the writer from the self-paralyzing effects of excessive thought. As we saw with Donald Hall, immersing oneself in activities creates a flow experience in which one loses all sense of time. Writing about death also has value for the reader, creating a bond of fellowship that would otherwise not exist. Calvin Trillin intimates this when he observes in *About Alice* that he was "touched" by the outpouring of letters he received from readers after his wife's death. "She got engaged with people's lives" (7), he tells us, modestly neglecting to point out the equally important observation that most of these people would not have heard about Alice were it not for his many published stories about her.

Alice Stewart Trillin reveals in "Of Dragons and Garden Peas" other aspects of her life that her husband never discloses in his books. She refers to Kierkegaard's "irrational leap toward faith" in the face of death but then states, simply and nondogmatically, that she is not religious and therefore cannot use this talisman. She is more sympathetic to skepticism than to mysticism, recognizing that we all need to confront what Joseph Conrad calls in *Heart of Darkness* "the horror, the horror" that underlies the abyss of nothingness. She also refers to what Ernest Becker calls the "rumble of panic underneath everything" (701)—a line her husband also cites in *About Alice*.

We hear the rumble of panic in "Of Dragons and Garden Peas" in a way that we do not in *About Alice*, but we also hear a calm, steady voice, determined to engage life to the fullest with a minimum of self-deception. The prose is luminescent, evocative, eloquent. She never lets us forget the dragon's glinting eye, but that only deepens her own unflinching gaze. There is a literary richness here, a seemingly effortless integration (which usually requires much effort) of writers as diverse as Leo Tolstoy, Susan Sontag, William Saroyan, Soren Kierkegaard, Ernest Becker, Joseph Conrad, and William Shakespeare. One writer whom she doesn't quote, but whose spirit casts a magical spell over her prose, is John Keats, who knew that an awareness of death only heightens our appreciation of life. Another writer whose philosophical spirit pervades the article is Voltaire. The desire to resume her life after treatment so that she and her family could travel to Nova Scotia, where they have a summer home, and tend to her "garden peas," recalls the end of *Candide*, where Voltaire's protagonist intends to cultivate his own garden. There is nothing provincial or self-absorbed about this wish. Cultivating garden peas allows her to escape from her worries and fears. Concentrating "on the details of when to plant them and how much mulch they would need" allowed her to forget about the thought of platelets and white blood cells. "I cherished the privilege of thinking about trivia" (701).

No less than *About Alice*, "Of Dragons and Garden Peas" affirms the transformative power of love—and its healing powers as well. "The strength of my love for my children, my husband, my life, even my garden peas has probably been more important than anything in keeping me alive. The intensity of this love is also what makes me so terrified of dying" (701). The article's penultimate paragraph contains a barely perceptible tinge of wry irony that banishes sentimentality. "It astonishes me that having faced the terror, we continue to live, even to live with a great deal of joy. It is commonplace for people who have cancer—particularly those who feel as well as I do—to talk about how much richer their lives are because they have confronted death. Yes, my life is very rich. I have even begun to understand that wonderful line in *King Lear*, 'Ripeness is all.' I suppose that becoming ripe means finding out that none of the really important questions have answers. I wish that life had devised a less terrifying, less risky way of making me ripe. But I wasn't given any choice about this" (701).

Dear Bruno

If cancer is terrifying to an adult, how much more terrifying is it to a child? Calvin Trillin tells us in *About Alice* that when he and his wife learned that the twelve-year-old son of their friends Victor and Annie Navasky had a malignant tumor in his chest, Alice wrote him a letter that was later published as *Dear Bruno*. The book was dedicated to the "kids at the Hole in the Wall Gang Camp [where the Trillins had worked as volunteer camp counselors] and to their special friends, Paul Newman and Joanne Woodward." In the foreword, Paul Newman comments on the book's "patience and generosity, wonderfully relaxed humor, sensible instruction, and, I am happy to note, no sufferance at all for idiots." The author writes from the point of view of cancer patient, survivor, friend, educator, and, mother. Everything she tells the boy is both truthful and reassuring—no easy feat with respect to life-threatening disease. She reveals at the end of the book, in the author's note, that she read aloud the letter to Bruno to the ten-year old girls in her cabin at The Hole in the Wall Gang Camp. "Amazingly, one of my campers had had a neuroblastoma, a tumor closely related to the neuroepithelioma Bruno named a 'Brunoma.' She told me, rather matter-of-factly, that she was one of the rare children to survive this particularly virulent form of cancer, and I was pleased to be able to introduce her to Bruno, whose experience had been so much like hers" (31). No children's story about cancer can be delightful, but *Dear Bruno* comes close. The opening paragraph, written from Nova Scotia in August 1979, reflects the gentle humor of the book:

> Dear Bruno,
>
> Bud has already written and told you all our jokes (not quite—did you hear the one about the fog?—oh well, it's probably too dense for you) and he has told you about what happens in Nova Scotia in the summer, and he has sent you an arrow-through-the-head to wear when you tell the doctors you have a little headache, and so I thought that there wasn't much left for me to write you, but there is one thing I know about that Bud doesn't know about, and that is what it is like to have a tumor in your lung. (6)

The paragraph is deceptively simple. Beginning with a light-hearted joke that will inevitably bring a smile to the reader, it then refers to another playful joke characteristic of her husband's humor, all the while demonstrating the closeness between husband and wife. The paragraph ends bluntly with the words "tumor in your lung." She uses no euphemism to soften the seriousness of Bruno's cancer or her own; she regards Bruno as an intellectual and emotional equal to whom she will tell the unvarnished truth. As close as she is to her husband, she knows that he can never understand what it is like to live with cancer—only other cancer patients can understand this. Some knowledge cannot be gleaned from books. Yet she is writing a book for readers who may not have cancer, and she does everything she can to convey her experience to them. She "wanted very badly to talk to someone who had the same thing I had" when she was ill (8), and she assumes Bruno also wants to talk about his illness. That's why she is writing to him—and to us: to relate her experiences and to answer whatever questions he may want to ask.

She uses humor whenever possible to demystify and detoxify the frightening experience of cancer treatment. What she most remembers about radiation therapy was the "awful Muzak" they played while they were "zapping" her (*Dear Bruno* 10). The radiologists were "nice," but they were always talking about real estate: "They were having trouble evicting the tenants next door so they would have room for the new CAT scanners" (12). She remembers that she was "incredibly well-behaved" during treatment, but occasionally she became "very angry" that she was sick while everyone she knew was well. She was also angry about getting lung cancer because she had never smoked. She makes no effort to minimize her anger or confusion—this, too, must be reassuring to Bruno, who will realize after reading her letter that these feelings are normal. She also discloses "an incredible question" that a medical student asked her after she gave a talk—presumably, the talk that was the basis for "Of Dragons and Garden Peas." "He said, if I knew that I would be OK, that I wouldn't be sick again, and if I could choose, would I choose to have been sick, to have gone through the experience I had gone through, as awful as it had been" (24). Stunned by the question, she never tells us whether she answered it in her talk. Nor does she include this question, or her response, in the article for the medical journal. But she answers the question in *Dear Bruno*. "That was a secret. I had never said it out loud. Of course, I would never choose to have cancer—that's just silly—but you don't get to choose, and the secret he had guessed was that there were things about having had cancer that I liked" (24). Calvin Trillin may be referring to a similar question when he states in *About Alice* that his wife said that "there was some relief at surviving what you might have thought was not survivable" (8).

She ends the letter to Bruno with the line from *King Lear* that she has used in "Of Dragons and Garden Peas": "Ripeness is all," adding that although it must be difficult to see anything good about getting cancer, "some day, when you are better—and riper—we should talk about it"

(26). The book closes with Bruno's letter to her, written sixteen years later, when he is indeed better—and riper. She then closes the author's note with a final reference to the dragon, still sleeping but perhaps not yet dead: "There are worse things to be than a fighter-of-dragons" (32).

"Betting Your Life"

The dragon appeared to spring to life again in 1990 when Alice Stewart Trillin found herself suffering from flulike symptoms and could not stop coughing. She describes this experience in her riveting essay aptly titled "Betting Your Life" that appeared in the January 29, 2001, issue of the *New Yorker.* A chest X-ray at Memorial Sloan-Kettering Cancer Hospital indicated fluid inside the lower lining of both her lungs—an ominous development because she had had malignant lymph nodes removed during the cancer surgery. Her oncologist ordered a needle aspiration of the fluid, and though it revealed nothing alarming, Alice could not stop worrying about the possibility that the lung cancer from fourteen years ago had returned. When she felt a sharp pain in her back that didn't go away, it seemed that the "dragon started breathing smoke" (38). Another chest X-ray indicated what appeared to be a fracture in one of the vertebrae in her thoracic spine—"the part of the spine that lies over the lungs" (38). Her neurologist and friend Kathleen Foley ordered an MRI—at which point Alice "started, finally, to get really scared" (38). The results indicated a likely possibility of a tumor, requiring still more tests: a needle biopsy of the suspicious vertebra and then a bone scan.

Now terrified, Alice agreed with her physician on the need to act quickly. "My imagination can always conjure up images that are scarier than any produced by an X-ray machine" ("Betting Your Life" 39)—a character trait her husband doesn't mention in any of his writings about her. The 1990 crisis reminded her of the medical scare that had followed the 1976 surgery, when she felt a spasm "like an electric current" moving along her back from the base of her skull to her toes. Noting that lung cancer often spreads to the brain and spine, she did not convey her fears to her family. "I spent the week trying not to tell my husband what I thought was happening" (39). Fortunately, the 1976 scare turned out to be something called Lhermitte's sign, a "not unusual side effect of radiation to the chest" (39). The new scare, however, seemed more menacing, especially when the bone scan indicated five "lights" that showed up—two in her ribs, two in her hips, and one in her spine.

What followed was a seemingly endless series of consultations with oncologists, radiologists, surgeons, and orthopedists, each of whom seemed to have a different explanation of and treatment plan for the five mysterious lights. The medical situation was frightening and bewildering. "I am known among my friends and family as an incorrigible, even ridiculous optimist," she observes, a statement her husband quotes in *About Alice*. "I think all optimists fear that one day they will wake up and won't be able to put a hopeful spin on anything ever again" ("Betting Your Life" 40). Unable to imagine a good outcome to the meaning of the bone scan lights, she began to dwell on death and her family's survival without her. "I did manage to imagine uplifting conversations I might have with my daughters about how it was O.K. for me to die this time, as it absolutely had not been when they were four and seven, and I had foreseen their adoring but occasionally absent-minded father getting them the wrong kind of sneakers or losing track of their dental appointments after I was gone. Now one of them was in college, and the other was teaching in California, and I was sure that I had told them everything of importance I knew; they had understood it all and figured out a lot on their own, and were as close to perfect as they could possibly be" (40).

After thinking about which of her friends could help her daughters pick out wedding dresses, Alice begins to cry and then imagines her husband's life after her death. What comes next is one of the most autobiographically revealing—and wry—disclosures in the article, all the more intriguing because part of it is expressed parenthetically: "Then I cried and decided that I really wanted to stay around, particularly when I started to think about the women who might come after my husband when I was gone. (The best description of this feeling came from my friend Josie Mankewitz Davis, who died young in a traffic accident, and who had said to her husband, years earlier, that if anything happened to her she'd certainly expect him to marry again, particularly because he would need help raising their children. Then she paused for a beat, and added, 'Just don't sleep with her!'") ("Betting Your Life" 40). Not only is the parenthetical observation unexpected and funny, worthy of Burns and Allen at their best, but it is the kind of comic statement that would, in a different situation, with a different person, appeal to Calvin Trillin. She portrays her husband as susceptible to pursuing females—as we see in John Bayley's comic memoir *Widower's House*, when he becomes the object—almost the victim—of two women's unsolicited attentions. That Trillin omits this passage from *About Alice* can probably be explained by the fact that it hits too close to home. The passage describes a future without his wife—a subject that is strictly out of bounds for this "moderate" self-discloser. But his wife cannot resist this self-disclosure, which lightens the mood of her essay and brings much-needed humor to an otherwise terrifying situation.

This passage also conveys the importance of family. Alice is closely connected to her daughters, who, with her husband, are the center of her world. That she can think about their wedding gowns as she is staring at death demonstrates her lack of self-absorption, her ability to focus on others, her faith in the future. I recall my wife's similar joy, two months after her diagnosis, during our younger daughter's wedding. Like Alice, Barbara was attentive to the hundreds of details that went into the planning of the wedding. (Barbara had actually made our older daughter's exquisite wedding gown, a project that took months.) One could never tell, from her smiling face and radiant eyes, that she was close to the dragon.

No less than her husband, Alice Stewart Trillin could be a humorist when she wanted to, yet there are several sardonic moments in "Betting Your Life" that Calvin Trillin chose not to include in *About Alice*—moments in which she exploits the grim humor of the situation. For example, amid the conflicting medical advice she receives, including the need for immediate, radical surgery that might leave her crippled, she recalls a statement made by the physician Jerome Groopman in an earlier issue of the *New Yorker*. While a medical student, he had received the ironic admonishment: "Don't just do something—stand there" (38). The advice proved to be especially relevant to Alice's 1990 crisis. Her orthopedist and bone specialist, Joseph Lane, "known both for his brusqueness and for his diagnostic skill" (41), reviewed her medical charts, checked her back and chest, and then uttered, in "words that came in bursts," the correct diagnosis: "Nope, this doesn't look like tumor to me. Radiation necrosis—a lot of that now in women radiated for breast cancer. Not so much in lung cancer, not that many live long enough." His treatment plan was simple to follow: "Take calcium, and a multivitamin to support the calcium. Nope, definitely not tumor." Stunned, her husband spoke—and joked—for the first time: "You're our favorite doctor so far." When Alice asks what kind of vitamin she should take, the physician's reply is short and to the point. "Dr. Lane seemed to consider this seriously. 'El cheapo is el besto,' he answered with a grin, as if he had just closed the deal on a color television" (42).

Why does Calvin Trillin omit these funny moments from *About Alice*? They would have enriched the story and portrayed another fascinating side to his wife's complex character. We can only speculate on why he chose not to use this material. He certainly did not have to worry about space considerations, since *About Alice* is one of the shortest books he or anyone else has published. Nor did he need to worry about getting permission from the *New Yorker* to reprint the material, since nearly all of the book appeared in the magazine months earlier. He may have decided not to use the material about Josie Mankewitz Davis because he would then have to confront in print the complicated subject of life without Alice. Yet it appears likely that she would have given her blessing for him to do this. In the memoir he refers to her directness, her lack of shyness in bringing up touchy subjects, her "instinctual attraction for avoided subjects" (43), and her characteristic statement, "You have to open all of this up" (8). What could be a more avoided subject in a memoir about spousal loss than whether the author has a desire to marry again? By quoting her parenthetical statement in "Betting My Life," Trillin would open up a subject best left closed for him. This doesn't explain, admittedly, his decision not to use for his book the material about Alice's encounter with his favorite doctor. For whatever reason, that part of the story is missing from *About Alice*. It might be that the optimistic final paragraph, written only months before her unexpected death from heart failure, is simply too painful for Calvin Trillin to contemplate. "The dragon had gone back to sleep for a while longer," Alice writes. "Almost ten years have passed. One of my daughters got married last summer, and the other will be married in May. I helped them pick out their dresses" ("Betting Your Life" 42).

"Betting Your Life" is compelling enough to deserve discussion by Jonathan Cohen in the *Journal of Bone and Joint Surgery*. "For the general reader and for orthopaedic surgeons, several questions arise. Why did so many experts not think of radiation necrosis as a possible cause? One wonders if the other consultants knew of osteonecrosis as a sequel to the type of radiation that was administered ten to twenty years previously for certain cancers." It is impossible to disagree with Dr. Cohen's conclusion. "The correct diagnosis was elicited by those physicians who listened to the patient's story, examined her, and put the pieces of evidence together in proper perspective."

While reading the Trillins' stories, I was struck by the many parallels between their family and my own. Both families emphasize the importance of education. Calvin Trillin's two daughters both went to his alma mater, Yale, and both of my daughters went to the university where I did my graduate work, Cornell. Their daughters and ours have gone into identical fields. Their daughter Abigail and son-in-law Brian are both lawyers whom Trillin describes in *Feeding a Yen* as of the "humanity-helping rather than the disgustingly lucrative sort" (190). The same is true of our daughter Jillian and son-in-law Alex, who are both federal prosecutors in Manhattan. The Trillins' other daughter, Sarah, is a clinical social worker, and our daughter Arielle is a clinical psychologist. Alice and Barbara were fiercely protective of their children. Sarah said in her eulogy that she thought "Alice had toughed it out until she was sure her girls had married the sort of husbands she considered good for the long haul. 'I know my mom's main goal in life was to protect my sister, my father, and me,' Sarah said. 'She wanted to protect us from worry, from sadness, from loneliness—things her parents had not been able to protect her from'" (*About Alice* 77). Jillian expressed similar feelings in her eulogy. "As many of you know, my mom did not want to go. She was devoted to her family and friends, and she had an amazing will to live and a love for life. To the end, she was interested in our future, even though she could not be part of it" (*Dying to Teach* 169). Amid all the controversies over child-rearing theories, Trillin captures in a few words what he and Alice and Barbara and I believed in and practiced: "We agreed on a simple notion: your children are either the center of your life or they're not, and the rest is commentary" (*About Alice* 60).

Like Alice, Barbara wanted to protect her children from the worries and fears from which she felt her parents were not able to protect her. Barbara was herself a "worrier-warrior," as our friend Judith Harris observed. Alice was also a worrier. Her father was an inventor who struggled financially his entire life. Barbara's father was a lawyer who struggled after World War II and went into his brother's clothes business, a decision he later regretted. Alice's mother developed Alzheimer's disease, as did Barbara's mother. Some of the parent-child dynamics in the Trillin and Berman families are similar. Our daughters regarded their mother as a perfectionist, as the Trillins' daughters regarded their mother. It is hard living with a perfectionist, and sometimes this caused strains in the mother-daughter relationship. "My mom was a perfectionist in everything she did," Jillian observed in her eulogy. "She always supported our efforts to learn her skills, but we didn't share her perfectionist tendencies" (*Dying to Teach* 168). Barbara would have agreed with every word of Alice's comment to her daughters: "As you get older . . . you will begin to understand that we love you not because you are perfect, but because you are decent and loving and honest and will always deal with what life brings you with courage" (*About Alice* 64).

Calvin Trillin met Alice at a party in 1963, the same year that I met Barbara in our freshman English class at the University of Buffalo. He was smitten by Alice, as I was by Barbara: it was love at first sight for him and me. The Trillins were married for thirty-six years, one year longer than we were. He and I each have four young grandchildren, one of whom is named Nate. Calvin Trillin and I have both written memoirs celebrating our wives' accomplished lives. Both women were stunningly beautiful, devoted to family and friends, successful in their careers. Both were secular Jews who were proud of their heritages but skeptical of the existence of God. Both began their careers as educators and never lost faith in the power of knowledge. Both were optimistic about the future without being Pollyannaish. Both were highly cultured yet also pragmatic and sensible. Both were problem-solvers and helped their parents during times of financial crisis. Both loved to travel, garden, attend concerts and plays, dine in restaurants, cook, and read. Both developed diseases few would have predicted: Alice was a nonsmoker who developed lung cancer, and Barbara was diagnosed with pancreatic cancer despite the fact that cancer was absent from both sides of her long-lived family. Both women battled valiantly to stay alive, sought out experimental medical treatments, and did their best to avoid burdening their families with grief. I believe that Barbara and Alice would have become warm and trusted friends.

Calvin Trillin and I are both authors. He is a world-class author, and I am not, but we are both committed to writing. He is able to make his living from his royalties. I'm fortunate that I can depend upon a steady if modest university salary; otherwise, I would not have the time and freedom to write. He writes on a much wider range of topics than I do, and he is an incomparable humorist, one of the funniest contemporary writers. He is also a novelist as well as a journalist. By contrast, all of my books are on "academic" subjects, thus guaranteeing a limited audience. He and I have both written books about suicide. He wrote *Remembering Denny* about his Yale classmate' suicide; I wrote *Surviving Literary Suicide* because of my mentor's suicide in 1968, two weeks after Barbara and I married. Our wives were our best readers and the first to read our manuscripts. He and I have dedicated many of our books to our wives, children, and now grandchildren. Like him, I wrote everything for my wife. Both of us were adoring husbands and fathers who could also be clueless, absent-minded, and eccentric. Like him, I thought I could protect my wife. As he writes in *About Alice*, "I somehow thought I could keep her alive because I wouldn't accept the possibility that she was going to die" (69). I did everything in my power to keep Barbara alive, but I discovered how limited that power is in the face of death. Trillin and I knew how lucky we were to be married to our soul mates—and both of us remind ourselves how fortunate we have been. Like him, I try to think of Barbara's death in these terms. Some days I can and some days I can't.

"*Grandfather Knows Best*"

Since Alice's death, Trillin has written several books, but apart from *About Alice*, only one of them is autobiographical—*Feeding a Yen*, published in 2003. In the chapter called "Grandfather Knows Best," Trillin talks about flying to San Francisco to see Abigail's first child—his first grandchild. We learn her name from the author's note, which is also a dedication: Isabelle Alice Trillin-Lee. The chapter is vintage Trillin, focusing on the cultural differences between Manhattan and San Francisco Chinese "takeout" (called "carryout" in the latter city), and reminiscing fondly about past Chinese-restaurants in the New York City area. He revels in expressing gluttony for food, as when he informs us that "*Out to Eat*, the Lonely Planet guidebook to San Francisco restaurants, describes a Mission burrito as 'a perfect rolled-up meal,' and I would differ only in describing a Mission burrito as 'two or three perfect rolled-up meals" (194–95). Impressed with San Francisco carryout restaurants in the Mission section—"Some of them were outposts of gentrification, described by Abigail as 'in the Mission but not of the Mission'" (195)—he tells her, patronizingly, on the way to the airport to return to New York City, "It was okay for out of town" (196). Returning home, he sorts his take-out menus, imagines Abigail looking through these menus on her next trip home, and happily visualizes all the enticing restaurants the two of them can visit in Manhattan.

"Grandfather Knows Best" is a delightful and entertaining story, but I can't help being struck by the absent presence of Alice that must have shadowed Trillin's every step in San Francisco. I'm disappointed that he decided not to mention his wife even momentarily when he saw his first grandchild for the first time. Even if he and his daughter managed to avoid invoking Alice's name—*especially* if they avoided mentioning her name—they must have both been thinking about her. How could they not? Indeed, he intimates this in a brief parenthetical sentence in *About Alice*, when he tells us that his granddaughter's coloring resembles Alice's. Recalling his first sight of Alice at a 1963 party, he writes: "She had blond hair, worn straight in those days, and a brow just a shade darker than her hair. (Our oldest grandchild, Isabelle Alice, who was born in 2002, has precisely that coloring, which may be one reason I sometimes have trouble taking my eyes off her)" (12). Surely that poignant parenthesis is as pregnant with meaning as Alice's about her friend Josie Mankewitz Davis's sardonic comment. And yet there is no mention of Alice in "Grandfather Knows Best," nothing about her recent death. In looking at his new granddaughter, Trillin must have thought about the first times he looked at his own infant daughters, decades earlier. Abigail must also have been conscious of her mother's absent presence the first time Calvin sees Isabelle Alice, who bears her grandmother's coloring and name. No family could be as tight-knit as theirs without feeling overwhelmed by these intense emotions of love and loss, joy and sorrow. These emotions are especially powerful when a widow or widower's first grandchild is born. It's hard to think of a more emotionally charged situation than the one Trillin describes, without comment, in "Grandfather Knows Best." One suspects that it was more difficult for Trillin *not* to write about Alice than to write about her, however briefly.

Alice Stewart Trillin died on September 11, 2001, a detail that her husband curiously omits in his memoir. Was it because of the fear that if he included this fact, some readers might believe that he was somehow equating, in an overstated or exploitative way, his personal loss with the nation's tragedy? He need not have worried about this. Mark Singer suggests, in a brief postscript to the "Talk of the Town" column in the October 1, 2001, issue of the *New Yorker*, that the staff's "overwhelming agony" of the terrorist attack "gave way to a particularized sadness and grief" when they heard about Alice Trillin's death. He quotes from "Of Dragons and Garden Peas": "It astonishes me that having faced the terror, we continue to live, even to live with a great deal of joy" (701)—a statement that continues to resonate with truth.

I admire Trillin as a writer and as a person, and I look forward to reading his future books, but I would like to tell him that if he is to remain faithful to his muse, his golden grail, the woman about whom he said, "I wrote everything for Alice," then he should not avoid writing about her in his post-Alice stories. I realize that it is presumptuous for a reader to tell an author what to write on, but Trillin's most profound books are about people. He admitted in an interview with the *Akron Beacon Journal* that his work has suffered since his wife's death. If so, he might continue to draw inspiration from her in future books. Has he been, as Alice wondered, pursued by women? Has he done the pursuing? Has Alice's experience with her dragon changed his attitude toward his own dragon? Alice would have emboldened him to write about these and related questions. Has he read any of his contemporaries' memoirs about their deceased spouses? Has he found value in observing his grief, as we have seen with C. S. Lewis? Is he interested in writing a second or third memoir, as John Bayley has done, with spectacular results? Would he agree with Donald Hall that writing about a deceased spouse leads to companionship in grief? Can he imagine, as do Bayley and Hall, companionship in joy with his deceased spouse? Has he experienced the magical thinking about which Joan Didion writes in her memoir? Does his silence reveal that he accepts Freud's theory of bereavement in which survivors detach themselves from deceased spouses, thus letting go of the past? Or does his silence simply indicate that there are certain subjects that he cannot write about, including spousal loss? There is a wealth of material in these questions for future writings.

It may be that *About Alice* offers companionship in grief only for those readers who label themselves as moderate on the reveal-o-meter of self-disclosure, as Trillin himself is, and who neither want nor expect a memoirist—especially a *comic* memoirist—to offer a graphic portrait of a dying spouse's suffering. Such readers may be content to infer a memoirist's grief: in some situations, silence is eloquent. Indeed, such readers may admire Trillin's tact and discretion in refusing to grieve publicly or to burden the reader with his own sorrow. These readers do not have an almost instinctual attraction for avoided subjects.

I realize that many people will disagree with my criticism of Trillin. A trusted colleague who read *Companionship in Grief* before I submitted it for publication felt that there is "something unyielding" about my desire to "remake Trillin" in the image of the other writers in this study. She also believed that many of my self-disclosures seem "out of place" in this book, more like a "holdover" from *Dying to Teach*. I also realize that my reading of Trillin may reflect more about me than about him. My reading reflects my inability to stop thinking or talking or writing about Barbara. How can I not recall our own parenting experiences when I am in the presence of my children and grandchildren? Living with the dead is an ever-present reality for so many people, especially as they get older and grow closer to death themselves. I can't help thinking about how Barbara would have been so proud of our children and grandchildren, how she would have rejoiced in seeing her children become extraordinary mothers, as she was. Nor can I stop thinking about the continuity of life and death, one generation following another. A beloved spouse's death does not simply result in a huge void in the survivor's life. One's lifelong memories have the paradoxical effect of both filling and widening the void. If I project these emotions onto Trillin's story, searching for the missing story he has not written, I suspect other readers will too.

I'm not suggesting that Trillin should end every story with the Burns and Allen equivalent of "Good night, Alice," though I'm sure he could do so in his own inimitable way. One can honor one's muse without talking incessantly about her, yet not to talk about her in a story about visiting one's grandchild for the first time strikes a jarring chord. In a February 15, 2007, NPR interview with Jeffrey Brown, Trillin said that he was afraid people wouldn't be interested in reading a book about his deceased wife. He expressed this fear to his daughters, who urged him to write the book anyway. "And my older daughter said, 'Well, even if they don't, it will be good for the kids.' And my younger daughter, who is a clinical social worker who does psychotherapy, said, 'Probably a good idea for you to write it anyway.'" They were right. One need not specialize in "tragic characters," as he claims in *Family Man*, to write candidly and movingly about being a family man. Trillin has the insight, compassion, humor, and courage to do so. Then he will truly demonstrate that grandfather knows best.

CONCLUSION

"It Is Possible to Be Bereft and Not Bereft Simultaneously"

> "Jason! Grief is the most powerful emotion a man or child or animal can feel. It's a *good* feeling."
>
> "In what fucking way?" he said harshly.
>
> "Grief causes you to leave yourself. You step outside your narrow little pelt. And you can't feel grief unless you've had love before it—grief is the final outcome of love, because it's love lost."

I can't imagine anyone choosing to be grief-stricken (except, perhaps, a masochist), and yet grief can be *good*, as we see from the dialogue in Philip K. Dick's 1975 novel *Flow My Tears, the Policeman Said* (102). Now that I'm completing *Companionship in Grief*, I can see how other memoirists have discovered the ways in which grief can be not only good but also transformative, allowing them to commemorate and honor the memories of their loved ones. To be sure, it is impossible not to feel ambivalent about grief, for it may be disabling or enabling, leading to callousness or compassion, selfishness or selflessness, self-preoccupation or self-transcendence. Grief can turn us away from the world, to avoid further losses, or compel us to memorialize those who have enriched our lives. In an unpublished essay quoted by Robert C. Solomon, Janet McCracken uses the term "dedicatory grief" to describe the ways in which grief may compel us to honor our lost loved ones: "When someone we love has died, we desire to *do honor to*, to *show appreciation for*, that life as a whole, differently from and more importantly than the honors or rewards she may have received for particular accomplishments during her life"(Solomon, *In Defense of Sentimentality*, 92; emphasis in original).

Spousal loss memoirists demonstrate the value of dedicatory grief, for they honor and commemorate their deceased partners while at the same time maintaining their attachment to them. They not only remember the dead but also show how the deceased may help the living. My own dedicatory grief takes the form of writing books and teaching courses on death education that honor my wife's memory. I see examples of dedicatory grief everywhere. Each year my former student Julia Florer sends me the sign she wears, "In Memory of Barbara," when she participates in a benefit for the American Cancer Society. Other students who have read *Dying to Teach* send me sympathy cards on October 17, Barbara's birthday. My dedicatory grief encourages students to honor their own loved ones, living and dead. Students who have taken my Love and Loss courses send me emails when their relatives or friends die. They tell me that, as a result of my course, they are able to write eulogies for their loved ones, speak more freely and openly about dying and death, and console others who have suffered loss. Witness the following email I received from a student as I was completing this book:

> Hi Prof. Berman, it's Steve from your first Love and Loss course. During my time in college, whenever we had our meetings in your office I remember always telling you how fortunate I was that at that point in my life I had never had a close loved one die. That changed this Tuesday morning, as my grandfather passed away. We were extremely close, and I was a mess the following day. I thought about our class, and more specifically the eulogy you wrote for your wife. I remembered how your eulogy painted a picture of your relationship with her while balancing tears and smiles. I tried to do something similar and wrote something to be read at my grandfather's funeral. I don't think I will be able to get through reading it. I just wrote it, and have only read it once so I'm not sure if it is the best piece of writing I have ever done. I just wanted to tell the stories so people can remember the relationship I had with my grandfather and maybe bring some smiles to people's faces on what is going to be a really sad day. I have attached what I wrote if you're interested in reading it. I just want to thank you again for your Love and Loss class. In a way it did prepare me for this, and hopefully I will make my grandfather proud.

"Everyone can master a grief but he that has it," Shakespeare observes shrewdly in *Much Ado about Nothing.* Even if one could choose to give up grief, it would not be easy to do, if only because grief may include many positive memories. "A widow or widower may remember times of intense passion, of youthful play, or caresses and kind words," Paul C. Rosenblatt states. "Thus, recurrent grief is not like recurrent illness. It can be a link with the best of life, an affirmation of light and joy. This is not to say that recurrent grief is not difficult for many people but to say that there is much more to it than sorrow" (55). "Where would I be without my sorrow," Eurydice asks pitifully in Louise Gluck's poem "Relic," adding that her song of sorrow is "of all gifts the most lasting" (36). Mourning offers us hidden consolation and is "immensely reassuring," Adam Phillips declares, "because it convinces us of something we might otherwise easily doubt: our attachment to others" (78). Mark Doty points out in his AIDS memoir *Heaven's Coast* that being in grief is like being in love. "In both states, the imagination's entirely occupied with one person. The beloved dwells at the heart of the world, and becomes a Rome: the roads of feeling all lead to him, all proceed from him. Everything that touches us seems to relate back to that center; there is no other emotional life, no place outside the universe of feeling centered on its pivotal figure" (38). Spousal loss memoirs chart the joyful journey to the heart of our world, the roads of feeling that lead to our life companions and soul mates; they also chronicle the dark journey following the loss of our loves, when we feel bereft and lost ourselves. Maintaining our attachment to the deceased is part of the larger task of maintaining our attachment to the past, as Donald Hall reminds us in *Eagle Pond*, for "if there is no connected past, we lack the implication of persistence after our own death. The preserved or continuous past implies the possibility that oneself may continue, in place or object or even in spirit, a ring of time that resolves, revisits, and contains" (98).

Why read the memoir? Sven Birkerts offers a succinct reason. "The point—the glory—of memoir is that it anchors its authority in the actual life; it is a modeling of the process of creative self-inquiry as it is applied to the stuff of lived experience. *This really happened* is the baseline contention of the memoir" (190; emphasis in original). Why read the spousal loss memoir? For an additional reason: the spousal loss memoir anchors its authority in both life and death—the stuff of actual living and dying. We usually see two views of the world, an egocentric view of the memoirist, who shows us what it is like to lose a loved one, and an allocentric view, concerned with the interests of others, the lost spouse. We see companionship in grief as well as, in many cases, companionship in joy. Spousal loss memoirs dramatize both personal and cultural mourning, casting much light on the nature and process of bereavement. These memoirs can help to humanize dying and death, one of the goals of death education, as Lynne Ann DeSpelder and Albert Lee Strickland observe in *The Last Dance*. We need spousal loss memoirs for the same reasons Jahan Ramazani suggests we need elegies: "because our society often sugarcoats mourning in dubious comfort, or retreats from it in embarrassed silence, or pathologizes it, even locking it up in medical institutions. We need them because people die around us every day and neither science nor technology can fix death, reverse loss, or cure bereavement" (ix).

Spousal loss memoirs contain words of wisdom and words of grief. The two are often inseparable. "For in much wisdom is much grief," Ecclesiastes (1:18) tells us, "and he that increaseth knowledge increaseth sorrow." Kafka did not have spousal loss memoirs in mind when he said that we should read books that "wound and stab us . . . , that affect us like a disaster, that grieve us deeply, like the death of someone we love more than ourselves, like being banished into forests far from everyone, like a suicide. A book must be the axe for the frozen sea inside us" (16). Nevertheless, Kafka's words characterize spousal loss memoirists, who write about people whom they love more than themselves, and whose deaths grieve us deeply. Sometimes we may find ourselves overwhelmed by these stories of love and loss, reminding us of T. S. Eliot's statement in the *Four Quartets* that "human kind cannot bear very much reality" (118). I suspect we read spousal loss memoirs, unlike other genres, slowly, in small doses. We pause when we find ourselves too grief-stricken to continue, and we resume our reading a few hours or days later when we are psychologically ready.

David E. Balk, the editor of *Handbook of Thanatology*, notes that "widows comprise the great numbers of persons who have participated in bereavement research and upon whom generalizations have been formed about loss, grief, and mourning" (161). Four of the five spousal loss memoirists in my study are males, from whom we learn much about widowers' lives, thus adding to our understanding of the aftermath of grief as experienced by men and the possibility of postbereavement growth.

"Bereavement," Ned H. Cassem writes, "may, in spite of itself, prove to be a good teacher for some, but few of us seek it out" (9). So, too, are spousal loss memoirs good teachers for some; paradoxically, many readers seek them out. The best spousal loss memoirs teach us while at the same time they move us aesthetically. We read them for their insights into life and death, their portrayals of love and loss, their depictions of wounding and healing, and their strategies for comfort and survival. Spousal loss memoirs are, unexpectedly, stories of recovery—how the authors survived devastating losses and were able later to find consolation, and, in some cases, joy in the aftermath of grief. Spousal loss memoirs are about death education and life education.

Spousal loss memoirs are also about connection. The Australian poet A. D. Hope's reference to moving "closer and closer apart," which John Bayley quotes in *Elegy for Iris*, is an apt metaphor for the ways in which memoirists remain attached to their deceased spouses. Memoirists write about absent presences who served as muses first in life and then in death. Writing about the dead is a way to bring them to life verbally and to reflect on their continuing impact on our lives. Robert Kastenbaum, a leading thanatologist, has suggested in *On Our Way* that terminally ill people draw strength from their closest companions and desire their continued companionship to the end (125). So, too, do memoirists draw strength from their deceased spouses. Writing maintains this companionship even after a spouse's death.

I have followed Alice Stewart Trillin's advice to her husband, when he was working on *Remembering Denny*, to write it "less as an observer and more as someone who had a lot in common with the subject" (*About Alice* 32). Social scientists call the person who writes from this dual perspective a "participant-observer." The challenge is to focus on self and other simultaneously without confusing the two. While writing this book, I found myself engaged with the lives of all five authors in my study, as well as their spouses. It was fascinating to learn about these ten people: their lives were so different from my own, and yet there were also many similarities as a result of our spouses' deaths. Writing this book was a pleasure, never a chore, and though I often teared up while reading the memoirs, I never found myself becoming depressed. Sad, yes; depressed, no. And more glad than sad. There were many more smiles than tears.

There were a few surprises while I was writing this book. I was surprised that none of the memoirists worried about how their deceased spouses would feel reading the books about them. Consequently, I have stopped worrying about how Barbara would feel if she read *Dying to Teach*. I'm struck by the irony of an agnostic/atheist who disbelieves in the possibility of life after death worrying so much about what a dead person may or may not feel. Either I'm deceiving myself about my religious disbeliefs or my worrying is misplaced.

Another surprise is that despite the devastation I experienced during Barbara's illness and following her death, I was never rendered speechless or wordless, as many of the other memoirists were. I never missed a day of teaching during Barbara's illness, and my life never threatened to spiral out of control. A friend told me that he couldn't understand how I wrote *Dying to Teach*. I wasn't exactly sure what he meant, but I told him that I *had* to write it. (There were many times when I wondered whether what I was writing was publishable, but that is a different question.) Teaching and writing helped to ground me, creating a continuity between my life with Barbara and my life without her. I was never close to a breakdown, as some of the memoirists were. I never experienced a crisis of faith, as C. S. Lewis dramatizes, never felt myself becoming suicidal or homicidal, as John Bayley admits, never found myself living a "scattery and hectic life, filled with misadventure," as Donald Hall confesses, never found myself engaged in prolonged magical thinking, as Joan Didion describes, and never stopped writing about spousal loss, as Calvin Trillin does.

I suspect that Lewis, Bayley, Hall, Didion, and Trillin would all have been stunned to hear that late in their lives they would author memoirs honoring their beloved deceased spouses. Few of them or their spouses were temperamentally inclined to self-disclosing writing or highly subjective, expressive writing. If writing about disaster represents, in Maurice Blanchot's words, the "limits of writing," insofar as the "disaster de-scribes," then writing about spousal loss requires the memoirist to express the inexpressible, that which "escapes the very possibility of experience" (7). Citing the poet Valery, Blanchot opines that "optimists write badly," adding, "but pessimists do not write" (113). If this is true, the writers in my study were all realists.

I was not surprised to discover that nearly all the memoirists affirmed the power of writing not only to memorialize loss but also to work through their own grief. With the possible exception of Joan Didion, all the writers in my study would agree with John Bayley's observation in

Widower's House: "Writing about the dead is a way not only of continuing to feel in touch with them but of expiating guilt" (108) the guilt being, I presume, survivor guilt. Bayley shows how writing is one of the "friends" not only of Alzheimer's disease, in particular, but also of spousal loss, in general, a solitary consolation, if not pleasure, that helps the survivor endure the unendurable. Regardless of their religious beliefs or disbeliefs, Lewis, Bayley, Hall, Didion, and Trillin turned to writing as a solemn death ritual. Writing was their grief work, the way in which they honored their spouses and remained attached to them. One of the most intriguing statements about writing as a form of grief work comes from Donald Hall in *Unpacking the Boxes*: "When I write every morning, making poetic lines about pain is a way of avoiding pain. Or maybe I transfer my pain onto others. . . . I turned my memories and feelings into language and by old habit tried to make my words into art—into the object called a poem, something that may exist outside my messy self and its pains or angers in the granite of art" (155–56).

To write about grief is, paradoxically, to overcome grief, if only temporarily. Such writing can either unburden or burden readers, sensitizing or desensitizing them to the suffering of others. I suspect that even Didion would agree that writing about spousal loss enabled her to transmute the pains and angers of the messy self into the granite of art. And she would also agree with her husband's statement that clarity comes only when pen is in hand. Spousal loss memoirists write because they *must* write, because they must bear testimony, and because writing is part of their life support system. It matters little whether one is a writer or a painter: one attempts to transmute one's suffering into art, as Mark Doty recognizes: "His wife Camille on her deathbed, Monet writes, 'I found myself, without being able to help it, in a study of my beloved wife's face, systematically noting the colors.'" Doty then adds, "What does a writer do, when the world collapses, but write?" (263). It is a conclusion that Carl H. Kraus also reaches in his epistolary memoir *Letters to Kate*, a moving tribute to his deceased wife. "How strange that I, a so-called writer and sometime writing teacher, would be so late in realizing that when everything else is gone, words and memories matter more than ever before. Why else am I writing you these letters?" (16).

Admittedly, not all memoirists are so unambiguous in their endorsement of writing. Paul Auster states in *The Invention of Solitude* that writing about his troubled childhood causes a "rift" between thinking and writing. "For the past few days, in fact, I have begun to feel that the story I am trying to tell is somehow incompatible with language, that the degree to which it resists language is an exact measure of how closely I have come to saying something important, and that when the moment arrives for me to say the one truly important thing (assuming it exists), I will not be able to say it." Writing for Auster is a form of wounding: "Instead of healing me as I thought it would, the act of writing has kept this wound open" (32). Kathlyn Conway would agree, claiming that "for those who are ill or disabled, writing frustrates as much as it heals" (3). That writing is *sometimes* painful or frustrating is beyond question, but statements made by C. S. Lewis, John Bayley, Donald Hall, and Alice Stewart Trillin give us a far more affirmative view of writing as a way to memorialize loss and work through grief.

Sven Birkerts's observation that "we are experiencing a crisis of representation in the arts, literature included" (21), does not appear to be true for memoirists of spousal loss, who spend little time bemoaning the limitations of language or, in Andrew Hudgins's words, worrying about the "lies of the autobiographer." These writers have stories to tell, about their own lived experiences, and they seldom retreat into highly theoretical or abstract discussions of the nonrepresentability of reality. They know, as Hall admits in *Unpacking the Boxes*, that "language explains us to ourselves and conceals us from ourselves" (126), and they do their best to find the words to tell their stories of love and loss.

The spousal loss memoirs in my study are all portraits of courage, not in a political but in a personal sense. The memoirists write unflinchingly about their spouses' lives and deaths. The memoirists come across as deeply human, unafraid to show how the loss of the most important persons in their lives darkened their vision and irrevocably changed their lives. So, too, do the deceased spouses confront unflinchingly their expected or unexpected deaths. We see in the memoirs, in varying degrees, an ethics of caring, demonstrating the truth of Ira Byock's statement that "caring for a dying loved one is a powerful way to express love, devotion, and reverence. Allowing a spouse or grown child to care for one becomes a final gift from the person dying" (160). The memoirist's "final gift" to the deceased is the memoir itself, a loving tribute that will live for decades if not centuries.

Death, particularly unexpected death, as in the cases of John Gregory Dunne and Alice Stewart Trillin, challenges our assumptions about life, and survivors must create new assumptions to guide them for the rest of their lives. And yet no matter how shaken they are by their spouses' expected or unexpected deaths, the memoirists affirm life. The memoirs are valuable not only for those who find themselves caring for or mourning the loss of a loved one but also for other readers who will surely find themselves confronting future losses. Spousal loss memoirs offer us insight into surviving what is, for most married people, life's greatest fear: a husband's or wife's death. I suspect that all of the memoirists in my study would agree with Daphne du Maurier's statement: "The husband I had loved and taken for granted for thirty-three years of married life, father of my three children, lay dead. If by writing about it now I expose myself and my feelings, it is not from a sense of self-advertisement, but because by doing so I may be able to help those readers who, like myself, have suffered the same sense of shock" (149).

The hardest death to endure, Simon Critchley asserts in *The Book of Dead Philosophers*, is not our own death but those of our loved ones. "It is the deaths of those we are bound to in love that undo us, that unstitch our carefully tailored suit of the self, that unmake whatever meaning we have made" (xxx). There is no way to test this claim until we ourselves die. I cannot imagine that my own death will be as wrenching as watching Barbara slowly waste away. Clinicians remind us that spousal death is the most devastating loss a person is likely to experience. Bernie Siegel notes that losing one's husband or wife heightens the risk of cancer and other serious illnesses (74) for the surviving spouse, and Lynn Caine quotes a 1984 study indicating that the "mortality rate for widowed persons under the age forty-seven is seven times higher than for non-widowed persons" (20).

My life is so different now without Barbara. I cry less often than I did a year or two ago, but there are times when I find myself unexpectedly wailing, when I cannot recognize the weeper I have become. Am I the same person or not? I often wonder about this question. During the winter of 2007–2008, I watched the horror film *Cloverfield* with my friend and colleague Mort Schoolman. While reptilian aliens destroy Manhattan, toppling skyscrapers as if they were erector sets and laying siege to the horrified population, the film's hero, played by Michael

Stahl-David, wanders through empty subway tunnels searching for his dying girlfriend, whom he had jilted earlier at a party. The movie is so flawed that it became for me an unconscious self-parody, but instead of laughing because it was so bad, I found my body quaking as I struggled to avoid bursting into tears. The shaky Camcorder technique, reminiscent of the *Blair Witch Project*, produced nausea and dizziness in thousands of viewers; the scenes of mass destruction in Manhattan, reminiscent of the destruction of the World Trade Center Towers during September 11, produced feelings of terror and helplessness in me. Mort noticed my difficulty watching the film. Later that evening, when we were having hot chocolate at Starbucks, I told him about my feeling that I have become a "different" person. John Bayley makes a similar observation about himself in *Widower's House*: "In widowhood you lose not only your loved one but much of yourself" (3–4). I might have also cited Dennis Klass's remark in *Parental Grief*: "The resolution of grief is . . . not a return to life as it was before, for there is no going back. The resolution of bereavement is a sense of a new self" (120). Seeing only my "old" self, Mort replied, "I don't think you're different, but Barbara's death has brought to the surface the primitive feelings inside of you—helplessness, sadness, terror." I think we're both right: I'm the same person *and* a different one. That's what happens during bereavement.

Barbara has been dead now for five years, and while grief accompanies me everywhere, it is not as wrenching as it was. I am struck by the truth of Phyllis R. Silverman and Steven L. Nickman's observation about the "continuing bonds" phenomenon: "The deceased are both present and not present at the same time. It is possible to be bereft and not bereft simultaneously, to have a sense of continuity and yet to know that nothing will ever be the same" (351). Living with grief combined with the responsibility to remain with the living means learning to survive the changes brought about by loss. Survival requires the existence of hope even when there is no hope of recovery, as Sherwin B. Nuland points out in *How We Die*: "The greatest dignity to be found in death is the dignity of the life that preceded it. This is a form of hope we can all achieve, and it is the most abiding of all. Hope resides in the meaning of what our lives have been" (242). Survival requires, in addition, a different kind of hope, what Jonathan Lear calls, in a slightly different context, "radical hope," hope that is "directed toward a future goodness that transcends the current ability to understand what it is" (103). Survival also requires gratitude for what we have experienced and hope for what we are capable of experiencing in the future.

Like the other memoirists in my study, I am learning to live with the dead, a process that is clearly ongoing. I still find myself making Freudian slips, as when I refer to my "deceased life." I still wear my wedding ring, though now it's on my right hand. I am the same and yet different. Spousal loss reminds us that to "live fully," to quote Calvin Trillin quoting Alice Stewart Trillin quoting Ernest Becker, "is to live with an awareness of the rumble of terror that underlies everything." That rumble becomes deafening when we lose our spouses, the most important people in our lives. Life after this loss is never the same. Now that Barbara is gone, the challenge is not only to imagine a fulfilling life without her but also to pursue actively a fulfilling life in her physical absence so that I can, perhaps, move from mere survival to living fully again, even with that "rumble of terror."

Indeed, over time, like Lewis, Bayley, and Hall, I have found myself moving from companionship in grief to companionship in joy. I have even found myself capable of feeling romantic joy again—unexpected but appreciated. Like Bayley and Hall, I am grateful for being alive and for being able to experience a new (and different) love that in no way threatens or disrespects my attachment to Barbara nor diminishes the importance of the new relationship. Barbara will forever be in my heart, and the life that we lived and loved together will always be the life we lived and loved together. She will always be a part of the life I am now living, even as I experience what Bayley and Hall describe as the sometimes painful, awkward, confusing, and funny process of falling in love again. I am the same and different; bereft and not bereft. I am a realist—with hope. I think of Ezra Pound's brief poem "Erat Hora," in which the speaker realizes that though he has lost his beloved, "one hour was sunlit and the most high gods/May not make boast of any better thing/Than to have watched that hour as it passed." (150). Spousal loss memoirists are in a unique position to bring to life that hour of sunlight and to demonstrate by word and deed that the remaining hours of the day are still worth living.

WORKS CITED

Adams, Tim. "Marriage Made in Heaven." *Observer*, March 18, 2001.

Adler, Jeremy. Afterword. In *Party in the Blitz: The English Years*, by Elias Canetti, translated by Michael Hofmann. New York: New Directions, 2005.

Ainsworth, M. D. S. "John Bowlby (1907–1990): Obituary." *American Psychologist* 47 (1992).

Albom, Mitch. *Tuesdays with Morrie: An Old Man, a Young Man, and Life's Greatest Lesson*. New York: Doubleday, 1997.

Arendt, Hannah. *The Human Condition*. Chicago: University of Chicago Press, 1958.

Ariès, Philippe. *The Hour of Our Death*. New York: Knopf, 1981.

Ashenburg, Katherine. *The Mourner's Dance: What We Do When People Die*. New York: North Point Press, 2002.

Attig, Thomas. *The Heart of Grief: Death and the Search for Lasting Love*. New York: Oxford University Press, 2000.

Auden, W. H. *The English Auden: Poems, Essays, and Dramatic Writings, 1927–1939*. Edited by Edward Mendelson. London: Faber and Faber, 1977.

Auster, Paul. *The Invention of Solitude*. New York: Sun, 1982.

Bayley, John. *Alice*. London: Duckworth, 1994.

———. *The Character of Love: A Study in the Literature of Personality*. New York: Collier, 1963.

———. *Elegy for Iris*. New York: Picador, 1999.

———. *An Essay on Thomas Hardy*. Cambridge: Cambridge University Press, 1978.

———. *Iris and Her Friends: A Memoir of Memory and Desire*. New York: Norton, 2000.

———. *Selected Essays*. Cambridge: Cambridge University Press, 1984.

———. *Shakespeare and Tragedy*. London: Routledge and Kegan Paul, 1981.

———. *Widower's House: A Study in Bereavement, or How Margot and Mella Forced Me to Flee My Home*. New York: Norton, 2001.

Bayley, Peter. "From Master to Colleague." In *C. S. Lewis at the Breakfast Table and Other Reminiscences*, edited by James T. Como, 77–86. New York: Macmillan, 1979.

Becker, Ernest. *The Denial of Death*. New York: Free Press, 1973.

Bellamy, Michael O. "An Interview with Iris Murdoch." In *From a Tiny Corner in the House of Fiction*, edited by Gillian Dooley, 44–55. Columbia: University of South Carolina Press, 2003.

Berman, Jeffrey. *Death in the Classroom: Writing about Love and Loss*. Albany: SUNY Press, 2009.

———. *Dying to Teach: A Memoir of Love, Loss, and Learning*. Albany: SUNY Press, 2007.

Bigsby, Christopher. "Interview with Iris Murdoch." In *From a Tiny Corner in the House of Fiction*, edited by Gillian Dooley, 97–119. Columbia: University of South Carolina Press, 2003.

Birkerts, Sven. *The Art of Time in Memoir: Then, Again*. Saint Paul, Minn.: Graywolf Press, 2008.

Blanchot, Maurice. *The Writing of the Disaster*. Translated by Ann Smock. Lincoln: University of Nebraska Press, 1995.

Bowlby, John. *Attachment and Loss*. 3 vols. New York: Basic Books, 1969–80.

Bremer, John. "Clive Staples Lewis, 1898–1963: A Brief Biography." In *The C. S. Lewis Readers' Encyclopedia*. Edited by Jeffrey D. Schultz and John G. West Jr., 9–65. Grand Rapids, Mich.: Zondervan Publishing House, 1998.

Breslin, Paul. "Jane Kenyon's 'Manners toward God': Gratitude and the 'Anti-Urge.'" In "*Bright Unequivocal Eye*," edited by Bert Hornback, 39–46. New York: Peter Lang, 2000.

Burns, George. *Gracie: A Love Story*. New York: Signet, 1991.

Byock, Ira. *Dying Well: Peace and Possibilities at the End of Life*. New York: Riverhead Books, 1997.

Caine, Lynn. *Being a Widow*. New York: Penguin, 1988.

Caldwell, Christopher. Review of *After Henry*, by Joan Didion. *American Spectator* 25 (1992): 62–64. Reprinted in *The Critical Response to Joan Didion*, edited by Sharon Felton, 243–48. Westport, Conn.: Greenwood Press, 1994.

Camus, Albert. *The Myth of Sisyphus and Other Essays*. Translated by Justin O'Brien. New York: Vintage, 1955.

Canetti, Elias. *Party in the Blitz: The English Years*. Translated by Michael Hofmann. New York: New Directions, 2005.

Cassell, Eric J. *The Nature of Suffering and the Goals of Medicine*. 2nd ed. New York: Oxford, 2004.

Cassem, Ned H. "Bereavement as Indispensable for Growth." In *Bereavement: Its Psychosocial Aspects*, edited by Bernard Schoenberg, Irwin Gerber, Alfred Wiener, Austin H. Kutscher, David Peretz, and Arthur C. Carr, 9–17. New York: Columbia University Press, 1975.

Christopher, Joe R. *C. S. Lewis*. Boston: Twayne, 1987.

Cohen, Jonathan. "Commentary on 'Betting Your Life.'" *Journal of Bone and Joint Surgery*.

Coles, Joanna. "The Joanna Coles Interview: Duet in Perfect Harmony." In *From a Tiny Corner in the House of Fiction*, edited by Gillian Dooley, 245–50. Columbia: University of South Carolina Press, 2003.

Como, James T., editor. *C. S. Lewis at the Breakfast Table and Other Reminiscences*. New York: Macmillan, 1979.

Conrad, Joseph. *Chance*. London: 1913; reprint, Dent, 1969.

Conradi, Peter J. *Iris Murdoch: A Life*. New York: Norton, 2001.

———. *The Saint and the Artist: A Study of the Fiction of Iris Murdoch*. 1989. 2nd ed. New York: HarperCollins, 2001.

Conway, Kathlyn. *Illness and the Limits of Expression*. Ann Arbor: University of Michigan Press, 2007.

Corr, Charles A., and Donna M. Corr. "Historical and Contemporary Perspectives on Loss, Grief, and Mourning." In *Handbook of Thanatology: The Essential Body of Knowledge for the Study of Death, Dying, and Bereavement*, edited by David Balk, 131–42. New York: Routledge, 2007.

Critchley, Simon. *The Book of Dead Philosophers*. New York: Vintage, 2009.

Csikszentmihalyi, Mihaly. *Creativity*. New York: HarperCollins, 1996.

Davidman, Joy. *Anya*. New York: Macmillan, 1940.

———. *Letter to a Comrade*. With a foreword by Stephen Vincent Benét. New Haven: Yale University Press, 1938.

———. "The Longest Way Round." In *These Found the Way: Thirteen Converts to Protestant Christianity*, edited by David Wesley Soper, 13–26. Philadelphia: Westminster Press, 1951.

———. *Smoke on the Mountain: An Interpretation of the Ten Commandments*. Philadelphia: Westminster Press, 1954.

———. *War Poems of the United Nations*. New York: Dial Press, 1943.

———. *Weeping Bay*. New York: Macmillan, 1950.

de Beauvoir, Simone. *Adieux: A Farewell to Sartre*. Translated by Patrick O'Brien. New York: Pantheon, 1984.

DeSpelder, Lynne Ann, and Albert Lee Strickland. *The Last Dance: Encountering Death and Dying*. Palo Alto, Calif.: Mayfield, 1983.

Dick, Philip K. *Flow My Tears, the Policeman Said*. New York: Daw Books, 1974.

Didion, Joan. *After Henry*. New York: Simon and Schuster, 1992.

———. *A Book of Common Prayer*. New York: Simon and Schuster, 1977.

———. *Democracy*. New York: Simon and Schuster, 1984.

———. *Fixed Ideas: America since 9.11*. New York: New York Review Books, 2003.

———. *The Last Thing He Wanted*. New York: Vintage, 1997.

———. *Miami.* New York: Simon and Schuster, 1987.
———. *Play It as It Lays.* New York: Farrar, Straus and Giroux, 1970.
———. *Political Fictions.* New York: Alfred Knopf, 2001.
———. *Run River.* 1963; reprint, New York: Vintage Books, 1994.
———. *Salvador.* New York: Vintage, 1983.
———. *Slouching towards Bethlehem.* New York: Farrar, Straus and Giroux, 1968.
———. *Vintage Didion.* New York: Vintage, 2004.
———. *We Tell Ourselves Stories in Order to Live: Collected Nonfiction.* New York: Everyman's Library, 2006.
———. *Where I Was From.* New York: Vintage, 2003.
———. *The White Book.* New York: Simon and Schuster, 1979.
———. "Why I Write." In *Joan Didion: Essays and Conversations*, edited by Ellen G. Friedman, 5–10. Princeton: Ontario Review, 1984.
———. *The Year of Magical Thinking.* New York: Alfred Knopf, 2005.
Dillard, Annie. *The Writing Life.* New York: Harper Perennial, 1990.
Dorsett, Lyle W. *And God Came In.* New York: Ballantine Books, 1984.
Doty, Mark. *Heaven's Coast: A Memoir.* New York: HarperPerennial, 1997.
Du Maurier, Daphne. "Death and Widowhood." In *In the Midst of Winter: Selections from the Literature of Mourning*, edited by Mary Jane Moffat, 147–55. New York: Vintage, 1992.
Dunn, Douglas. *Elegies.* London: Faber and Faber, 1985.
Dunne, John Gregory. *Crooning.* New York: Simon and Schuster, 1990.
———. *Delano.* New York: Farrar, Straus and Giroux, 1971.
———. *Dutch Shea, Jr.* New York: Linden Press/Simon and Schuster, 1982.
———. *Harp.* New York: Simon and Schuster, 1989.
———. *Monster: Living Off the Big Screen.* New York: Vintage, 1997.
———. *Nothing Lost.* New York: Knopf, 2004.
———. *Playland.* New York: Random House, 1994.
———. *Quintana and Friends* New York: Dutton, 1978.
———. *The Red White and Blue.* New York: Simon and Schuster, 1987.
———. *Regards: The Selected Nonfiction of John Gregory Dunne.* Foreword by Calvin Trillin. New York: Thunder's Mouth Press, 2006.
———. *The Studio.* New York: Farrar, Straus and Giroux, 1969.
———. *True Confessions.* 1977; reprint, New York: Thunder's Mouth Press, 2006.
———. *Vegas: A Memoir of a Dark Season.* New York: Random House, 1974.
Edelman, Hope. *Motherless Daughters: The Legacy of Loss.* New York: Delta, 1994.
Edgers, Geoff. Review of *About Alice*, by Calvin Trillin. *Boston Globe*, January 6, 2007.

Edgerton, Becky. "Attention as a Palliative for Depression: The Poems of Jane Kenyon." In "*Bright Unequivocal Eye*," edited by Bert Hornback, 77–86. New York: Peter Lang, 2000.

Eliot, T. S. *The Complete Poems and Plays, 1909–1950*. New York: Harcourt, Brace, and World, 1952.

Empson, William. *The Complete Poems of William Empson*. Edited by John Haffenden. Gainesville: University Press of Florida, 2001.

Fitzgerald, F. Scott. *The Crack-Up*. Edited by Edmund Wilson. New York: New Directions, 1956.

Freud, Sigmund. *Beyond the Pleasure Principle*. In *The Standard Edition of the Complete Psychological Works of Sigmund Freud*, translated by James Strachey. Vol. 18. London: Hogarth Press, 1955.

———. "Mourning and Melancholia." In *The Standard Edition of the Complete Psychological Works of Sigmund Freud*, translated by James Strachey, 243–58. Vol. 14. London: Hogarth Press, 1957.

———. *Notes upon a Case of Obsessional Neurosis*. In *The Standard Edition of the Complete Psychological Works of Sigmund Freud*, translated by James Strachey. Vol. 10. London: Hogarth Press, 1955.

———. "On Transience." In *The Standard Edition of the Complete Psychological Works of Sigmund Freud*, translated by James Strachey, 305–7. Vol. 14. London: Hogarth Press, 1957.

———. *Studies on Hysteria*. In *The Standard Edition of the Complete Psychological Works of Sigmund Freud*, translated by James Strachey. Vol. 2. London: Hogarth Press, 1955.

———. *Totem and Taboo*. In *The Standard Edition of the Complete Psychological Works of Sigmund Freud*, translated by James Strachey. Vol. 13. London: Hogarth Press, 1953.

Friedman, Ellen G. "The Didion Sensibility: An Analysis." In *Joan Didion: Essays and Conversations*, edited by Ellen G. Friedman, 81–90. Princeton, N.J.: Ontario Review Press, 1984.

Gilbert, Sandra M. *Death's Door: Modern Dying and the Ways We Grieve*. New York: Norton, 2006.

———. *Wrongful Death: A Medical Tragedy*. New York: Norton, 1995.

———, editor. *Inventions of Farewell: A Book of Elegies*. New York: Norton, 2001.

Glick, Ira, Robert Weiss, and Colin Murray Parkes. *The First Year of Bereavement*. New York: Wiley, 1974.

Gluck, Louise. "Relic" in *Vita Nova*. Hopewell, N.J.: Ecco, 1999.

Goleman, Daniel. *Emotional Intelligence*. New York: Bantam Books, 1995.

Gopnik, Adam. "Prisoner of Narnia." *New Yorker*, November 21, 2005.

Gorer, Geoffrey. *Death, Grief, and Mourning in Contemporary Britain.* 1965; reprint, Salem, N.H.: Ayer, 1987.

Green, Roger Lancelyn, and Walter Hooper. *C. S. Lewis: A Biography.* Revised edition. New York: HarperCollins, 2002.

Gresham, Douglas H. *Lenten Lands: My Childhood with Joy Davidman and C. S. Lewis.* San Francisco: HarperSanFrancisco, 1988.

Gunther, John. *Death Be Not Proud.* New York: Perennial Classics, 1949.

Haffenden, John. "Interview with Iris Murdoch." In *From a Tiny Corner in the House of Fiction*, edited by Gillian Dooley, 124–38. Columbia: University of South Carolina Press, 2003.

Hall, Donald. *The Best Day the Worst Day:; Life with Jane Kenyon.* Boston: Houghton Mifflin, 2005.

———. *Breakfast Served Any Time All Day: Essays on Poetry New and Selected.* Ann Arbor: University of Michigan Press, 2003.

———. *Eagle Pond.* Boston: Houghton Mifflin, 2007.

———. *Fathers Playing Catch with Sons.* San Francisco: North Point Press, 1985.

———. "Ghost in the House." In *Simply Lasting*, edited by Jane Peseroff, 83–93. Saint Paul, Minn.: Graywolf Press, 2005.

———. *Goatfoot Milktongue Twinbird: Interviews, Essays, and Notes on Poetry, 1970–76.* Ann Arbor: University of Michigan Press, 1978.

———. *Henry Moore: The Life of a Great Sculptor.* New York: Harper and Row, 1966.

———. *Life Work.* Boston: Houghton Mifflin, 1993.

———. *Milkman's Boy.* New York: Walker, 1997.

———. *The Museum of Clear Ideas.* New York: Ticknor and Fields, 1993.

———. *Old Home Day.* San Diego: Browndeer Press, 1996.

———. *The Old Life.* Boston: Houghton Mifflin, 1996.

———. *The One Day: A Poem in Three Parts.* Boston: Houghton Mifflin, 1988.

———. *The Painted Bed.* Boston: Houghton Mifflin, 2002.

———. *Principal Products of Portugal: Prose Pieces.* Boston: Beacon Press, 1995.

———. *Their Ancient Glittering Eyes: Remembering Poets and More Poets.* New York: Ticknor and Fields, 1992.

———. "Two Poets in One House." In "*Bright Unequivocal Eye*," edited by Bert Hornback, 1–2. New York: Peter Lang, 2000.

———. *Unpacking the Boxes: A Memoir of Life in Poetry.* Boston: Houghton Mifflin, 2008.

———. *The Weather for Poetry: Essays, Reviews, and Notes on Poetry, 1977–81.* Ann Arbor: University of Michigan Press, 1982.

———. *When Willard Met Babe Ruth.* Illustrated by Barry Moser. San Diego: Browndeer Press, 1996.

———. *White Apples and the Taste of Stone: Selected Poems, 1946–2006*. Boston: Houghton Mifflin, 2006.

———. *Willow Temple: New and Selected Stories*. Boston: Houghton Mifflin, 2003.

———. *Without*. Boston: Houghton Mifflin, 1998.

———. *Writing Well*. 3rd ed. Boston: Little, Brown, 1979.

———, editor. *The Modern Stylists: Writers on the Art of Writing*. New York: Free Press, 1968.

Hazan, Cindy, and Phillip Shaver. "Romantic Love Conceptualized as an Attachment Process." *Journal of Personality and Social Psychology* 52 (1987): 511–24.

Hemingway, Ernest. *A Farewell to Arms*. New York: Scribner's, 1929.

Heusel, Barbara Stevens. "Interview with Iris Murdoch." In *From a Tiny Corner in the House of Fiction*, edited by Gillian Dooley, 194–208. Columbia: University of South Carolina Press, 2003.

Hill, Laban. "Jane Kenyon." In *Simply Lasting*, edited by Joyce Peseroff, 113–44. Saint Paul, Minn.: Graywolf Press, 2005.

Holmes, Thomas, and Richard Rahe. "The Social Readjustment Rating Scale." *Journal of Psychosomatic Research* 11 (1967): 213–18.

Hornback, Bert, editor. *"Bright Unequivocal Eye": Poems, Papers, and Remembrances from the First Jane Kenyon Conference*. New York: Peter Lang, 2000.

Horowitz, Mardi, Nancy Wilner, Charles Marmor, and Janice Krupnick. "Pathological Grief and the Activation of Latent Self-Images." *American Journal of Psychiatry* 137 (1980): 1157–62.

Hotchner, A. E. *Papa Hemingway*. New York: Bantam, 1973.

Hudgins, Andrew. *The Glass Anvil*. Ann Arbor: University of Michigan Press, 1997.

Hughes, Ted. *Birthday Letters*. New York: Farrar Strauss Giroux, 1998.

Jacobs, Alan. *The Narnian: The Life and Imagination of C. S. Lewis*. San Francisco: HarperSanFrancisco, 2005.

Jamison, Kay Redfield. *Touched with Fire: Manic Depressive Illness and the Artistic Temperament*. New York: Free Press, 1993.

Jones, Ernest. *The Life and Work of Sigmund Freud*. 3 vols. New York: Basic Books, 1953–57.

Kafka, Franz. *Letters to Friends, Family, and Editors*. Translated by Richard Winston and Clara Winston. New York: Schocken, 1977.

Kakutani, Michiko. "Joan Didion: Staking out California." In *Joan Didion: Essays and Conversations*, edited by Ellen. G. Friedman, 29–42. Princeton, N.J.: Ontario Review Press, 1984.

Kastenbaum, Robert. *On Our Way: The Final Passage through Life and Death.* Berkeley: University of California Press, 2004.

———. *The Psychology of Death.* 2nd ed. New York: Springer, 1992.

Kennedy, David. *Elegy.* London: Routledge, 2007.

Kenyon, Jane. *A Hundred White Daffodils: Essays, the Akhmatova Translations, Newspaper Columns, Notes, Interviews, and One Poem.* Saint Paul, Minn.: Graywolf Press, 1999.

———. *Jane Kenyon: Collected Poems.* Saint Paul, Minn.: Graywolf Press, 2005.

Klass, Dennis. *Parental Grief: Solace and Resolution* New York: Springer, 1988.

Klass, Dennis, Phyllis R. Silverman, and Steven L. Nickman. *Continuing Bonds: New Understandings of Grief.* Washington, D.C.: Taylor and Francis, 1996.

Kottler, Jeffrey. *The Language of Tears.* San Francisco: Jossey-Bass, 1996.

Kramer, Peter D. "The Anatomy of Grief." *Slate,* www.slate.com/id/2128095, Monday, October 17, 2005.

———. "Unequivocal Eye." In *Simply Lasting,* edited by Joyce Peseroff, 251–55. Saint Paul, Minn.: Graywolf Press, 2005.

Kraus, Carl H. *Letters to Kate: Life after Life.* Iowa City: University of Iowa Press, 2006.

Kübler-Ross, Elisabeth. *On Death and Dying.* New York: Macmillan, 1970.

Kuehl, Linda. "Interview with Joan Didion." *The Paris Review* 20 (1978): 142–63.

Lambert, Ellen Zetzel. *Placing Sorrow: A Study of the Pastoral Elegy Convention from Theocritus to Milton.* Chapel Hill: University of North Carolina Press, 1976.

Larson, Thomas. *The Memoir and the Memoirist: Reading and Writing Personal Narrative.* Athens: Swallow Press/Ohio University Press, 2007.

Lear, Jonathan. *Radical Hope: Ethics in the Face of Cultural Devastation.* Cambridge: Harvard University Press, 2006.

Lewis, C. S. *The Allegory of Love: A Study in Medieval Tradition.* London: Oxford University Press, 1936.

———. *Collected Letters.* Edited by Walter Hopper. 3 vols. New York: HarperCollins, 2004.

———. *The Four Loves.* New York: Harcourt, Brace, 1960.

———. *A Grief Observed.* 1963; reprint, San Francisco: Harper San Francisco, 1994.

———. *Letters of C. S. Lewis.* Edited and with a memoir by W. H. Lewis. London: Geoffrey Bles, 1968.

———. *Letters to an American Lady.* Edited by Clyde S. Kilby. Grand Rapids, Mich.: William B. Eerdmans, 1967.

———. *Letters to Malcolm: Chiefly on Prayer.* New York: Harcourt, Brace and World, 1964.

———. *The Problem of Pain.* London: Centenary Press, 1940.

———. *Surprised by Joy: The Shape of My Early Life.* London: Geoffrey Bles, 1955.

———. *Till We Have Faces: A Myth Retold.* London: Geoffrey Bles, 1956.

Lindemann, Erich. "Symptomatology and Management of Acute Grief." *American Journal of Psychiatry* 101 (1944): 141–48.

Lutz, Tom. *Crying: The Natural and Cultural History of Tears.* New York: Norton, 1999.

Maher, Jane. *Mina P. Shaughnessy: Her Life and Work.* Urbana, Ill.: National Council of English Teachers, 1997.

Mann, Thomas. *The Magic Mountain.* Translated by H. T. Lowe-Porter. New York: Vintage, 1952.

Malcolm, Janet. *The Journalist and the Murderer.* New York: Knopf, 1990.

McCabe, Marilyn. *The Paradox of Loss: Toward a Relational Theory of Grief.* Westport, Conn.: Praeger, 2003.

Miller, Nancy K. *Bequest and Betrayal: Memoirs of a Parent's Death.* New York: Oxford University Press, 1996.

Monette, Paul. *Borrowed Time: An AIDS Memoir.* San Diego: Harcourt Brace Jovanovich, 1988.

Montaigne, Michel de. "To Philosophize Is to Learn How to Die." In *The Essays of Montaigne*, translated by E. J. Trechmann. Vol. 1. New York: Oxford University Press, 1946.

Moyers, Bill. *The Language of Life: A Festival of Poets.* New York: Doubleday, 1995.

Murdoch, Iris. *Acastos: Two Platonic Dialogues.* London: Chatto and Windus, 1986.

———. *Jackson's Dilemma.* New York: Viking, 1996.

———. *Metaphysics as a Guide to Morals.* New York: Allen Lane/Penguin Press, 1993.

———. *The Sacred and Profane Love Machine.* London: Chatto and Windus, 1974.

———. *The Sea, the Sea.* London: Chatto and Windus, 1978.

Neimeyer, Robert. "Reauthoring Life Narratives: Grief Therapy as Meaning Reconstruction." *Israel Journal of Psychiatry and Related Sciences* 38 (2001): 171–83.

Nietzsche, Friedrich. *The Philosophy of Nietzsche.* New York: Modern Library, 1954.

Nuland, Sherwin B. *How We Die: Reflections on Life's Final Chapter.* New York: Vintage, 1995.

Nussbaum, Martha C. "Love and Vision: Iris Murdoch on Eros and the Individual." In *Iris Murdoch and the Search for Human Goodness*, edited by Maria Antonaccio and William Schweiker. Chicago: University of Chicago Press, 1996.

O'Connor, Flannery. *Mystery and Manners*. Edited by Sally Fitzgerald and Robert Fitzgerald. New York: Farrar, Straus and Giroux, 1969.

Oltjenbruns, Kevin Ann, and David Balk. "Life Span Issues and Loss, Grief, and Mourning." In *Handbook of Thanatology: The Essential Body of Knowledge for the Study of Death, Dying, and Bereavement*, edited by David Balk, 151–63. New York: Routledge, 2007.

Oz, Amos. *A Tale of Love and Darkness*. Translated by Nicholas de Lange. Orlando, Fla.: Harcourt, 2003.

Parkes, Colin Murray. *Bereavement: Studies of Grief in Adult Life*. 3rd ed. Madison, Conn.: International Universities Press, 1998.

Pausch, Randy. *The Last Lecture*. With Jeffrey Zaslow. New York: Hyperion, 2008.

Pennebaker, James. "Writing about Emotional Experiences as a Therapeutic Process." *Psychological Science* 8 (1997): 162–66.

Phillips, Adam. *Terrors and Experts*. Cambridge: Harvard University Press, 1996.

Pound, Ezra. "Erat Hora." In *Collected Early Poems of Ezra Pound*, edited by John King. New York: New Directions, 1976.

Prescott, Peter S. "Didion's Grace." Review of *A Book of Common Prayer*, by Joan Didion. *Newsweek*, March 21, 1977, 81.

Ramazani, Jahan. *Poetry of Mourning: The Modern Elegy from Hardy to Heaney*. Baltimore: Johns Hopkins University Press, 1994.

Rosenblatt, Paul C. "Grief Does Not End." In *Continuing Bonds: New Understandings of Grief*, edited by Donald Klass, Phyllis R. Silverman, and Steven L. Nickman, 45–58. Washington, D.C.: Taylor and Francis, 1996.

Roth, Philip. *Patrimony: A True Story*. New York: Vintage, 1996.

Ryerson, Marjorie. *Companions for the Passage: Stories of the Intimate Privilege of Accompanying the Dying*. Ann Arbor: University of Michigan Press, 2005.

Sacks, Peter. *The English Elegy: Studies in the Genre from Spenser to Yeats*. Baltimore: Johns Hopkins University Press, 1985.

Sayer, George. *Jack: C. S. Lewis and His Times*. London: Macmillan, 1988.

Schenck, Celeste Marguerite. *Mourning and Panegyric: The Poetics of Pastoral Ceremony*. University Park: Pennsylvania State University Press, 1988.

Schowalter, John E. "Parent Death and Child Bereavement." In *Bereavement: Its Psychosocial Aspects*, edited by Bernard Schoenberg, Irwin Gerber, Alfred Wiener, Austin H. Kutscher, David Peretz, and Arthur C. Carr, 172–79. New York: Columbia University Press, 1975.

Shuchter, Stephen, and Sidney Zisook. "Treatment of Spousal Bereavement: A Multidimensional Approach." *Psychiatric Annals* 16 (1986): 295–305.

Sibley, Brian. *Through the Shadowlands: The Love Story of C. S. Lewis and Joy Davidman*. Grand Rapids, Mich.: Revell, 2005.

Siegel, Bernie. *Love, Medicine, and Miracles*. New York: Perennial Library, 1988.

Silverman, Phyllis R., and Steven L. Nickman. "Concluding Thoughts." In *Continuing Bonds: New Understandings of Grief*, edited by Donald Klass, Phyllis R. Silverman, and Steven L. Nickman, 349–55. Washington, D.C.: Taylor and Francis, 1996.

Singer, Mark. "The Talk of the Town—Postscript." *New Yorker*, October 1, 2001, 42.

Solomon, Andrew. *The Noonday Demon: An Atlas of Depression*. New York: Touchstone, 2001.

Solomon, Robert C. *In Defense of Sentimentality*. New York: Oxford University Press, 2004.

———. *True to Our Own Feelings: What Our Emotions Are Really Telling Us*. New York: Oxford University Press, 2007.

Soper, David Wesley. *These Found the Way: Thirteen Converts to Protestant Christianity*. Philadelphia: Westminster Press, 1951.

Spence, Donald B. *Narrative Truth and Historical Truth: Meaning and Interpretation in Psychoanalysis*. New York: Norton, 1984.

Spiro, Howard. "Facing Death." In *Facing Death: Where Culture, Religion, and Medicine Meet*, edited by Howard Spiro, Mary McCrea Curnen, and Lee Palmer Wandel, xv–xx. New Haven: Yale University Press, 1996.

Stade, George. Review of *Dutch Shea, Jr.*, by John Gregory Dunne. *New York Times*, March 28, 1982.

Stamberg, Susan. "Cautionary Tales." In *Joan Didion: Essays and Conversations*, edited by Ellen G. Friedman, 22–28. Princeton, N.J.: Ontario Review Press, 1984.

Stewart, Garrett. *Death Sentences: Styles of Dying in British Fiction*. Cambridge: Harvard University Press, 1984.

Stone, Ruth. *What Love Comes To: New and Selected Poems*. Port Townsend, Wash.: Copper Canyon Press, 2008.

———. *Who Is the Widow's Muse?* Cambridge, Mass.: Yellow Moon Press, 1991.

Stroebe, Margaret, and Henk Schut. "The Dual Process Model of Coping with Bereavement: Rationale and Description." *Death Studies* 23 (1999): 197–224.

Styron, William. *Darkness Visible*. New York: Random House, 1990.

Talbott, Thomas. "A Grief Observed." In *The C. S. Lewis Readers' Encyclopedia*, edited by Jeffrey D. Schultz and John G. West Jr., 193–94. Grand Rapids, Mich.: Zondervan Publishing House.

Timmerman, John. *Jane Kenyon: A Literary Life*. Grand Rapids, Michigan: William B. Eerdmans, 2002.

Trillin, Alice Stewart. "Betting Your Life." *New Yorker*, January 29, 2001, 38–42.

———. *Dear Bruno*. Illustrated by Edward Koren, with a foreword by Paul Newman. New York: New Press, 1996.

———. "Of Dragons and Garden Peas: A Cancer Patient Talks to Doctors." *New England Journal of Medicine* 304 (1981): 699–701.

———. "Stalking the Greasy Kid Stuff." *Nation*, October 21, 1978, 414–15.

Trillin, Alice Stewart, and Associates. *Teaching Basic Skills in College*. San Francisco: Jossey-Bass, 1980.

Trillin, Calvin. *About Alice*. New York: Random House, 2006.

———. *Alice, Let's Eat*. New York: Vintage, 1978.

———. "Alice, Off the Page." *New Yorker*, March 27, 2006, 44–57.

———. *American Fried*. Garden City, N.Y.: Doubleday, 1974.

———. *Family Man*. New York: Farrar Straus Giroux, 1998.

———. *Feeding a Yen*. New York: Random House, 2003.

———. *Floater*. New Haven: Ticknor and Fields, 1980.

———. *A Heckuva Job: More of the Bush Administration in Rhyme*. New York: Random House, 2006.

———. *Killings*. New York: Ticknor and Fields, 1984.

———. *Messages from My Father*. New York: Farrar, Straus and Giroux, 1996.

———. *Obliviously on He Sails*. New York: Random House, 2004.

———. *Remembering Denny*. New York: Farrar, Straus and Giroux, 1993.

———. *Tepper Isn't Going Out*. New York: Random House, 2001.

———. *Third Helpings*. New Haven: Ticknor and Fields, 1983.

———. *Too Soon to Tell*. New York: Farrar Straus Giroux, 1995.

———. *Travels with Alice*. New York: Farrar, Straus and Giroux, 1989.

———. *Uncivil Liberties*. New Haven: Ticknor and Fields, 1982.

———. *With All Due Disrespect*. New York: Ticknor and Fields, 1985.

Vanauken, Sheldon. *A Severe Mercy*. San Francisco: HarperCollins, 1987.

Vidal, Gore. Preface. In *The Norton Book of American Autobiography*, edited by Jay Parini. New York: Norton, 1999.

Volkan, Vamik D. "Individuals and Societies as 'Perennial Mourners': Their Linking Objects and Public Memorials." In *On Deaths and Endings: Psychoanalysts' Reflections on Finality, Transformations, and New Beginnings*, edited by Brent Willock, Lori C. Bohm, and Rebecca C. Curtis, 42–59. London: Routledge, 2007.

———. "'Re-Grief' Therapy." In *Bereavement: Its Psychosocial Aspects*, edited by Bernard Schoenberg, Irwin Gerber, Alfred Wiener, Austin H. Kutscher, David Peretz, and Arthur C. Carr, 334–50. New York: Columbia University Press, 1975.

Weil, Robert. "Memories of Iris." In *From a Tiny Corner in the House of Fiction*, edited by Gillian Dooley, 251–55. Columbia: University of South Carolina Press, 2003.

Whitehead, Alfred North. *Dialogues of Alfred North Whitehead.* As recorded by Lucien Price. New York: Mentor Books, New American Library, 1956.

Wiener, Alfred, Irwin Gerber, Delia Battin, and Arthur M. Arkin, "The Process and Phenomenology of Bereavement." In *Bereavement: Its Psychosocial Aspects*, edited by Bernard Schoenberg, Irwin Gelber, Alfred Wiener, Austin H. Kutscher, David Peretz, and Arthur C. Carr, 58–65. New York: Columbia University Press, 1975.

Wilber, Ken. *Grace and Grit: Spirituality and Healing in the Life and Death of Treya Killam* Wilber. Boston: Shambhala, 2000.

Wilson, A. N. *C. S. Lewis: A Biography*. London: Collins, 1990.

Winchell, Mark Royden. *Joan Didion*. Revised Edition. Boston: Twayne, 1989.

Wogrin, Carol. "Professional Issues and Thanatology." In *Handbook of Thanatology: The Essential Body of Knowledge for the Study of Death, Dying, and Bereavement*, edited by David Balk, 371–86. New York: Routledge, 2007.

Worden, J. William. *Grief Counseling and Grief Therapy: A Handbook for the Mental Health Practitioner.* 3rd ed. New York: Springer, 2002.

Zeiger, Melissa F. Beyond Consolation: Death, Sexuality, and the Changing Shapes of Elegy. Ithaca: Cornell University Press, 1977.

Zinsser, William, editor. *Inventing the Truth: The Art and Craft of Memoir.* Revised and expanded edition. Boston: Houghton Mifflin, 1998.

INDEX